WILLIAMS-SONOMA

eating by color

for maximum health

RECIPES

Georgeanne Brennan

Dana Jacobi

Annabel Langbein

GENERAL EDITOR

Chuck Williams

PHOTOGRAPHY

Dan Goldberg

Oxmoor House®

8 Introduction

22 Purple & blue

27 Eggplant crisps with yogurt dipping sauce

Roasted purple carrots & fennel

28 Grilled pizzas with blue potatoes & onions

31 Purple asparagus with orange vinaigrette

Scallops with bell pepper dressing

32 Grilled eggplant & feta cheese rolls

Purple carrots glazed with red wine

37 Fig & purple endive salad

Halibut & purple grapes

38 Roasted tuna with olives, grapes & pine nuts

Roasted turkey breast with figs & lavender

41 Chicken & eggplant salad

Chicken & fig skewers

42 Roasted pork & prunes

47 Baked pilaf with currants, lavender & almonds

Herbed blue potatoes

48 Salmon with wild blueberry & rhubarb sauce

51 Stir-fried pork with black plums

Duck with purple cabbage, blackberries & port

52 Sichuan beef with eggplant

57 Wild rice with purple bell pepper & pecans

Pan-fried blue potatoes with sage

58 Grilled plums with kirsch cream

Grilled berry parcels

61 Purple fruits with lavender syrup

Roasted black plums with star anise

62 Blackberry crêpes

Pomegranate-glazed figs

64 Green

69 Belgian endive with blue cheese & walnuts

Green onions with anchovy sauce

70 Grilled fish tacos with green cabbage salad

73 Roasted broccolini with lemon

Roasted zucchini with anchoïade

74 Spinach soufflé

79 Stir-fried chicken with broccoli & mushrooms

Dry-fried long beans

80 Chicken breasts stuffed with goat cheese & arugula

83 Trout & green pear salad

Grilled halibut with limes

84 Chicken, avocado & spinach salad

89 Roasted asparagus with eggs & parmesan

Cod on a bed of cucumbers

90 Baked pasta with dandelion greens & sausage

93 Lamb chops with arugula pesto

Broccoli gratin

94 Fettuccine with fava beans, artichokes & asparagus

Lemon sole with peas

97 Duck & Brussels sprouts

101 Stir-fried calamari & pea shoots

Chicken with tomatillo sauce

102 Okra with yellow plum tomatoes

Swiss chard with lemon & anchovy

105 Green figs with almond custard

106 Green apples baked with dried cranberries

Green pear & grape clafoutis

108 White & tan

113 Mushroom bruschetta

Mustard-honey leeks

114 Baked onion & white eggplant purée

Mashed Jerusalem artichokes with truffle oil

117 White asparagus mimosa with browned butter

Potato galettes with smoked salmon

118 Turkey sandwiches with sweet onions

Grilled white corn salad

123 Pork pot roast with parsnips, carrots & apples

124 Sicilian shrimp with cauliflower & almonds

Potatoes with chorizo & parsley

127 Turkey fricassee with kohlrabi, pears & mushrooms

Pork chops smothered in onions & apples

128 Monkfish with roasted white corn salsa

133 White eggplant & green onion salad

Grilled fennel with Indian spices

134 Cuban-style pork & plantains

137 Mu shu pork

138 Spicy cauliflower gratin

Parsley portobellos

143 Roasted fennel with fennel seed

Celery root & potato gratin

144 Turnips with peas & mushrooms

Chicken with caramelized shallots & wine

147 White nectarines with raw sugar & rum

Baked bananas & tapioca pudding

contents

148 Yellow & orange

153 Yellow tomatoes with mint & pecorino

Grilled pumpkin with pumpkin seed dressing

154 Corn & crab quesadillas

Scallops with golden beets

157 Spanish tortilla with golden potatoes

158 Grilled salmon, yellow potato & corn salad

163 Grilled duck breast with papaya

164 Grilled snapper & mandarin salad

Mahimahi & mango salsa

167 Halibut with roasted nectarine chutney

Roasted sea bass with carrot purée

168 Rack of lamb with orange bell pepper relish

Baked sweet potato & rutabaga mash

173 Spaghetti squash aglio e olio

Turban squash with honey butter

174 Baked stew of curried root vegetables

177 Chicken with yellow peppers & passion fruit

Stuffed squash blossoms

178 Shrimp with papaya & coconut

Apricot-stuffed chicken breasts

183 Rutabaga & golden beets with pomegranate seeds

Indian-spiced squash with cashews

184 Ham & sweet potato hash

Butternut squash & pears with rosemary

187 Grilled apricots with sabayon

188 Pumpkin flan

191 Winter peach shortcake

192 Red

197 Grilled radicchio

Liver & onion bruschetta

198 Grilled calamari

Romesco sauce

201 Roasted tomato tart

Tart shell

202 Warm tomato & olive bruschetta

Red wine spaghetti with red bell pepper & onion

207 Shrimp with watermelon, feta & mint

Grilled cherry tomatoes

208 Sautéed trout with red grape sauce

211 Mahimahi with red potato, red bell pepper & rosemary

Baked mackerel with red currants

212 Game hens with pears

Roasted chicken & red onion

215 Duck with blood orange sauce

Turkey tenderloin with cranberry compote

219 Pork tenderloin with sour cherry sauce

Red-hot hash browns

220 Lamb kebabs with blood orange salad

223 Veal with red plum sauce

Chicken with cherry salsa

224 Baked pasta with radicchio & blue cheese

229 Rib-eye steaks with baked plums

Roasted beets with Indian spices

230 Berry gratin

Deep-dish cherry pie

233 Caramelized red pears with cinnamon

Broiled grapes in yogurt & sour cream

234 Strawberries in red wine

Cherries & pound cake

236 Brown

241 Broiled polenta with mushroom ragout

242 Chicken thighs with lima bean purée

245 Broiled tuna with cannellini bean salad

246 Chicken, mushroom & barley casserole

251 Duck sausage, tomato & cranberry bean casserole

252 Turkey with red mole

255 Cashew chicken stir-fry

259 Bulgur salad with zucchini, asparagus & green onions

260 Pork, quinoa & chile casserole

263 Lima beans baked with ham

Tamarind shrimp with peanuts

264 Ginger couscous with dried fruit

Split peas with yogurt & mint

269 Black bean & white corn salad

Lentils with shallots & serrano ham

270 Mango chicken with toasted quinoa

Kasha with walnuts & pasta

273 Maple panna cotta with candied walnuts

274 Pear, cranberry & walnut crisp

Oatmeal & dried peach muffins

276 Reference

About this book

This colorful cookbook was created to offer simple and appealing ways to enjoy a diet rich in fruits, vegetables, legumes, and grains.

In our modern world, we have a multitude of choices when it comes to food, from locally grown fruits and vegetables to a vast array of processed convenience items. With so many options comes a responsibility to choose wisely and well. It's a proven fact that the foods you eat directly affect your overall health and energy level. One of the best ways you can ensure that you experience the benefits of good health and plenty of energy is to add an array of fresh produce and whole grains to your diet.

The recipes in *Eating by Color* are organized in a new way: by the color of the key fruits or vegetables used in the dish. This approach highlights the different nutritional benefits that each color group contributes to your overall health. By thinking about the color of foods, you can be sure to include all the fresh produce you need in your diet. If you consume at least one vegetable or fruit from each color group daily, you can feel confident you are getting the number of servings required for optimum health. Whole grains and legumes have a chapter of their own and, like fresh produce, form the foundation of a wholesome diet.

Eating by Color will help you prepare a wide range of fresh fruits, vegetables, and whole grains using different healthy cooking techniques, bringing beautiful color to every meal you make.

Chuck Williams

Eating the rainbow

Purple and blue fruits and vegetables contain fiber, vitamins, and phytochemicals that promote heart health; help memory function; lower the risk of some cancers; promote urinary tract health; and boost immunity

Green fruits and vegetables contain fiber, vitamins, and phytochemicals that lower the risk of breast, prostate, lung, and other cancers; promote eye health; help build strong bones and teeth; and boost immunity

Adapted from educational materials of the Produce for Better Health Foundation

White and tan fruits and vegetables contain fiber, vitamins, and phytochemicals that promote heart health; help maintain healthful cholesterol levels; lower the risk of breast, lung, and other cancers; and slow cholesterol absorption

Red fruits and vegetables contain fiber, vitamins, and phytochemicals that promote heart health; help memory function; lower the risk of certain cancers; promote urinary tract health; and boost immunity

Yellow and orange fruits and vegetables contain fiber, vitamins, and phytochemicals that promote heart health; promote eye health; lower the risk of some cancers; and boost immunity

Brown whole grains, legumes, seeds, and nuts include fiber, vitamins, and phytonutrients that lower blood cholesterol levels and reduce the risk of colon and other cancers, diabetes, heart disease, and stroke

Eating by color

Initially, a cookbook organized by color that promotes a healthy diet sounds like a flight of fancy. Focusing on the red of tomatoes or the yellow of squash seems like a distraction when you are trying to cut out "bad" foods and fill up on "good" ones on your path to healthier eating. But in fact, the best and most natural way to improve your diet is to start thinking about the colors on your plate.

The philosophy of this cookbook is simple and straightforward: the consumption of moderate amounts of a wide range of foods, especially peak-of-season produce and whole or minimally processed grains and legumes, is the key to a healthy diet. Instead of laboriously counting calories, fat grams, or carbohydrates, simply focus on maintaining a constantly varied diet rich in fresh vegetables, fruits, grains, and legumes. If consuming such foods is the first priority of your daily regimen, a healthier balance of other foods will naturally follow.

Humans are omnivores, but the modern diet is remarkably restricted in the kind of plant foods we eat. Instead of having to forage for our next meal, we are able to surround ourselves with every possible food luxury—and under these circumstances it's hard not to overindulge in the concentrated sources of energy our bodies crave, especially animal fats. Our appetites also naturally gravitate toward carbohydrates, which are excellent sources of quick energy. Unfortunately, our most common modern forms of carbohydrates, such as white bread and white rice, are stripped of the wholesome nutrients found in whole grains.

While taking a daily multivitamin is a good insurance policy, taking pills and supplements isn't a good solution to an ongoing lack of vitamins and minerals in your diet. Your body

can make better use of these compounds when it extracts them in their natural state from food. Eating a wide variety of plant foods, rounded out with modest portions of protein-rich foods such as meat and seafood, is the best way of getting what you need, in a form in which your body is designed to use it.

Surprisingly, the colors of plant foods are an important part of the healthy eating equation. Some of the benefits of eating fruits and vegetables come from the vitamins, minerals, and fiber they contain, but others come from a more recently discovered class of compounds called phytonutrients, or phytochemicals. These plant compounds work in a number of ways to protect our bodies and fight disease. In many cases, they are also the elements in plant foods that give them their distinctive

colors and flavors. So the dazzling hues of vegetables and fruits, from bright red strawberries to dark green spinach to deep purple eggplant (aubergine), give clues to the particular phytonutrients each plant contains. Eating a rainbow of produce will give you the broadest array of health benefits from all these various compounds.

Aside from colorful fruits and vegetables, your daily diet should also include members of another important group of plant foods: grains and legumes. These foods are rich in fiber, protein, complex carbohydrates, and minerals, and offer phytochemicals of their own. For the greatest nutritional benefit, grains should be eaten whole or in a minimally processed form.

This volume shows how to enjoy this wholesome natural bounty using some of the

most healthful cooking methods: grilling. roasting, and sautéing. These cooking methods use only small amounts of added fat and bring out the inherent flavors in different foods.

To guide your meal planning, the chapters in this cookbook are organized by the five prominent color groups of vegetables and fruits: purple and blue, green, white and tan, yellow and orange, and red. Each chapter begins with a chart showing which fruits and vegetables are at their peak of ripeness each season. A sixth chapter focuses on "brown" foods, including whole grains, legumes, nuts, and seeds. The recipes are simple and straightforward, designed for real-life cooks who haven't much time to spare, but who want to use the time they do have to cook and eat creatively, colorfully, and—above all—*well*.

Fruits & vegetables

Fruits and vegetables are the cornerstones of a healthy diet. They are also some of the most beautiful and delicious foods on the planet—a boon to both the eye and the palate, with tastes and textures that range from sweet and juicy to bitter and crisp. The recipes in *Eating by Color* will inspire you to try new fruits and vegetables and reap all the benefits of their vitamins, minerals, and phytochemicals.

In the early years of the twentieth century, scientists discovered, one by one, the many different vitamins and minerals we now know are essential to maintaining good health and fighting disease. Today, we are entering into a similarly exciting era of discovery as we learn about the roles that colorful phytonutrients play in our bodies.

These protective compounds, which are believed to number in the thousands, work alone and in combination with one another and with nutrients. They work in different ways. For example, some phytochemicals act as antioxidants, protecting the body by neutralizing unstable oxygen molecules (known as free radicals) that damage cells and promote disease. Regularly eating plant foods rich in antioxidants is believed to reduce the incidence of various cancers, heart disease, impaired vision, and other health problems.

Fruits and vegetables from different color groups provide us with different assortments of phytonutrients, each playing a unique role in fighting disease and promoting health and well-being.

By eating fruits and vegetables at their peak of ripeness, you will be both pleasing your palate and giving your body the benefit of all the healthy nutrients that these plant foods contain.

Grains & legumes

Grains and legumes have long played key roles in the human diet. In Asia, a meal is not a meal without rice, while beans are seldom absent from the Mexican table. American diners are accustomed to eating white rice or a white bread roll as part of dinner. Lately, however, there has been a rising interest in healthier whole grains, from nutty brown rice to homey barley and exotic amaranth.

Perhaps the interest in whole grains emerged as part of the low-carb diet craze, which made white breads and pastas taboo. Whatever the cause of this trend, making a shift from refined white grains to unrefined brown ones is a welcome development for everyone's health.

Whole grains and legumes are good sources of fiber, which keeps our digestive system in good working order and helps regulate the cholesterol levels in our blood. They also contain many proteins, vitamins, minerals, and their own phytochemicals. But in our modern diet, grains are usually refined, lacking the fiber-rich hull and the nutrient-rich germ.

In *Eating by Color*, recipes that feature grains and legumes are grouped in a chapter called Brown. These foods come in a variety of colors, but you can think of them as brown to remind yourself that they should be as close to their natural state as possible, rather than stripped of nutrients, texture, flavor, and color.

The recipes in this book encourage you to try a variety of grains, such as bulgur and rice, in their whole forms. It is worthwhile experimenting with other, less common whole grains, too, such as quinoa, an ancient South American grain.

Legumes include peas, beans, lentils, and peanuts. They contain fiber, complex carbohydrates, phosphorus, and iron, plus plenty of protein. And they are available in a wide range of appealing colors and shapes, from yellow chickpeas and green split peas to red, green, yellow, brown, and tiny black lentils.

Grains and legumes are both seeds, which are an especially nutritious type of plant food. Other seeds include flaxseed, sesame seeds, and all types of tree nuts, from almonds to walnuts. These are rich in omega-3 fatty acids and high in fiber. Nuts are also a good source of heart-healthy vitamin E.

All about grilling

Whether the product of a happy accident or clever invention, grilling is the oldest cooking method. There is a primal satisfaction in preparing food over an open flame that is difficult to find in any other cooking technique. We have refined the method over the centuries, with the use of grills, racks, charcoal, and now gas grills, but the essential spirit of grilling remains the same.

Most people associate grilling with warm summer weather, and this is often one of the best parts of the experience: cooking and eating in the open air. However, the advent of the popular gas grill has made cold-weather grilling more widely possible. It's a time-saver, too, eliminating the time needed to wait for the coals to heat up.

Even during the most inclement weather, however, remember that you have an indoor substitute for the barbecue: your broiler (grill). While it does not impart the same smoky flavor, it does cook foods quickly using high heat, and almost any grilling recipe can be adapted to the broiler. Moving the oven racks closer to or farther away from the heat element gives you

the same type of control as arranging coals in a kettle grill or turning the knobs of a gas grill.

The grilling recipes in this volume take a straightforward approach: most call for direct grilling over medium heat. The heat level is a little lower than in some grilling cookbooks, in the interest of keeping the recipes as healthful as possible. When meat is cooked at high temperatures over hot coals, carcinogens are created both by an amino acid reaction in the food and by fat dripping onto the coals and releasing smoke.

Try a chimney starter to start a charcoal fire. This simple contraption allows you to light coals without using chemicals. The coals burn in the chimney until they are covered with white ash, at which point you spread them evenly over the bottom of the grill. It is useful to leave a section of the grill empty of coals to create a cooler area, so that if flare-ups occur, you can move the food to the cooler area temporarily. If you want to grill food over an indirect fire, set the food over the empty area and close the lid of the grill to create an ovenlike environment.

To test the accurate temperature level of a charcoal grill, hold your hand about 4 inches (10 cm) above the coals and count the number of seconds you can keep it there comfortably: 1 to 2 seconds means a hot fire, 3 to 4 seconds is a medium fire, and 5 seconds or more is a low fire. Or, use an oven thermometer to check the temperature by setting the thermometer on the rack and closing the lid.

Using a gas grill for direct grilling is simple: turn the knobs to light the burner(s) the food will sit over and adjust the heat level. For indirect grilling, place the food over the unlit burner(s), light the burner(s) on the opposite side, and close the lid.

Gas grills tend to produce less intense heat than grills fired with live coals, so they benefit

from at least 15 minutes of preheating with the lid closed before you start cooking.

Whether you are grilling with charcoal or with gas, be sure to clean the grill rack with a wire brush after heating, and oil both food and rack to prevent sticking. The easiest way to do this is to pour a little oil onto a wadded paper towel and use tongs to rub the rack with it.

Many recipes in this book call for grilling delicate or small pieces of food that can easily slip through the rack. For these items you will want to use a basket—either a fish basket, which allows you to turn fish without fear of losing it, or a shaker basket, which holds small pieces. Or, you can line a portion of the grill with heavy-duty foil and place the food on it. This may extend cooking times slightly.

All about roasting

Roasting or baking vegetables, fruits, and grains—on their own or in combination with meats, poultry, or fish—is a healthy way to cook. Dry-heat cooking forms a crust that helps to retain natural juices and nutrients, resulting in flavorful and wholesome dishes. And unlike other techniques, such as frying or braising, roasting incorporates little additional fat into the dish.

In this book, the terms *roasting* and *baking* are used to cover a variety of oven-cooked dishes. Although definitions vary, in general *roasting* is used to describe cooking a larger piece of meat or vegetables in an uncovered pan in the dry heat of the oven. *Baking* has a variety of different meanings, from cooking small pieces of savory foods, sometimes covered, to

cooking desserts in the oven. A handful of the dishes included here are cooked covered, but most are not. The recipes may be as simple as baked squash or roasted potatoes or as special as a berry gratin or a tomato tart. In general, little liquid is used in roasting or baking. Instead, the dry heat of the oven cooks the food.

In some cases, recipes begin with a stove-top treatment, such as searing, boiling, or steaming, and then the dish is placed in the oven and roasted or baked. Searing is sometimes desirable for meat and poultry dishes. It browns them more fully than roasting alone, thereby enhancing both flavor and appearance. Other types of foods might need to be boiled or steamed to cook them partially before they are combined with other ingredients and baked. For example, spinach and dandelion greens are boiled and drained, and then used in a savory soufflé (page 74) and a baked pasta dish (page 90), respectively.

Conversely, foods might first be roasted or baked, and then used as a component in a finished dish, such as Rib-eye Steaks with Baked Plums (page 229) or Baked Onion and White Eggplant Purée (page 114). Monkfish with Roasted White Corn Salsa (page 128) is another example, with the corn roasted and then used in a salsa.

In most cases, however, fruits or vegetables are roasted directly in the oven, in recipes such as in Roasted Tuna with Olives, Grapes, and Pine Nuts (page 38) or Roasted Turkey Breast with Figs and Lavender (page 38).

Keep in mind these few tips for success. Make sure your ingredients, especially meat, poultry, or fish, are patted dry before seasoning and cooking. This will prevent them from steaming and looking pale instead of roasting and browning well. When oiling food for roasting, use only enough fat to keep the food from sticking to the pan or rack. Most of the ingredients used in these recipes have natural juices that keep them moist. Letting meat and poultry rest for several minutes after roasting will allow these juices to distribute evenly so the food is moist.

For the best results, always make sure your oven is set at the temperature indicated in the recipe. Cooking temperatures vary depending on what you are cooking and the desired texture of the finished dish. For example, to cook firm, dense winter squash all the way through requires long, slow cooking at a relatively low temperature, but raspberries and other tender fruits are best cooked quickly using high heat, so that they hold their shape and retain their flavor. Many ovens heat inaccurately. Use an oven thermometer to check yours and then adjust the setting if needed. Allow the oven to preheat for at least 20 minutes to ensure that it has reached the full temperature before roasting.

Whether you use a roasting pan or a baking dish, make sure it is solid and heavy, with shallow sides for good air circulation.

All about sautéing

Sautéing is an ideal cooking technique for healthy meals because it cooks food quickly, preserving flavors, and uses no liquid, which can leach out nutrients. By intensifying the flavors in foods, sautéing increases the pleasure of eating healthy vegetables, fruits, and even grains. Although generally used for main dishes, this cooking method is also good for making starters, sides, and desserts.

Sautéing calls for cooking food rapidly over high heat in a small amount of fat. The technique—the name of which derives from the French word for "jump"—has been traditionally described as tossing and stirring small pieces of food in a hot pan. The definition has expanded to include larger pieces of fish, poultry, and meat, which are sometimes cut or pounded thin to keep the cooking time short. These larger pieces don't need to be kept moving constantly, though they are sometimes turned several times.

Since there is no water involved, sautéing is known as a dry-heat cooking method, like grilling and roasting. The dry heat and fat create appealing and delicious browning. As food browns, its juices concentrate and caramelize. Adding liquid to the pan at the end of sautéing dissolves these juices and produces a delicious sauce in minutes.

Successful sautéing requires a heavy-bottomed pan that conducts heat evenly. Enameled steel, lined copper, high-quality nonstick, and cast iron are all good choices for materials. You can use either a shallow frying pan with sloping sides or a deeper sauté pan with straight sides, depending on the food. It is important to select a pan size that holds the food comfortably. If the pan is too small, the liquid will collect rather than evaporate and the food will steam rather than sear. If the pan is too big, both the food and pan will dry out and possibly scorch or burn.

As a rule, start sautéing over medium-high or high heat, to ensure a nice browned surface, and then lower the heat so that the food will cook through without burning.

To lessen the risk of foods sticking to the pan, always heat the pan slightly before you add the fat, and then warm up the fat before you add the food. Swirl the pan to coat it evenly with the fat. When sautéing a larger piece of poultry or meat, let it cook undisturbed for a few minutes to brown well on the first side.

There are a few variations on sautéing. Dry sautéing uses no fat and is particularly good for fruits and onions, giving the foods an appetizing flavor and color by searing the surface but not cooking them through. Wet sautéing in a little broth is another way of concentrating flavors without using fat. Shallow frying uses more fat than typical sautéing but far less than deep-frying. It makes foods like potatoes golden and crisp.

Stir-frying, a cousin to sautéing that originated in Asia, calls for cooking small pieces of food in a little oil over the highest possible heat. A flat-bottomed wok works best on conventional stoves because it conducts heat well and evenly. A large, deep, heavy frying pan can also be used. All of your ingredients must be chopped and your sauce ingredients combined before you start to cook because the cooking goes quite quickly. To test the oil, flick a drop of water into the pan; it should sizzle. As you cook, keep the food moving constantly.

The best fats for sautéing are ones that won't burn easily. Canola and grape seed oils are rich in monounsaturated fats that help lower the level of bad cholesterol and increase the good cholesterol. Olive oil has a lower smoke point but is healthful as well. For stir-fries, beneficial peanut oil heats well and gives a traditional flavor. Butter, used in moderation, also adds good flavor to sautéed dishes.

Creating the healthy meal

A commitment to eating a healthful diet based on vegetables, fruits, legumes, and whole grains may mean making some lifestyle changes. For example, you may need to modify your shopping habits, visiting the market more often for seasonal fresh produce, or to reduce the amount of meat and poultry you eat if you have grown accustomed to supersizing. But the rewards will quickly be evident.

To find the best fresh produce, seek out just-harvested, locally grown vegetables and fruits in season at a good produce market or a natural-foods store. Or, better yet, make a visit to a farmers' market part of your weekend recreation. Although organic produce costs more, pesticide-free vegetables and fruits picked at the peak of ripeness on farms in your area also taste better and are more densely packed with nutrients.

The colorful eating philosophy of this cookbook emphasizes fruits, vegetables, and grains, but it doesn't exclude a variety of meats and dairy products. These ingredients add flavor, interest, texture, and nutrients to a wide selection of healthy dishes.

Meat, dairy, and other animal foods appeal to our bodies' craving for nutrient-rich calories, but it is easy to overindulge in these items, especially when you lead a typically sedentary modern life. The secret is to find balance in enjoying these ingredients. Animal foods contribute important proteins and vitamins to the diet, so they have an important place in the healthy kitchen. But they should play a costarring role alongside grain and vegetables rather than dominating the dinner plate. Keep your portions modest: a reasonable portion of cooked, boneless meat, poultry, or seafood is about the size of a deck of playing cards. Remember, too, that certain meats and many cheeses can act as seasoning elements, rather than main events.

While too much fat adds excessive calories to the diet, a certain amount of fat is essential for the body to function properly. Fat also gives the body the sensation of being satiated, which helps us to avoid overeating. Most of the recipes in this book use olive or canola oil as the primary fat for cooking food. These oils are high in monounsaturated fat, which raises the level of good cholesterol and lowers the bad. Fish and shellfish contribute healthy fats and play a key role in the colorful kitchen.

Herbs and spices are essential flavor boosters in creating healthful dishes. A simple scattering of minced fresh parsley adds not only color and intense flavor to many different foods, but also valuable green antioxidants. Vinegar, citrus juice, and citrus zest are other important flavorings in the healthy kitchen. They contribute an acidic note that heightens other flavors without making a dish taste too rich or heavy.

The simple decision to cook your meals at home, rather than loading up on takeout or eating in restaurants, is an important step toward healthier eating. The recipes in this cookbook are deliberately easy to prepare and streamlined. Preparation and cooking times are listed at the beginning of each recipe to help you fit their assembly into your daily routine. Many dishes can be prepared in a half hour or a little more, making them perfect for a midweek family supper. If you shop and cook more frequently, you will find that both activities become more of a habit, even if you a lead a busy life. And the rewards are great. Eating meals at home is often the highlight of the day. It bonds friends, couples, and families together and makes us appreciate all the wonderful foods nature has provided us.

eggplants prunes blackberries

PURPLE AND BLUE FRUITS AND VEGETABLES PROMOTE

purple carrots black currants

MEMORY FUNCTION • HELP PROMOTE URINARY TRACT

lavender blue potatoes purple

HEALTH • BOOST THE IMMUNE SYSTEM • HELP PROMOTE

cabbage raisins black grapes

HEALTHY AGING • OFFER ANTIOXIDANTS FOR HEALING

purple figs black plums purple

AND PROTECTION • HELP REDUCE THE RISK OF SOME

bell peppers purple asparagus

CANCERS • PURPLE AND BLUE FRUITS AND VEGETABLES

Purple & blue

Rich-hued blueberries, eggplants (aubergines), purple cabbages, black plums—the purple and blue members of the produce world offer wonderful flavors and create a gorgeous effect on the dinner plate. And this color family includes some intriguing surprises: fruits and vegetables that are better known in other shades, such as purple asparagus, carrots, potatoes, and dusky sweet peppers (capsicums).

All the purple and blue vegetables and fruits are gems because they are both alluring to the senses and packed with potent health benefits. Their intense and unusual color—a sure sign of abundant antioxidants that protect the heart and memory—can add vivid hues to dishes all year round.

In spring, purple asparagus glistens in a warm citrus dressing (page 31), while on a balmy summer night, the sweet-tart flavors of wild blueberries and rhubarb make the perfect foil to salmon quickly seared in a hot pan, the fish delivering both beneficial omega-3 fatty acids and delicious flavor (page 48). When the

weather cools, a lean duck breast, served over sautéed purple cabbage seasoned with the warm flavors of rosemary and ginger, goes well with a robust red wine (page 51), while pan-fried blue potatoes topped with crisp sage prove the perfect partner for a thick veal chop or a tender rib-eye steak (page 57).

SPRING	SUMMER	AUTUMN	WINTER
purple asparagus	purple bell peppers	purple-tipped Belgian endive	purple-tipped Belgian endive
purple-tipped Belgian endive	blackberries	purple bell peppers	purple cabbage
blueberries	black currants	blueberries	purple carrots
purple cabbage	blueberries	purple cabbage	dried currants
purple carrots	eggplant	purple carrots	dried figs
fresh black currants	purple figs	dried currants	purple grapes
dried currants	lavender	eggplant	black olives
prunes	black plums	purple figs	blue potatoes
raisins		purple grapes	prunes
		black plums	raisins
		blue potatoes	
		prunes	
		raisins	

eggplant crisps with yogurt dipping sauce

2 very firm Asian eggplants (slender aubergines)

2 Tbsp olive oil

1 cup (8 oz/250 g) plain low-fat or whole yogurt

1 cucumber, peeled and coarsely chopped

8 oil-packed sun-dried tomatoes, finely chopped

2 cloves garlic, minced

Preheat oven to 400°F (200°C).

Using a mandoline or a sharp knife, cut eggplant into very thin rounds about ⅛ inch (3 mm) thick. Arrange on a baking sheet in a single layer, using a second baking sheet if necessary. Drizzle with olive oil and turn to coat evenly.

Roast eggplant until golden on bottom, about 15 minutes. Turn slices and roast until golden brown on second side and crisp, about 15 minutes more.

Meanwhile, in a bowl, combine yogurt, cucumber, sun-dried tomatoes, garlic, and ¼ tsp salt and stir to mix well.

Remove eggplant crisps to paper towels to drain. Sprinkle with 2 tsp salt. Serve warm or at room temperature with yogurt sauce.

To prepare: 10 minutes

To cook: 30 minutes

4 starter servings

roasted purple carrots & fennel

1 large or 2 medium fennel bulbs, trimmed (see Note)

½ lb (250 g) purple carrots, trimmed

1½ Tbsp olive oil

1 tsp fresh thyme leaves

1½ Tbsp Pernod

Preheat oven to 375°F (190°C). Cut fennel bulb(s) in half from top to bottom, then cut each half into wedges about ½ inch (12 mm) thick. Cut carrots in half crosswise if quite long; otherwise, leave whole. Arrange carrots and fennel in a baking dish just large enough to hold them in a single layer. Drizzle with olive oil, sprinkle with thyme and ½ tsp salt, and turn to coat evenly.

Roast until fennel has caramelized slightly and carrots have begun to wrinkle slightly, about 35 minutes. Remove from oven, pour Pernod over, and carefully light fumes with a long match. Shake pan slightly until flames go out. Serve at once.

Note: To trim fennel bulbs, cut off stems, feathery tops, and any bruised outer stalks.

To prepare: 5 minutes

To cook: 35 minutes

4 side-dish servings

grilled pizzas with blue potatoes & onions

Pizza Dough

1²/₃ cups (13 fl oz/410 ml) warm water (about 105°F/40°C)

1 package (2¼ tsp) active dry yeast

1 tsp sugar

1 tsp salt

2 Tbsp olive oil

About 4 cups (20 oz/625 g) all-purpose (plain) flour

Caramelized Onions

2 Tbsp olive oil

3 large red onions, halved and each half thinly sliced

1 Tbsp dark brown sugar

1 Tbsp balsamic vinegar

1 tsp fresh rosemary leaves, chopped

1 lb (500 g) blue potatoes, steamed until tender and sliced

8 oz (250 g) mozzarella cheese, shredded (2 cups)

6 oz (185 g) fresh goat cheese or feta cheese, crumbled (1¼ cups)

¼ cup (1¼ oz/40 g) pine nuts, toasted (see Note, page 37)

Minced fresh rosemary for garnish

For Dough: Put warm water in a small bowl and stir in yeast and sugar. Let stand until foamy, about 5 minutes. Transfer to a food processor and add salt, olive oil, and 3 cups (15 oz/470 g) flour. Process until a ball forms, 2–3 minutes. If dough is too sticky, add a little more flour. Dough should be slightly sticky and soft. Alternatively, mix in a stand mixer or in a bowl with a wooden spoon. Place dough on a lightly floured work surface and knead until smooth and elastic, about 7 minutes. Put dough in an oiled bowl, turn to coat, and cover with a damp towel. Let rise in a warm place until doubled in bulk, 1½–2 hours.

For Onions: Heat olive oil in a large sauté pan over medium heat. Add onions, brown sugar, vinegar, rosemary, ½ cup (4 fl oz/125 ml) water, ½ tsp salt, and several grindings of pepper and stir to mix. Cover and cook until onions are soft, about 15 minutes. Uncover and cook until all liquid has evaporated and onions are golden, 3–5 minutes more. Remove from heat.

Build a fire in a charcoal grill for cooking over medium-high heat or preheat a gas grill to 375°F (190°C). Line a baking sheet with a double layer of heavy-duty aluminum foil and sprinkle lightly with flour. For easy assembly, arrange onions, potatoes, mozzarella and goat cheeses, and pine nuts on a platter. Punch dough down and divide into 12 balls. Roll out each into a thin round 6 inches (15 cm) in diameter. Place 3 or 4 dough rounds on prepared pan. Slide foil onto grill and cook, uncovered, until bottoms of crusts are lightly golden, about 2 minutes.

Turn crusts and sprinkle with mozzarella. Add a layer of potato slices, then caramelized onions, and then goat cheese, dividing evenly. Sprinkle with pine nuts and season with salt and pepper. Cover grill and cook until crust is crisp and cooked through and edges are golden and mozzarella is melted, 2–3 minutes more. Repeat to cook other pizzas. As pizzas are cooked, sprinkle with rosemary, cut into wedges, and serve at once.

Notes: If you prefer pizza topping to be crusty and browned, slide grilled pizzas under a preheated broiler (grill) for a couple of minutes.

To prepare: 45 minutes, plus 2 hours for dough to rise

To cook: 35 minutes

12 starter servings (twelve 6-inch/15-cm pizzas)

purple asparagus with orange vinaigrette

14 spears fat purple or green asparagus (about 1 lb/500 g), tough ends trimmed

½ tsp olive oil

2 tsp minced shallot

Juice of 1 navel orange

1 Tbsp lime juice

1 tsp lavender honey

2 Tbsp fresh chervil leaves for garnish (optional)

Cut asparagus tips on the diagonal and set aside. Cut 10 stalks on the diagonal into slices ¼ inch (6 mm) thick. Using a vegetable peeler, remove the colored outside of the remaining 4 stalks in long strips. Discard interior of the spears or reserve for another use.

Blanch asparagus tips and strips in boiling water for 30 seconds. Remove with a slotted spoon and cool in ice water. Spin in a salad spinner or pat dry with paper towels.

Heat oil in a nonstick frying pan over medium-high heat. Add shallot and sauté until starting to soften, about 30 seconds. Add citrus juices, then stir in honey until it dissolves. Remove pan from heat.

To serve, arrange asparagus slices and shaved strips on 4 salad plates. Spoon on warm dressing and garnish with chervil, if using.

To prepare: 10 minutes

To cook: 3 minutes

4 starter or side-dish servings

scallops with bell pepper dressing

16 fresh sea scallops

3 Tbsp extra-virgin olive oil

1½ tsp ground cumin

¼ tsp red pepper flakes

Zest and juice of 1 lime

Sugar

1 large purple bell pepper (capsicum), seeded and very finely diced

1 green (spring) onion, thinly sliced

1 small clove garlic, crushed

2 tsp white wine vinegar

Put scallops in a bowl. Add 2 Tbsp olive oil, 1 tsp cumin, red pepper flakes, lime zest, a pinch of sugar, and salt and black pepper to taste. Turn to coat evenly. Cover and refrigerate for 30 minutes–6 hours.

In another bowl, stir together bell pepper, green onion, garlic, remaining 1 Tbsp olive oil, vinegar, remaining ½ tsp cumin, and a pinch of sugar to make a dressing. Taste and adjust seasoning. Let stand for 30 minutes.

Build a fire in a charcoal grill for cooking over high heat or preheat a gas grill to 400°F (200°C). Oil grill rack. Grill scallops for about 1 minute per side, just to sear. Do not overcook, or they will be rubbery.

Divide dressing among 4 warmed plates. Top each serving with 4 scallops. Drizzle with lime juice and serve at once.

To prepare: 10 minutes, plus 30 minutes to marinate

To cook: 2 minutes

4 servings

grilled eggplant & feta cheese rolls

2 medium globe eggplants (aubergines), about 1½ lb (750 g) total

2 Tbsp extra-virgin olive oil, plus extra as needed

8 oz (250 g) feta cheese, crumbled (1½ cups)

Zest of 1 lemon, plus lemon juice for drizzling

2 Tbsp chopped fresh parsley

1 tsp fresh thyme leaves

Chopped red onion and green (spring) onion for garnish

Build a fire in a charcoal grill for cooking over medium heat or preheat a gas grill to 350°F (180°C). Oil grill rack. Cut eggplants lengthwise into slices about ¼ inch (6 mm) thick. Brush slices on both sides with olive oil and sprinkle with salt and pepper. Grill, turning once, until golden and softened, 4–5 minutes per side. Remove from heat and place in a paper bag or sealed container to steam and cool (this softens them fully and makes them more tender). Let cool to room temperature, about 20 minutes.

In a bowl, toss feta with 2 Tbsp olive oil, lemon zest, parsley, and thyme. Place about 2 Tbsp of feta mixture along short edge of a grilled eggplant slice and roll up tightly to enclose. Repeat to make remaining rolls.

Arrange rolls, seam side down, on a serving platter or individual plates. Drizzle with olive oil and lemon juice and serve at room temperature, garnished with bell pepper and green onion.

To cook: 10 minutes, plus 20 minutes to cool

To prepare: 10 minutes

6 starter servings (12–14 rolls)

purple carrots glazed with red wine

2 tsp butter or canola oil

24 young, slender purple or orange carrots

½ cup (4 fl oz/125 ml) fruity red wine such as Beaujolais

⅓ cup (3 fl oz/80 ml) low-sodium chicken broth

1 tsp peppercorns, coarsely cracked

Melt butter or heat oil in a nonstick frying pan over medium-high heat. Add carrots, stir to coat, and cook for 2 minutes. Add wine, broth, and peppercorns. Reduce heat to medium and cook until most of the liquid has evaporated and carrots are fork-tender, about 10 minutes. Serve carrots hot or warm.

Note: Since their purple color and many of their nutrients are in the skin, do not peel carrots. If only large carrots are available, cut them on the diagonal into slices ½ inch (12 mm) thick.

To prepare: 5 minutes

To cook: 12 minutes

4 side-dish servings

bacon-wrapped prunes

Wrap pitted prunes in bacon, securing the bacon with toothpicks. Grill wrapped prunes over medium-high heat, turning them often, until the bacon is crisp. Prunes get very hot on the grill, so let cool a little before serving.

grilled blue potatoes

Dice blue potatoes and mound on squares of heavy-duty foil. Season with olive oil, chopped garlic, fresh rosemary and thyme, lemon juice, salt, and pepper. Close into pouches and grill over medium heat until tender, about 15 minutes.

grilled purple cabbage

Thinly slice a head of purple cabbage and toss with grape seed oil, grated ginger, salt, and pepper. Put in an oiled basket and grill over medium-high heat, shaking often, until wilted. Garnish with rice vinegar, sesame oil, and sesame seeds.

figs with ricotta

Halve purple figs and brush cut sides with canola oil. Grill over medium-high heat until softened and lightly browned. Place atop small scoops of ricotta cheese mixed with a little lemon zest and vanilla extract (essence) and drizzle with honey.

fig & purple endive salad

2 Tbsp dried currants

2 Tbsp orange juice

4 Tbsp extra-virgin olive oil

1 Tbsp balsamic vinegar

1 tsp sugar

1 tsp Dijon mustard

6 ripe but firm purple figs, halved

2 large heads purple-tipped Belgian endive (chicory/witloof), cores intact, cut into 1-inch (2.5-cm) wedges

1 fennel bulb (about ½ lb/250 g) trimmed and thinly sliced lengthwise

1 Tbsp lemon juice

2 Tbsp pine nuts, toasted (see Note)

Build a fire in a charcoal grill for cooking over medium heat or preheat a gas grill to 350°F (180°C). Oil grill rack.

Combine currants and orange juice in a microwave-safe bowl, cover, and microwave on high for 1 minute. In a large bowl, whisk together 3 Tbsp olive oil, vinegar, sugar, mustard, ½ tsp salt, and a few grindings of pepper. Stir in currant mixture. Let dressing stand for 15 minutes.

In a bowl, combine figs, endive, fennel, remaining 1 Tbsp olive oil, and lemon juice and toss to coat evenly. Grill, turning often, until vegetables are wilted and figs are softened, about 5 minutes. Remove to bowl with dressing and toss gently to mix. Taste and adjust seasoning. Arrange on a serving platter and serve at once, garnished with pine nuts.

Note: To toast pine nuts, put them in a small, dry frying pan over medium heat. Stir often until just starting to turn golden, about 2 minutes; watch carefully, or they may burn. Remove at once to a plate to cool.

To prepare: 10 minutes, plus 15 minutes to stand

To cook: 6 minutes

4–6 side-dish servings

halibut & purple grapes

1½ lb (750 g) skinless halibut or other firm white fish fillets, cut into 1½-inch (4-cm) pieces

Zest of 1 lime

16 large seedless purple grapes

¼ cup (2 fl oz/60 ml) orange juice

2 Tbsp lime juice

4 tsp chopped fresh dill

2 tsp butter

Build a fire in a charcoal grill for cooking over medium heat or preheat a gas grill to 350°F (180°C).

Put fish in a bowl. Add lime zest, ¾ tsp salt, and several grindings of pepper. Turn fish to coat evenly. Cut out four 12-inch (30-cm) squares of heavy-duty aluminum foil. Arrange squares on a work surface and divide fish and grapes evenly among them, mounding in centers. Stir orange and lime juices together in a bowl and spoon 1½ Tbsp over each portion. Sprinkle each with 1 tsp dill and dot with ½ tsp butter. Fold foil over fish and crimp edges to seal.

Arrange parcels on grill and cook for 7 minutes. Remove one parcel, open carefully, and test for doneness; fish should just flake in center when prodded with a fork and should be opaque throughout. If not done, reseal, return to grill, and cook all parcels 1–3 minutes more. Open the parcels and arrange the contents on warmed serving dishes.

To prepare: 10 minutes

To cook: 10 minutes

4 servings

roasted tuna with olives, grapes & pine nuts

3 Tbsp olive oil

1 cup (6 oz/185 g) seedless purple grapes, some cut in half

½ cup (2½ oz/75 g) pitted oil-cured black olives, coarsely chopped

4 ahi tuna steaks, each about 5 oz (155 g) and ½ inch (12 mm) thick

3 Tbsp pine nuts

Preheat oven to 450°F (230°C). Pour 1 Tbsp olive oil into a shallow baking dish just large enough to hold tuna steaks in a single layer. Add grapes and olives and turn to coat evenly with oil. Arrange tuna steaks among olives and grapes, season with 1 tsp salt and 1 tsp pepper, and drizzle with 2 Tbsp olive oil. Sprinkle pine nuts over all. Roast until lower one-third of tuna steaks are opaque, about 10 minutes. Turn tuna steaks and cook until second side is opaque but tuna is still pink in center for medium-rare, 5–8 minutes more.

To serve, place a tuna steak on each warmed plate and spoon grape and olive mixture alongside.

To prepare: 5 minutes

To cook: 15 minutes

4 servings

roasted turkey breast with figs & lavender

1 turkey breast, 2½ lb (1.25 kg)

1 tsp dried lavender blossoms, crushed

¾ cup (4 oz/125 g) dried purple figs, coarsely chopped

2 Tbsp minced shallot

½ cup (4 fl oz/125 ml) low-sodium chicken broth

1 Tbsp balsamic vinegar

Preheat oven to 375°F (190°C). Rub turkey with lavender, 1 tsp salt, and 1 tsp pepper. Place in a shallow, flameproof roasting pan and roast, basting occasionally with pan juices, until skin is golden brown and juices run clear when pierced to bone with a sharp knife, about 40 minutes.

Remove from oven and remove turkey from pan. Make a bed of figs and shallot in roasting pan, then put turkey on top and add 3 Tbsp of chicken broth to the pan. Return pan to oven and roast until figs are soft and shallot is translucent, 10–15 minutes.

Remove turkey breast to a carving board, tent loosely with foil, and let rest for 10 minutes. Place roasting pan on a burner or two over medium-high heat. Add remaining 5 Tbsp (2½ fl oz/75 ml) chicken broth and the vinegar and cook, stirring to scrape up browned bits from bottom of pan and mashing figs to make a thick sauce, about 1 minute.

Carve turkey into thick slices, drizzle with pan sauce, and serve at once.

To prepare: 10 minutes

To cook: 1 hour, plus 10 minutes to rest

6 servings

chicken & eggplant salad

⅓ cup (3 fl oz/80 ml) olive oil

⅓ cup (3 fl oz/80 ml) lemon juice

3 Tbsp homemade or purchased basil pesto

Zest of 1 lemon

4 skinless, boneless chicken breast halves, sliced on diagonal

1 globe eggplant (aubergine)

2 cups (12 oz/375 g) black or red cherry tomatoes, halved

1 cup (5 oz/155 g) pitted Kalamata or other rich-flavored black olives

9 cups (9 oz/280 g) mixed tender salad greens

In a glass measuring pitcher, stir together olive oil, lemon juice, pesto, and lemon zest. Pour two-thirds of mixture into a bowl to use as a marinade; set aside remainder for dressing. Add sliced chicken to bowl and coat with marinade. Cover and refrigerate for 30 minutes–6 hours.

Build a fire in a charcoal grill for cooking over medium heat or preheat a gas grill to 350°F (180°C). Oil grill rack. Halve eggplant lengthwise, then cut each half crosswise into slices ½ inch (12 mm) thick. Brush eggplant slices on both sides with olive oil and sprinkle with salt and pepper. Remove chicken from marinade, discarding marinade. Arrange chicken and eggplant on hot grill. Grill, turning once, until eggplant is golden and chicken is opaque throughout, 3–4 minutes per side. Remove to a serving bowl and let cool completely.

Add reserved pesto mixture, tomatoes, olives, and salad greens. Toss gently to combine. Serve at room temperature.

To prepare: 10 minutes, plus 30 minutes to marinate

To cook: 10 minutes

4 servings

chicken & fig skewers

1 Tbsp olive oil

1 Tbsp balsamic vinegar

2 tsp maple syrup

¼ tsp Chinese five-spice powder

1½ lb (750 g) skinless, boneless chicken thighs or breasts, cut into 2-inch (5-cm) cubes

16 cipolline or boiling onions

4 large fresh purple figs, quartered

In a bowl, combine olive oil, vinegar, maple syrup, and five-spice powder. Add chicken and turn to coat. Cover and refrigerate for 30 minutes–4 hours. Remove from refrigerator 15–20 minutes before grilling.

Soak 8 wooden skewers in water to cover for 30 minutes. Build a fire in a charcoal grill for cooking over medium heat or preheat a gas grill to 350°F (180°C). Oil grill rack.

Bring a saucepan of water to a boil. Add onions, return to a boil, and cook for 2 minutes. Drain in a colander and place under cold running water until cool to the touch. Trim off ends and gently slip off skins, keeping onions intact. Thread onions, chicken, and figs onto skewers.

Grill, turning often, until chicken is opaque throughout, 10–12 minutes. Allow 2 skewers per serving, or remove chicken, figs, and onions from skewers and arrange on a warmed serving platter.

To prepare: 15 minutes, plus 30 minutes to marinate

To cook: 12 minutes

4 servings

roasted pork & prunes

**1 boneless pork loin roast,
1½–2 lb (750 g–1 kg)**

1 Tbsp olive oil

1 tsp paprika

1 tsp dried sage, crushed

4 slices bacon, coarsely chopped

2 Tbsp minced shallot

**4 tablespoons (2 fl oz/60 ml) dry
white wine**

1½ cups (9 oz/280 g) pitted prunes

Preheat oven to 400°F (200°C). Rub pork all over with ½ Tbsp olive oil, then rub with paprika, sage, 1 tsp salt, and 1 tsp pepper.

Heat ½ Tbsp olive oil in a frying pan over medium-high heat. Add bacon and sauté until it is sizzling, about 2 minutes. Reduce heat to low and continue cooking, stirring occasionally, until fat is rendered and bacon is crisp, about 5 minutes more. Remove from heat. Using a slotted spoon, remove bacon to paper towels to drain, leaving fat in pan.

Return pan to medium-high heat. When fat is hot, add pork and sear until bottom is browned, about 3 minutes. Using tongs to turn and hold pork, brown all other sides, 2–3 minutes per side. Add shallot while browning last side, stirring to coat. Remove pork to a platter. Raise heat to high, add 2 Tbsp wine, and stir to scrape up browned bits from bottom of pan. Return bacon to pan and stir to combine, then pour contents of pan into a shallow, flameproof roasting pan. Add pork and any accumulated juices from platter.

Roast for 15 minutes. Remove from oven, surround roast with prunes, add remaining 2 Tbsp wine to pan, and return to oven. Reduce heat to 375°F (190°C) and continue roasting until pork registers 140°–145°F (60°–63°C) on an instant-read thermometer, about 30 minutes more.

Remove roast to a carving board, tent loosely with foil, and let rest for 10 minutes. Carve roast into slices 1 inch (2.5 cm) thick. Arrange slices overlapping on a warmed platter. Place roasting pan on stove top over medium heat and gently reheat prunes and pan juices. Spoon prunes and juices down center or alongside sliced roast. Serve at once.

To prepare: 10 minutes

*To cook: 1 hour, plus
10 minutes to rest*

4–6 servings

roasted eggplant, asian style

Cut Asian eggplants (slender aubergines) in half lengthwise, drizzle with oil, sprinkle with minced garlic, and roast in a hot oven until tender. Drizzle with soy sauce and sprinkle with toasted sesame seeds and chopped basil before serving.

baked stuffed blue potatoes

Bake potatoes until tender. Cut in half lengthwise. Scoop out flesh and mix with butter, grated Gruyère cheese, and salt and pepper. Refill potato shells, then top with a little more grated cheese and put under broiler (grill) until tops are golden.

sweet blueberry
flat bread

Roll out your favorite pizza dough into a round. Transfer to a baking sheet. Sprinkle with sugar and cover with blueberries. Sprinkle with more sugar and dot with butter. Bake like a pizza until crust browns and berries bubble.

raisin & prune chutney
with lemon

In a baking dish, combine raisins, chopped prunes and onion, brown sugar, lemon juice and zest, balsamic vinegar, and a small amount of water. Cover and bake at 300°F (150°C), stirring occasionally, until juices thicken, about 40 minutes.

baked pilaf with currants, lavender & almonds

½ cup (3 oz/90 g) wild rice

½ cup (3½ oz/105 g) long-grain white rice

1 Tbsp butter

1 stalk celery, minced

2 Tbsp minced yellow onion

⅓ cup (2 oz/60 g) dried currants

½ cup (2½ oz/75 g) chopped almonds, toasted (see Note, page 84)

⅓ cup (3 fl oz/80 ml) orange juice

1 tsp dried lavender blossoms, crushed

1 orange, peeled and cut crosswise into slices ¼ inch (6 mm) thick

In a saucepan over medium-high heat, bring 1½ cups (12 fl oz/375 ml) water to a boil, stir in ½ tsp salt, and add wild rice. Return to a boil, cover, and reduce heat to low. Cook until rice grains have plumped and water is absorbed, about 45 minutes. Drain rice well in a colander.

Meanwhile, in another saucepan over medium-high heat, bring 1 cup (8 fl oz/250 ml) water to a boil and stir in ½ tsp salt. Add white rice, return to a boil, cover, and reduce heat to low. Cook until rice is tender and water is absorbed, about 20 minutes. Remove from heat and set aside.

Preheat oven to 375°F (190°C) and lightly butter a medium baking dish. In a frying pan over medium-high heat, melt butter. When it foams, add celery, onion, currants, and half the almonds. Reduce heat to medium and sauté until celery and onion are translucent, about 2 minutes. Add white rice and wild rice and cook, stirring, until rice glistens, 2–3 minutes more. Add orange juice, lavender, 1 tsp salt, and ½ tsp pepper. Taste and adjust seasoning.

Spoon pilaf into prepared baking dish. Spread evenly, then sprinkle with remaining almonds. Arrange orange slices on top. Bake until pilaf is heated throughout and orange slices have softened slightly, about 30 minutes. Serve hot, directly from baking dish.

To prepare: 10 minutes

To cook: 1 hour 20 minutes

4 side-dish servings

herbed blue potatoes

2 Tbsp olive oil

8 medium or 16 small blue potatoes, scrubbed and halved lengthwise

Leaves from 4–6 sprigs rosemary

Preheat oven to 375°F (190°C). Drizzle olive oil into a baking dish. Add potatoes and turn to coat on all sides. Remove to a baking sheet and arrange cut side up. Gently press 8–10 rosemary leaves onto surface of each in an attractive pattern. Sprinkle with 1 tsp salt.

Roast until potatoes are easily pierced through to their centers with the tip of a sharp knife, about 1 hour. Serve hot.

To prepare: 10 minutes

To cook: 1 hour

4 side-dish servings

salmon with wild blueberry & rhubarb sauce

Blueberry & Rhubarb Sauce

1 Tbsp canola oil

1 small onion, cut half, halves cut into slices

2–3 thin stalks rhubarb, about 6 oz/180 g, cut into slices ½ inch (12 mm) thick (1½ cups)

1½ cups (6 oz/185 g) fresh or frozen wild or cultivated blueberries

2 Tbsp blueberry or wildflower honey

½ cup (4 fl oz/125 ml) unsweetened blueberry juice (optional; see Note)

¼ tsp wasabi powder or paste

1 lb (500 g) wild king salmon fillet, cut crosswise into 4 equal pieces

For Sauce: Heat oil in a sauté pan over medium-high heat. Add onion and sauté until lightly browned, 4–5 minutes. Add rhubarb and cook, stirring, until bottom of pan looks syrupy, 3–4 minutes. Add blueberries and honey. Add blueberry juice if using wild berries (see Note). When berries start to soften, after about 1 minute, lower heat to medium. Simmer until rhubarb is tender and collapsing, about 5 minutes. Remove from heat and stir in wasabi. Transfer to a bowl and cover to keep warm.

Heat a dry nonstick frying pan over medium heat until hot. Sprinkle fish with ½ tsp salt and ⅛ tsp pepper. Arrange salmon in pan and cook until browned and crisp on bottom, about 4 minutes. Using a wide spatula, turn salmon and brown on second side, about 3 minutes, lowering heat if necessary to prevent burning. Fish should flake easily with a fork and still be translucent in the center only.

To serve, divide fish among warmed plates, spoon sauce in the center of each plate, and place fish atop sauce.

Note: If using fresh wild berries, include the blueberry juice. Fresh wild blueberries contain less moisture than cultivated ones or frozen ones.

To prepare: 10 minutes

To cook: 20 minutes

4 servings

stir-fried pork with black plums

1 Tbsp lime juice

1 tsp hoisin sauce

2 tsp cornstarch (cornflour)

2 tsp canola oil

12 oz (375 g) pork tenderloin, sliced on diagonal ½ inch (12 mm) thick

½ cup (4 fl oz/125 ml) apple juice

¼ tsp grated fresh ginger

1 small jalapeño chile, seeded and cut lengthwise into thin strips

2 large black plums, halved, pitted, and cut into ½-inch (12-mm) wedges

In a small bowl, mix together lime juice, hoisin sauce, and cornstarch. Set hoisin mixture aside.

Heat oil in a large frying pan over medium-high heat. Brown pork slices, turning once, 6–8 minutes total. Transfer meat to a plate. Add apple juice, ginger, and chile to pan and stir to scrape up browned bits. Boil until liquid is reduced by one-third, about 3 minutes. Add plums and hoisin mixture and return pork to pan. Stir until sauce thickens, coating meat, about 3 minutes. Arrange pork on a warmed serving platter, spoon sauce over, and serve at once.

Note: Serve with sautéed or steamed spinach.

To prepare: 15 minutes

To cook: 12 minutes

4 servings

duck with purple cabbage, blackberries & port

2 Tbsp plus 1 tsp canola oil

6 cups finely shredded purple cabbage (1 head, about 1¾ lb/875 g)

⅔ cup (5 fl oz/160 ml) unsweetened black cherry juice

⅓ cup (3 fl oz/80 ml) ruby port

1 Tbsp ginger marmalade or orange marmalade

1 tsp chopped fresh rosemary

1 cup (4 oz/125 g) fresh or frozen blackberries

1 whole boneless moulard duck breast, about 1¼ lb (625 g)

Preheat oven to 450°F (230°C). Heat 2 Tbsp oil in a sauté pan over medium-high heat. Sauté cabbage until wilted, about 5 minutes. Stir in cherry juice, port, marmalade, and rosemary and cook until cabbage is soft and most of liquid has evaporated, about 15 minutes. Add berries and cook about 2 minutes more.

Heat remaining 1 tsp oil in an ovenproof frying pan over medium heat. Sauté duck, skin side down, until skin is browned and fat is rendered, about 12 minutes. Discard fat and turn duck. Place duck in oven and roast until an instant-read thermometer inserted into thickest part registers 150°F (65°C), about 12 minutes. Let rest for 10 minutes.

Arrange cabbage on a warmed serving platter. Remove and discard duck skin. Slice breast crosswise and arrange over cabbage. Serve at once.

To prepare: 15 minutes

To cook: 1 hour

6 servings

sichuan beef with eggplant

¾ lb (375 g) flank steak

¾ lb (375 g) Asian eggplants (slender aubergines)

2 tsp sugar

¼ cup (2 fl oz/60 ml) low-sodium chicken broth

2 Tbsp low-sodium soy sauce

2 Tbsp sherry

2 tsp rice wine vinegar

¼ cup (2 fl oz/60 ml) peanut oil

3 Tbsp chopped garlic

½ cup (1½ oz/45 g) chopped green (spring) onions, including white and tender green parts

Steamed brown or white rice for serving

2 Tbsp chopped cilantro (fresh coriander) for garnish

Freeze meat for up to 1 hour to make it easier to slice. Thinly slice with the grain, then cut slices into pieces 2 inches (5 cm) long. Set aside.

Trim eggplants and cut on the diagonal into slices ½ inch (12 mm) thick. Stack and cut slices lengthwise into thirds. Set aside.

In a small bowl, mix together sugar, broth, soy sauce, sherry, vinegar, and ¼ tsp pepper. Set aside.

Heat oil in a wok over medium-high heat until almost smoking. Using a slotted spoon, transfer beef to hot oil. Stir-fry until color changes, about 1½ minutes. Remove to a plate using a slotted spoon. Add garlic and green onions to wok and stir-fry until fragrant, about 30 seconds. Remove to plate with beef. Pour off all but 2 Tbsp oil and add eggplant. Stir-fry until it starts to soften, about 2 minutes. Add soy sauce mixture and cook until eggplant is tender, about 2 minutes more.

Return beef, garlic, and green onions to wok. When beef is cooked through, about 2 minutes, spoon hot stir-fry hot over rice and garnish with cilantro. Serve at once.

To prepare: 35 minutes, plus 1 hour to freeze meat

To cook: 8 minutes

4 main-course servings, 6 with other dishes

savory & spicy blackberry sauce

After sautéing pork or turkey, add ½ cup (4 fl oz/125 ml) black currant juice and a minced shallot to pan over medium heat and deglaze. Add blackberries and a pinch of chipotle chile powder. Cook for 1 minute, and serve over meat.

eggplant caponata

Sauté diced red onion and eggplant (aubergine) in olive oil until softened. Add chopped tomato, raisins, capers, a dash of vinegar, and a smear of tomato paste. When eggplant is tender, season with salt and pepper. Serve at room temperature.

purple cabbage
with raisins

Sauté shredded purple cabbage in melted butter until limp. Add a handful of raisins, 1 or 2 cinnamon sticks, honey, a splash of balsamic vinegar, apple cider as needed to moisten, and salt and pepper. Cook until tender-crisp, then serve warm.

blueberries with lemon

Warm 1 cup (4 oz/125 g) fresh or frozen berries in butter. Add plenty of wild blueberry juice, a splash of lemon liqueur, and 1 tsp cornstarch (cornflour). Boil, stirring, until sauce is clear. Serve lukewarm over sliced angel food cake.

wild rice with purple bell pepper & pecans

2 Tbsp peanut oil

1 medium purple or green bell pepper (capsicum), seeded and diced

1 small red onion, chopped

2 cups cooked wild rice, frozen and thawed (see Note)

½ tsp grated orange zest

¼ cup (1 oz/30 g) coarsely chopped pecans

Heat oil in a wok over medium-high heat until almost smoking. Add bell pepper and onion and stir-fry until onion is translucent, about 2 minutes. Add rice and orange zest and stir-fry until rice is heated through, about 1½ minutes. Stir in pecans. Serve hot or warm.

Note: Freezing rice reduces sticking when it is stir-fried.

To prepare: 10 minutes

To cook: 4 minutes

4 side-dish servings

pan-fried blue potatoes with sage

¾ lb (375 g) small blue or red new potatoes

¼ cup (2 fl oz/60 ml) olive oil

10 medium fresh sage leaves

In a saucepan, cover potatoes with 2 inches (5 cm) cold water. Bring to a boil over high heat and cook until a thin knife inserted into potatoes meets only slight resistance, about 20 minutes. Drain potatoes and pat dry. Slice potatoes ⅜ inch (1 cm) thick, discarding any loose skin.

Heat oil in a medium sauté pan over medium-high heat. Arrange potatoes in a single layer, leaving ¼ inch (6 mm) between slices (you may need to cook them in 2 batches). Cook potatoes, turning once, until golden and crusty on both sides, 8–9 minutes total. Remove potatoes with slotted spoon and drain on paper towels, blotting dry.

Add sage leaves to pan; they will sizzle and curl slightly. In 10 seconds, turn leaves with tongs and fry for 5 seconds more. Drain sage on fresh paper towels.

Arrange potatoes on a warmed platter, sprinkle with 1 tsp salt, and top with sage leaves. Serve at once.

To prepare: 5 minutes

To cook: 30 minutes

6 starter servings or 4 side-dish servings

grilled plums
with kirsch cream

9 large black plums, halved and pitted

2 Tbsp superfine (caster) sugar

2 Tbsp kirsch

Canola or grape seed oil

2 tsp butter, cut into 18 tiny bits

1 cup (8 fl oz/250 ml) heavy (double) cream

1 Tbsp powdered (icing) sugar

1 tsp vanilla extract (essence)

Place plums cut side up in a shallow dish. Sprinkle with superfine sugar and drizzle with 1 Tbsp kirsch. Let stand for 30 minutes–4 hours.

Build a fire in a charcoal grill for cooking over medium heat or preheat a gas grill to 350°F (180°C). Oil grill rack. Arrange plums, cut side down, on grill. Cook until cut sides are lightly browned and caramelized, about 2 minutes. Turn plum halves over and put a bit of butter into each cavity. Cook until partially tender, 2–3 minutes more. Remove from heat and let cool slightly.

In a deep bowl, beat cream until soft peaks form. Using a rubber spatula, fold in powdered sugar, vanilla, and remaining 1 Tbsp kirsch.

Arrange 3 plum halves on each dessert plate. Dollop with kirsch cream and serve at once.

Note: Cover and refrigerate grilled plums for up to 12 hours. Bring to room temperature before serving. Whip cream just before serving.

To prepare: 10 minutes, plus 30 minutes to stand

To cook: 5 minutes

6 dessert servings

grilled berry parcels

4 cups (1 lb/500 g) fresh or frozen blackberries

2 cups (8 oz/250 g) fresh or frozen blueberries

2 just-ripe large bananas, peeled and thickly sliced on diagonal

1 tsp vanilla extract (essence)

⅓ cup (3 oz/90 g) sugar

1 Tbsp cornstarch (cornflour)

Build a fire in a charcoal grill for cooking over medium heat or preheat a gas grill to 350°F (180°C).

In a large bowl, combine berries, bananas, and vanilla and stir to combine. In another bowl, stir together sugar and cornstarch.

Cut out six 12-inch (30-cm) squares of heavy-duty aluminum foil. Arrange squares on a work surface and divide fruit mixture evenly among them, mounding in centers. Sprinkle with sugar mixture. Fold foil over fruit and crimp edges to seal.

Arrange parcels on grill and cook until fruit has softened, about 10 minutes. Remove parcels to dessert plates and serve at once.

To prepare: 5 minutes

To cook: 10 minutes

6 dessert servings

purple fruits with lavender syrup

½ cup plus 2 Tbsp sugar

6 fresh, pesticide-free lavender sprigs or 1 teaspoon dried lavender flowers, plus more for garnish

4 purple plums, halved and pitted

20 black grapes

1½ tsp butter

The day before serving, in a small saucepan, combine 1 cup (8 fl oz/250 ml) water and ½ cup sugar and bring to a boil over high heat. Reduce heat to medium and stir until sugar is dissolved, 10 minutes. Add lavender, cover, and let stand overnight. The following day, strain syrup through a fine-mesh sieve lined with several layers of damp cheesecloth. Return to a clean saucepan, bring to a boil, and cook until reduced by one-half, about 5 minutes. Remove from heat and let cool.

Preheat oven to 400°F (200°C).

Butter a baking dish just large enough to hold fruit in a single layer. Add plums, cut side down, and grapes. Sprinkle with 2 Tbsp sugar and dot with butter. Bake until butter and sugar have melted and the skin of the plums and grapes is just beginning to wrinkle, 8–10 minutes.

Remove and let stand for 10 minutes. Gently spoon fruit into dessert bowls or glasses and drizzle with lavender syrup. Garnish each with lavender and serve warm.

To prepare: 24 hours for syrup

To cook: 25 minutes

4 servings

roasted black plums with star anise

2 tsp butter

4 black plums, halved and pitted

4 tsp palm sugar (see Notes)

8 star anise pods (see Notes)

Preheat oven to 375°F (190°C). Lightly butter a baking dish just large enough to hold plum halves in a single layer. Arrange plums, cut side up, in prepared dish. Put ½ tsp sugar in cavity of each plum half, then place a star anise pod on top. Roast until sugar has melted, plums are heated through, and skins are just beginning to wrinkle a bit on the edges, about 15 minutes. Serve hot or warm.

Notes: Palm sugar, also called jaggery, can be found in Asian and Indian markets. Star anise is inedible but makes for a pretty presentation; instruct diners to remove before eating. Or, remove before serving.

To prepare: 5 minutes

To cook: 15 minutes

4 dessert servings

blackberry crêpes

Buckwheat Crêpes

⅓ cup (2 oz/60 g) buckwheat flour

⅓ cup (2 oz/60 g) all-purpose (plain) flour

½ cup (4 oz/125 g) plus 2 tsp sugar

1 cup (8 fl oz/250 ml) whole or reduced-fat (2 percent) milk

1 large egg plus 1 large egg white

¼ tsp salt

2 Tbsp clarified butter (see Note, page 208)

¼ cup (2 oz/60 g) Neufchâtel or low-fat cream cheese

¼ cup (2 fl oz/60 ml) low-fat or whole plain yogurt

1 Tbsp limoncello or other lemon liqueur

1½ cups (6 oz/185 g) fresh or unthawed frozen blackberries

½ cup (4 oz/125 g) sugar

For Crêpes: Whisk together flours, sugar, milk, whole egg, egg white, and salt in a bowl until smooth. Let batter stand for at least 30 minutes, or cover and refrigerate for up to 24 hours. Heat 2 tsp butter in a medium crêpe pan or medium frying pan over medium-high heat. When very hot, pour in a scant ⅓ cup (3 fl oz/80 ml) batter and quickly tilt pan to cover bottom evenly. Cook until crêpe is dark brown on bottom, about 3 minutes. Flip and cook on second side for 1 minute. Repeat to make 8 crêpes in all, brushing pan with more butter as needed. Stack cooked, cooled crêpes on a plate. If not using at once, cover with foil and let stand for up to 2 hours or refrigerate for up to 24 hours.

Combine cheese, yogurt, and liqueur in mini-food processor or blender and process to make a filling. If not using at once, cover and refrigerate (for up to 2 days).

To serve, wrap crêpes in foil and reheat in a 200°F (95°C) oven for 10 minutes. (If crêpes have been refrigerated, reheat for 15 minutes in a 350°F/180°C oven.) Fold each crêpe in half, spread with filling, and fold into quarters. Place 2 crêpes on each of 4 dessert plates. Combine blackberries and sugar in a medium nonstick frying pan over medium heat and sauté until berries are slightly soft and surrounded by syrup, about 3 minutes. Spoon hot berries and syrup over crêpes and serve.

To prepare: 20 minutes, plus 30 minutes to stand

To cook: 25–30 minutes

4 dessert servings

---

pomegranate-glazed figs

2 tsp butter

8 fresh purple figs, stemmed and halved lengthwise

½ cup (4 fl oz/125 ml) pomegranate juice

3 whole cloves

2 Tbsp mascarpone cheese

Unsweetened cocoa powder for garnish

Melt butter in a medium frying pan over medium-high heat. Add figs, cut side down, and sauté until golden, about 4 minutes. Using tongs, turn figs and cook for 1 minute more. Arrange 4 fig halves on each of 4 dessert plates, with bottoms toward the center to make a star.

Add pomegranate juice and cloves to pan and boil until liquid is syrupy, about 5 minutes. Discard cloves and spoon warm syrup over figs. Place 1½ tsp cheese in center of each plate and sprinkle with cocoa powder. Serve figs warm.

To prepare: 5 minutes

To cook: 10 minutes

4 dessert servings

avocados cucumbers spinach

GREEN FRUITS AND VEGETABLES BOOST THE IMMUNE

watercress arugula asparagus

SYSTEM • PROMOTE EYE HEALTH • HELP BUILD STRONG

kale broccoli snow peas leeks

BONES • BUILD STRONG TEETH • OFFER ANTIOXIDANTS

grapes zucchini green beans

FOR HEALING AND PROTECTION • REDUCE THE RISK OF

endive brussels sprouts limes

CERTAIN CANCERS • GREEN FRUITS AND VEGETABLES

green tea kiwifruits artichokes

BOOST THE IMMUNE SYSTEM • PROMOTE EYE HEALTH

Green

Green is the broadest band in the colorful produce spectrum, with flavors and textures ranging from creamy avocados to cool, crisp pears. We all know that it's healthy to eat our greens. In fact, the darker the leaves of the green vegetable—think kale, chard, and spinach—the more packed with nutrients it is. And the recipes in this chapter make eating your greens a pleasure rather than a chore.

Green vegetables vary in flavor from tangy tomatillos to robust broccoli to sweet sugar snap peas—in other words, a taste to complement every meal.

In this chapter, you'll find chicken breasts stuffed with arugula and goat cheese served with a quick medley of tomatoes and leeks (page 80), a pleasing pairing of contrasting red and green. You'll also discover an enlightened stir-fry that marries calamari rings with tender green pea shoots (page 101).

Classic French cooking is seldom labeled healthy, but green peas and tender lettuce sautéed in a modest amount of butter and then showered with a chiffonade of fresh mint prove that it can be just that (page 98).

For breakfast or dessert, reach for green grapes, kiwifruits, and green apples. Or, sauté green figs in a tiny nugget of butter and serve them in a pool of almond custard for a dessert that is both delicious and healthful (page 105).

SPRING	SUMMER	AUTUMN	WINTER
artichokes	arugula	green apples	green apples
asparagus	Hass avocados	artichokes	Fuerte avocados
green bell peppers	green beans	bok choy	bok choy
endive	green chiles	broccoli	broccoli
kiwifruits	cucumbers	broccoli rabe	broccoli rabe
lettuce	green grapes	Brussels sprouts	Brussels sprouts
Persian and Key limes	green herbs	green cabbage	green cabbage
green pears	Persian and Key limes	endive	celery
peas	green-fleshed melons	green beans	endive
snowpeas	okra	kale	kale
sugar snap peas	sugar snap peas	leeks	leeks
spinach	spinach	green pears	snow peas
watercress	zucchini	Swiss chard	spinach

belgian endive with blue cheese & walnuts

¾ cup (3 oz/90 g) walnut pieces

4 heads Belgian endive (chicory/witloof), cores intact, cut lengthwise into 6 wedges

2 Tbsp olive oil

2 Tbsp lemon juice

4 oz (125 g) blue cheese, crumbled (1 cup)

Place walnuts in a dry frying pan over medium heat. Stir until golden and toasted, 3–4 minutes. Remove at once to a plate. Set aside.

Put endives in a shallow dish. Stir olive oil, lemon juice, ½ tsp salt, and several grindings of black pepper together in a small bowl. Pour over endives and turn to coat evenly. Let marinate at room temperature for 30 minutes, or cover and refrigerate for up to 4 hours.

Preheat broiler (grill). Arrange endives on a baking sheet cut side up. Slide under broiler 4 inches (10 cm) from heat source and broil, turning once, until softened and starting to caramelize, about 2 minutes per side. Remove to a serving platter and scatter blue cheese and walnuts on top. Serve at once.

Note: This dish makes a nice starter and is also good as a side dish with grilled chicken or pork. Instead of broiling, you can grill the endives over medium-high heat for 2 minutes per side.

To prepare: 10 minutes, plus 30 minutes to marinate

To cook: 5 minutes

4 starter or side-dish servings

green onions with anchovy sauce

1 can (2 oz/50 g) olive oil-packed anchovy fillets, with oil

2 cloves garlic, crushed

2 pitted green olives

1 Tbsp red wine vinegar

2 Tbsp extra-virgin olive oil

16–20 green (spring) onions, trimmed of root ends and top thirds

Combine anchovies and their oil, garlic, olives, vinegar, and olive oil in a food processor or blender and process until smooth. Or, combine ingredients except for olive oil in a mortar and pound with a pestle until evenly mashed, then gradually stir in oil until smooth. Season with several grindings of pepper. Transfer sauce to a small serving bowl. Cover and refrigerate for 2 hours to meld flavors.

Build a fire in a charcoal grill for cooking over medium heat or preheat a gas grill to 350°F (180°C). Oil grill rack. Grill onions, placing them perpendicular to rack and turning often, until softened and lightly browned, about 7 minutes. Pile onions onto a serving plate and serve. Pass sauce at table.

To prepare: 10 minutes, plus 2 hours to marinate

To cook: 7 minutes

4 side-dish servings

grilled fish tacos with green cabbage salad

1 lb (500 g) skinless halibut or other firm white fish fillets, cut into strips about 3 inches (7.5 cm) long and 1 inch (2.5 cm) wide

2 tsp Cajun spice mix

2 tsp olive oil

4 cups (12 oz/375 g) finely shredded green cabbage

1 tsp sugar

1 small green chile, seeded and minced

2 green (spring) onions, including tender green parts, finely chopped

2 Tbsp finely chopped cilantro (fresh coriander)

4 Tbsp (2 fl oz/60 ml) lime juice

2 avocados, pitted and peeled

8–10 fresh corn or small flour tortillas, warmed

Put fish in a bowl. Sprinkle with spice mix, olive oil, and ½ tsp salt and turn fish to coat evenly. Cover and refrigerate for 30 minutes–4 hours. Remove from the refrigerator 15 minutes before grilling.

Build a fire in a charcoal grill for cooking over medium heat. If using a gas grill, preheat to high heat (400°F/200°C) and then reduce heat to medium (350°F/180°C) for cooking.

In a bowl, combine cabbage, sugar, and ½ tsp salt. Work cabbage between your fingers to soften and moisten. Add chile, green onions, cilantro, 2 Tbsp lime juice, and several grindings of pepper and toss to mix well. Taste and adjust seasoning. Set aside at room temperature to allow flavors to meld.

Mash avocados in a small bowl and stir in remaining 2 Tbsp lime juice. Cover and refrigerate until ready to serve.

Arrange fish in a single layer in an oiled grill basket or on oiled heavy-duty aluminum foil. Place basket on or slide foil onto grill. Grill, turning once, until fish just starts to flake when prodded with a fork and is opaque throughout, about 2 minutes per side. Divide cabbage salad among tortillas and top with fish and a dollop of avocado. Serve at once.

To prepare: 15 minutes, plus 30 minutes to marinate

To cook: 4 minutes

4 servings

roasted broccolini with lemon

1½ Tbsp olive oil

2 cloves garlic, minced

1 bunch broccolini, trimmed and coarsely chopped

½ lemon, not peeled, seeded and cut into ¼-inch (6-mm) dice

Preheat oven to 350°F (180°C). Heat 1 Tbsp olive oil in a frying pan over medium-high heat. Add garlic and sauté until lightly golden, about 1 minute, then add broccolini, lemon, and ½ tsp salt. Sauté just until color of broccolini deepens, about 1 minute more.

Remove contents of frying pan to a medium ovenproof baking dish, add ½ Tbsp olive oil, and turn to coat. Roast until broccolini is tender-crisp, 10–12 minutes. Remove to a bowl or platter and serve hot or cooled to room temperature.

To prepare: 5 minutes

To cook: 15 minutes

3 or 4 side-dish servings

roasted zucchini with anchoïade

2 zucchini (courgettes)

1 Tbsp olive oil

1 tsp fresh thyme leaves

Anchoïade
⅓–½ cup (3–4 fl oz/80–125 ml) extra-virgin olive oil

1 can (2½ oz/75 g) anchovy fillets, rinsed and drained

3 cloves garlic, minced

Preheat oven to 400°F (200°C).

Cut zucchini in half crosswise. Cut each half lengthwise into 3 even slices. Arrange slices in a baking dish just large enough to hold them in a single layer. Drizzle with olive oil and sprinkle with thyme. Season with ½ tsp salt and ½ tsp pepper and turn to coat evenly.

Roast until bottoms are golden brown, 15–20 minutes. Turn and roast until golden on second side and tender-crisp, 5–10 minutes more.

For Anchoïade: In a small frying pan over low heat, heat ⅓ cup olive oil. Add anchovies and garlic and cook, mashing anchovies until they dissolve into oil to make a paste, about 3 minutes. Gradually stir in enough of the remaining oil to give sauce the consistency of a thick vinaigrette.

Serve zucchini warm, accompanied with *anchoïade*.

To prepare: 10 minutes

To cook: 30 minutes

3 or 4 starter servings

spinach soufflé

1 Tbsp grated Parmesan cheese

6 cups (6 oz/185 g) packed spinach leaves (about 1 bunch)

4½ Tbsp (2¼ oz/70 g) butter

2 Tbsp minced shallot

¼ cup (1½ oz/45 g) all-purpose (plain) flour

⅛ tsp freshly grated nutmeg

1 cup (8 fl oz/250 ml) low-fat or whole milk

4 whole eggs, separated, plus 2 egg whites, at room temperature

Preheat oven to 375°F (190°C). Butter bottom and sides of a 1-qt (1-l) soufflé dish. Sprinkle bottom with Parmesan, then turn dish on its side, tapping and turning to coat all sides with cheese. Set aside.

In a large saucepan over high heat, bring 4 cups (32 fl oz/1 l) water to a boil. Add spinach, reduce heat to medium, and cook until spinach is wilted but still bright green, about 4 minutes. Remove to a colander and rinse under cold running water until cool. Drain thoroughly, squeeze out excess water, and chop coarsely. In a frying pan over medium-high heat, melt 1 Tbsp butter. When it foams, add shallot and cook, stirring, until translucent, about 1 minute. Add spinach and cook, stirring, until it glistens, about 2 minutes. Set aside.

In a medium saucepan over medium-high heat, melt 3½ Tbsp butter. When it foams, remove from heat and whisk in flour, nutmeg, 1 tsp salt, and ¼ tsp pepper. Return to medium-high heat and add milk slowly, whisking constantly. Cook, whisking occasionally, until taste of flour is gone and sauce is thickened and smooth, about 5 minutes. Remove from heat and let cool for 2–3 minutes.

In a bowl, using an electric mixer or a whisk, beat 6 egg whites until stiff peaks form when beater or whisk is lifted. In another bowl, beat 4 egg yolks until creamy.

Whisk egg yolks into cooled white sauce until well blended. Stir in spinach mixture. Stir about 3 Tbsp egg whites into spinach mixture to lighten it, then use a spatula to gently fold in remaining egg whites just until no white streaks remain. Scrape into prepared soufflé dish.

Bake until top has puffed and is golden brown, about 40 minutes. Serve hot, directly from dish.

To prepare: 20 minutes

To cook: 55 minutes

4 servings

crisp green apple & celery salad

Cut 2 cored, unpeeled green apples into matchsticks and toss with lemon juice, walnut oil, thinly sliced celery and green (spring) onions, salt, pepper, and toasted coriander seeds. Serve with grilled seafood or chicken.

grilled artichoke salad

Oil-packed artichoke hearts provide an easy alternative to trimming fresh ones for the grill. Drain and cut in half lengthwise. Grill over medium heat until lightly browned on all sides. Toss with a garlicky vinaigrette and chopped herbs.

honeydew prosciutto wraps

Wrap chunks of honeydew melon or green figs in prosciutto. Brush lightly with olive oil and grill over high heat until fruit is warm and prosciutto is lightly browned. Serve as a starter on a bed of arugula (rocket) leaves.

grilled favas

Grill fava (broad) beans in the pods over medium-high heat until pods are blackened and soft. Let cool, then shell beans and peel each one. Toss with olive oil, salt, and pepper. Top with toasted hazelnuts (filberts) and pecorino shavings.

stir-fried chicken with broccoli & mushrooms

1 Tbsp fermented black beans

2 Tbsp dry sherry

½ lb (250 g) ground (minced) chicken breast

⅛ tsp ground white pepper

1 tsp Asian sesame oil

¼ cup (⅓ oz/10 g) Thai basil leaves

2 Tbsp peanut or canola oil

2 Tbsp chopped garlic

1 Tbsp chopped fresh ginger

2 cups (6 oz/185 g) broccoli florets

½ cup (2 oz/60 g) chopped shallots

2 Tbsp chicken broth

1 can (15 oz/470 g) straw mushrooms, drained

Cooked rice noodles for serving

In a small bowl, soak black beans in sherry for 20 minutes. Drain, reserving sherry. In another bowl, mix chicken with ½ tsp salt, white pepper, and sesame oil and cover with plastic wrap. Let chicken stand for 20 minutes.

Stack the basil leaves and roll up lengthwise. With a sharp knife, cut crosswise into thin strips to make a chiffonade for garnish. Set aside.

Heat peanut oil in a wok over medium-high heat until almost smoking. Add chicken and stir-fry, breaking up meat with a spatula, until color changes from pink to brown, about 2 minutes. Remove chicken to a plate using a slotted spoon. Add garlic, ginger, and black beans and stir-fry until fragrant, about 30 seconds. Add broccoli and shallots and stir-fry for 1 minute. Add broth, reserved sherry, and ½ tsp salt and stir to combine. Return chicken to wok, add mushrooms, and stir-fry until wok is almost dry, 2–3 minutes.

To serve, spoon noodles into bowls or onto a platter and top with chicken and vegetables. Garnish with basil and serve at once.

To prepare: 10 minutes, plus 20 minutes to soak and marinate

To cook: 6 minutes

4 servings

dry-fried long beans

¼ cup (2 fl oz/60 ml) chicken broth

1 tsp sugar

½ cup (4 fl oz/125 ml) canola oil

¾ lb (375 g) Asian long beans, cut into 4-inch (10-cm) lengths

2 Tbsp finely chopped fresh ginger

1 red bell pepper (capsicum), chopped

1 Tbsp balsamic vinegar

1 tsp Asian sesame oil

In small bowl, mix together broth, sugar, and ½ tsp salt. Set aside.

Heat oil in a wok over medium-high heat until almost smoking. Add beans and cook, alternately stirring them and pressing them against wok, until skin wrinkles and brown spots appear, about 3 minutes. Remove beans to a plate using a slotted spoon. Pour off all but 1 Tbsp oil. Return wok to medium-high heat, add ginger, and stir-fry until fragrant, about 30 seconds. Add broth mixture, return beans to wok, and cook until wok is almost dry, 3–4 minutes. Stir in bell pepper, vinegar, and sesame oil. Serve warm or at room temperature.

To prepare: 10 minutes

To cook: 8 minutes

4–6 side-dish servings

chicken breasts stuffed with goat cheese & arugula

4 cups (8 oz/250 g) coarsely chopped arugula (rocket), rinsed and shaken

4 skinless, boneless chicken breast halves, about 6 oz (185 g) each

½ cup (3 oz/90 g) creamy fresh goat cheese

Sauce

2 Tbsp olive oil

½ cup (2 oz/60 g) chopped leek, white part only

¼ cup (1 oz/30 g) finely chopped red onion

1 clove garlic, finely chopped

2½ cups (15 oz/470 g) seeded and chopped plum (Roma) tomatoes

1 cup (8 oz/250 g) canned diced tomatoes

¼ cup (2 fl oz/60 ml) dry white wine such as Pinot Grigio or Sancerre

Cook damp arugula in a dry, nonstick frying pan over medium-high heat until it wilts and is dark green, about 3 minutes. Remove arugula to a plate and let cool.

While arugula cools, pound each breast half between 2 sheets of plastic wrap, using a mallet or rolling pin, until ¼ inch (6 mm) thick.

Squeeze water from arugula and chop finely. In a bowl, combine chopped arugula with goat cheese, ½ tsp salt, and a few grindings of pepper. Place one-fourth of goat cheese mixture in center of each breast half, spreading it with your fingers over the chicken and leaving a ¼-inch (6-mm) border uncovered all around. Starting at a narrow end, roll up each breast like a jelly roll. Set stuffed rolls, seam side down, on a plate and cover with plastic wrap.

For Sauce: Heat oil in a sauté pan over medium-high heat. Add leek and onion and sauté until onion is translucent, about 4 minutes. Add garlic and sauté for 1 minute more. Add plum tomatoes with their liquid and sauté until they start to soften, 3–4 minutes. Add canned tomatoes, cover, and simmer for 5 minutes.

Add stuffed chicken breasts to pan, cover, and cook over medium heat until opaque all the way through, 15–20 minutes. With tongs, remove chicken to a warmed serving platter and tent with foil. Add wine to sauce and cook over medium-high heat until it has a chunky, light consistency, about 5 minutes.

Serve chicken rolls whole or sliced, with sauce spooned alongside.

To prepare: 30 minutes, plus 15 minutes to cool

To cook: 40 minutes

4 servings

trout & green pear salad

4 skinless steelhead trout or salmon
fillets, each about ⅓ lb (155 g) and
1 inch (2.5 cm) thick

2 Tbsp finely chopped fresh chervil
or parsley

Olive oil

2 just-ripe crisp green pears, halved,
cored, and cut into thin wedges
(10–12 wedges per pear)

2 Tbsp lime juice

1 Tbsp lemon juice

1 bunch watercress, stemmed
(about 1 cup/1 oz/30 g)

2 Tbsp sliced (flaked) almonds,
toasted (see Note, page 84)

Build a fire in a charcoal grill for cooking over medium-high heat
or preheat gas grill to 375°F (190°C). Sprinkle fillets with chervil and
season with salt and pepper. Brush with a little oil.

Combine pears with lime and lemon juices in a mixing bowl and toss
to coat. Set aside. Arrange fish in a single layer in an oiled grill basket
or on oiled heavy-duty aluminum foil. Place basket or slide foil onto grill.
Cover grill and cook, turning once, until flesh just flakes when prodded
with a fork and is barely opaque in center, about 3 minutes per side.
Remove to a plate, tent with foil, and let rest for 5 minutes.

Add watercress to pears and toss gently to combine. Break trout into
salad in bite-sized chunks. Add almonds, season to taste with salt and
pepper, and toss again gently. Divide among individual plates and serve.

To prepare: 15 minutes

To cook: 6 minutes

4 servings

grilled halibut with limes

3 limes

1 Tbsp olive oil

1 tsp sugar

1 tsp whole-grain mustard

4 halibut or other firm white fish
fillets, about 6 oz (185 g) each

4 oz (125 g) watercress, tough
stems removed

Grate zest from 1 lime. Whisk olive oil, sugar, mustard, and zest together
in a small bowl. Brush fish on both sides with zest mixture. Cover and
refrigerate for 30 minutes–1 hour.

Build a fire in charcoal grill for cooking over medium heat or preheat
gas grill to 350°F (180°C). Arrange fish in an oiled grill basket and season
lightly with salt and pepper. Place basket on grill. Cover grill and cook,
turning once, until flesh just flakes in thickest part when prodded with
a fork and is still translucent only in the center, about 4 minutes per side.
Remove to a plate, tent with foil, and let stand for 5 minutes. Meanwhile,
cut remaining 2 limes in half and place on grill, cut side down. Heat
until lightly grill-marked, about 3 minutes.

Make a bed of watercress on each warmed plate and arrange fish
on top. Serve at once, garnished with grilled lime halves. Diners can
squeeze the lime juice or slice off the peel and eat the grilled fruit.

To prepare: 5 minutes,
plus 30 minutes to marinate

To cook: 12 minutes

4 servings

chicken, avocado & spinach salad

1 Tbsp cumin seeds

1 tsp fennel seeds

1 cup (8 oz/250 g) plain low-fat yogurt

4 Tbsp (2 fl oz/60 ml) olive oil

3 cloves garlic, crushed

2 tsp paprika

4 skinless, boneless chicken breast halves

5 cups (5 oz/155 g) baby spinach leaves

2 avocados, pitted, peeled, and cut into thin wedges

1 grilled or roasted red bell pepper (capsicum) (page 205), peeled, seeded, and thinly sliced (optional)

¼ cup (1 oz/30 g) sliced (flaked) almonds, toasted (see Note)

Juice of 1 lemon

Put cumin and fennel seeds in a small, dry frying pan over medium heat and toast, stirring often, until fragrant, about 1 minute; watch closely, as they can burn easily. Grind coarsely with a mortar and pestle or spice grinder. Combine ground seeds, yogurt, 2 Tbsp olive oil, garlic, paprika, and ½ tsp salt in a large bowl and stir to mix well. Remove and reserve one-third of mixture. Add chicken to bowl and stir to coat evenly. Cover and refrigerate for 30 minutes–12 hours.

Preheat broiler (grill). Remove chicken from marinade and discard remaining marinade. Cut chicken into long, thick slices (4 or 5 per breast). Spread slices in a single layer on a baking sheet lined with foil. Sprinkle with salt and pepper and brush with oil. Slide under broiler about 4 inches (10 cm) from heat source and broil (grill), turning once, until browned and opaque throughout, 10–12 minutes. Remove to a large bowl and let rest for 5 minutes. Add reserved yogurt mixture, stir to coat evenly, and let cool for 5–10 minutes more.

Add spinach, avocados, grilled or roasted pepper (if using), and almonds to bowl. Drizzle with remaining 2 Tbsp olive oil and the lemon juice and toss gently to combine. To serve, pile onto a platter or salad plates. Drizzle any dressing remaining in bowl over salads and serve.

Note: Toast almonds or small seeds in a small, dry frying pan over medium heat. Toast, stirring often, until just starting to turn golden, about 2 minutes; watch closely, as they burn easily. Remove at once to a plate.

To prepare: 10 minutes, plus 30 minutes to marinate

To cook: 15 minutes, plus 15 minutes to cool

4 servings

poblano chiles stuffed with goat cheese

Slit poblano chiles and remove seeds and membranes. Stuff with mashed mixture of goat cheese, milk, chives, shallot, and salt. Roast chiles at 400°F (200°C) in a lightly oiled baking dish until soft and slightly wrinkled, 30–40 minutes.

sautéed spinach with peanuts & soy sauce

Sauté minced shallot or onion in peanut oil until softened. Toss with spinach and chopped peanuts, drizzle with just enough soy sauce to season, and bake at 350°F (180°C) until spinach is dark and wilted, 11–15 minutes.

broccoli baked with garlic & chile

Chop broccoli and put in a baking dish. Add olive oil to come ¼ inch (6 mm) up sides of dish. Season with minced garlic, red pepper flakes, salt, and pepper. Turn to coat evenly. Cover and bake in a 250°F (120°C) oven until tender.

gratinéed swiss chard

Stem chard and cook in salted boiling water until tender. Chop, drain, and place in a baking dish. Sprinkle with olive oil, salt, and pepper and turn to coat. Top with grated Parmesan, dot with butter, and bake in a hot oven until golden.

roasted asparagus
with eggs & parmesan

1 lb (500 g) asparagus
spears, trimmed

1 Tbsp olive oil

1 tsp distilled white vinegar

4 eggs

1 Tbsp grated Parmesan cheese

Preheat oven to 450°F (230°C). Arrange asparagus in a single layer in a baking dish. Drizzle with olive oil, sprinkle with ¼ tsp salt and ¼ tsp pepper, and turn to coat evenly. Roast, turning occasionally, until tips are lightly browned and asparagus is tender-crisp, 15–20 minutes. Remove to a platter and tent loosely with foil.

Fill a deep sauté pan with cold water. Add vinegar and a pinch of salt and set pan over medium heat. When water begins to simmer, break eggs, one at a time, into a cup and slip each gently into the water. Keeping water at a low simmer, poach to desired doneness, 3–5 minutes. Using a slotted spoon, remove eggs and blot dry.

To serve, divide asparagus spears among plates and top each portion with a poached egg and a sprinkle of Parmesan, salt, and pepper.

To prepare: 10 minutes

To cook: 25 minutes

4 starter servings

cod on a bed
of cucumbers

1½ cucumbers, peeled, halved
lengthwise, and seeded

2 tsp Asian fish sauce

½ tsp palm or raw sugar
(see Notes, page 61)

2 Tbsp lime juice

1 stalk lemongrass

4 cod fillets, each about 5 oz (155 g)
and ½ inch (12 mm) thick

2 Tbsp chopped fresh Thai basil

1 Tbsp minced fresh chives

Preheat oven to 450°F (230°C). Cut cucumber halves on diagonal into long slices about ¼ inch (6 mm) thick. Overlap slices in bottom of a baking dish just large enough to hold cod fillets in a single layer.

In a small bowl, stir together fish sauce, sugar, and lime juice. Cut off and discard top of lemongrass stalk, then remove tough outer layer from bulbous lower portion. Crush lightly with flat side of a chef's knife to bruise, which releases flavorful oils. Tuck lemongrass into cucumber slices and arrange fillets in a single layer on top of cucumbers. Drizzle with fish sauce mixture. Cover dish tightly with foil and bake until fish is opaque throughout and flakes easily with a fork, 12–15 minutes.

Garnish with basil and chives and serve directly from baking dish, slipping a spatula beneath cucumbers.

To prepare: 10 minutes

To cook: 15 minutes

4 servings

baked pasta with dandelion greens & sausage

½ lb (250 g) orecchiette pasta

2 Tbsp olive oil

3 chicken-fennel or other mild sausages

1 bunch dandelion greens, about 12 oz (375 g), tough stems removed, leaves coarsely chopped

1 cup (8 oz/250 g) whole-milk ricotta cheese

1 Tbsp butter

¼ cup (½ oz/15 g) fresh bread crumbs (see Notes, page 251)

Bring a large pot of salted water to a boil over high heat. Add orecchiette and reduce heat to medium. Stir once or twice and cook until al dente, about 15 minutes. Drain thoroughly and place in a medium baking dish. Drizzle with 1 Tbsp olive oil, sprinkle with 1 tsp salt and 1 tsp pepper, and stir to mix well.

Preheat oven to 350°F (180°C).

In a frying pan, heat 1 Tbsp olive oil over medium-high heat. When oil is hot, add sausages and sauté, turning as needed, until browned on all sides, about 10 minutes. Remove to a cutting board and let cool slightly. Meanwhile, add dandelion greens to pan and sauté over medium-high heat until tender but still bright green, 5 minutes. Remove from heat.

Cut sausages into 1-inch (2.5-cm) slices and add to pasta with greens and pan juices. Toss and stir until ingredients are evenly distributed. Taste and adjust seasoning. Spoon ricotta onto pasta and spread it evenly over the top.

In a small frying pan over medium heat, melt butter. When it foams, add bread crumbs and cook, stirring often, until golden, 3–4 minutes. Sprinkle toasted crumbs evenly over ricotta.

Bake until cheese is lightly browned around edges, 25–30 minutes. Serve hot, directly from baking dish.

To prepare: 10 minutes

To cook: 1 hour

4 servings

lamb chops with arugula pesto

8 lamb loin or rib chops, trimmed of excess fat

2 Tbsp lemon juice

1 Tbsp olive oil

2 or 3 sprigs mint, lightly bruised

2 cloves garlic, crushed

Arugula Pesto

5 cups (5 oz/155 g) packed arugula (rocket) leaves

½ cup (½ oz/15 g) packed fresh mint leaves

½ cup (4 fl oz/125 ml) extra-virgin olive oil

1 clove garlic

Zest of 1 lemon

Put lamb chops in a bowl and sprinkle with lemon juice, olive oil, mint, garlic, and salt and pepper to taste. Toss to coat evenly. Cover and marinate at room temperature for 30 minutes, or in the refrigerator for up to 4 hours. Bring to room temperature before grilling.

For Pesto: In a food processor or blender, combine arugula, mint, olive oil, garlic, lemon zest, ½ tsp salt, and several grindings of pepper. Process until smooth. Taste and adjust seasoning. Spoon into a small serving bowl and refrigerate until ready to serve.

Build a fire in a charcoal grill for cooking over medium-high heat or preheat a gas grill to 375°F (190°C). Oil grill rack. Grill lamb chops, turning once, until nicely browned and done to your liking, about 3 minutes per side for medium-rare (an instant-read thermometer inserted in thickest part, away from bone, should read 130°F/54°C). Remove to a serving platter, tent with foil, and let rest for 5 minutes. Arrange 2 chops on each warmed plate and serve with pesto.

To prepare: 10 minutes, plus 30 minutes to marinate

To cook: 6 minutes

4 servings

broccoli gratin

2–4 slices sourdough or country-style bread

¼ cup (2 fl oz/60 ml) olive oil

½ cup (2 oz/60 g) grated Parmesan cheese

2 Tbsp capers, drained and finely chopped

2 cloves garlic, crushed

1½ lb (750 g) broccoli, stalks peeled and chopped, heads cut into small florets

3 Tbsp reduced-fat sour cream

Preheat broiler (grill). Remove crusts from bread slices and toast about 4 inches (10 cm) from heat source until golden on both sides, about 2 minutes total. Break into large pieces and process in a food processor just to form coarse crumbs. Measure 2 cups (6 oz/185 g) crumbs. Toss bread crumbs with olive oil, Parmesan, capers, and garlic.

Bring a saucepan three-fourths full of lightly salted water to a boil. Add broccoli and cook for 2 minutes. Drain in a colander and place under cold running water to cool. Drain again thoroughly and arrange in a shallow baking or gratin dish. Spread sour cream over broccoli and sprinkle with bread-crumb mixture. Slide under broiler about 6 inches (15 cm) from heat source and cook until gratin is heated through and bread crumbs are golden and crisp, 4–5 minutes. Serve at once.

To prepare: 15 minutes

To cook: 9 minutes

4 side-dish servings

fettuccine with fava beans, artichokes & asparagus

1 lemon

1¼ lb (625 g) baby artichokes

1 lb (500 g) fresh fava beans, shelled

8 spears thin asparagus, tough ends trimmed, spears cut into 2-inch (5-cm) pieces

3 Tbsp olive oil

2 cloves garlic, sliced lengthwise

¾ lb (375 g) dried farro or whole-wheat (wholemeal) fettuccine

¼ cup (1 oz/30 g) grated pecorino cheese

Squeeze lemon into large bowl and add squeezed halves and 2 cups (16 fl oz/500 ml) water. Cut off top of each artichoke, discard outer leaves, trim base, and add to lemon water. When all are trimmed, pour 1 cup (8 fl oz/250 ml) lemon water into steamer pan. Put artichokes, favas, and asparagus on rack. Cover, bring to boil, and steam until tender, about 6 minutes. Return vegetables to lemon water and let cool, then drain. Halve artichokes lengthwise and slip thick skins from favas.

Heat oil in a frying pan over medium-high heat. Add garlic and sauté until golden, about 4 minutes. Remove to a plate with a slotted spoon. Sauté artichokes in garlic oil until warmed through, about 3 minutes. Add favas and asparagus and sauté for 2–3 minutes more.

Meanwhile, cook pasta in salted boiling water until al dente, 12 minutes. Drain pasta and divide among warmed wide, shallow bowls. Spoon vegetables and oil over pasta, top with garlic and cheese, and serve.

To prepare: 30 minutes

To cook: 25 minutes

4 servings

lemon sole with peas

¼ lb (125 g) sugar snap peas

1 cup (5 oz/155 g) fresh or frozen baby green peas

4 sole fillets, 6 oz (185 g) each

⅓ cup (2 oz/60 g) all-purpose (plain) flour

2 Tbsp clarified butter (see Note, page 208)

Juice of 1 lemon

2 Tbsp dry white wine such as Sauvignon Blanc or dry Riesling

Blanch sugar snap peas for 30 seconds in boiling water. Add green peas and cook for 30 seconds more. Drain peas, remove to a warmed serving platter, tent with foil, and set aside.

Pat fish dry with paper towels. Season to taste with salt and pepper. Dredge in flour and gently tap off excess. Heat butter in a frying pan. Shaking pan, add fillets, placing the more attractive side down. Continue shaking for 1 minute to prevent sticking. Cook until fish is golden, 1–2 minutes. Using a wide spatula, turn fish and cook, shaking pan or sliding spatula underneath to keep it from sticking, until almost opaque in center at thickest point, 2–4 minutes. Arrange fish atop peas.

Add lemon juice and wine to pan and stir to scrape up browned bits. Spoon hot sauce over fish and serve at once.

To prepare: 8 minutes

To cook: 8 minutes

4 servings

duck & brussels sprouts

1 whole duck leg with thigh, about ½ lb (250 g)

1 Tbsp olive oil

3–4 Tbsp hazelnut oil

1 lb (500 g) Brussels sprouts, trimmed and quartered

⅓ cup (3 fl oz/80 ml) dry vermouth or white wine

⅓ cup (2 oz/60 g) skinned toasted hazelnuts (filberts) (see Note), chopped

Preheat oven to 350°F (180°C). Rub duck leg with olive oil, ½ tsp salt, and ½ tsp pepper. Place duck in a shallow roasting dish just large enough to fit it and roast until skin is golden brown and flesh is tender, about 1¼ hours. Remove from oven but leave oven on.

In an ovenproof sauté pan or Dutch oven, heat 1 Tbsp hazelnut oil over medium-high heat. Add Brussels sprouts and sauté just until beginning to turn golden, about 3 minutes. Add duck and any pan juices and turn to coat. Raise heat to high and add vermouth, stirring to scrape up any browned bits from bottom of pan.

Cover pan and place in oven. Bake until duck shreds easily and Brussels sprouts are tender, about 20 minutes. Remove from heat and remove duck to a cutting board. When duck is cool enough to handle, pull meat from bones and shred or chop coarsely. Discard skin and bones.

Add duck meat to pan with Brussels sprouts and toss to combine. Add toasted hazelnuts and drizzle with 2–3 Tbsp hazelnut oil. Season with salt and pepper to taste. Serve warm or at room temperature.

Note: To skin hazelnuts, place them on a baking sheet and toast in a 350°F (180°C) oven for 15–20 minutes, or until they are fragrant and the color deepens. After the nuts have cooled to the touch, rub them with firmly with a kitchen towel and pick off the remaining skins with your fingers.

To prepare: 25 minutes

To cook: 1 hour 35 minutes

3 or 4 servings

chinese broccoli with oyster sauce

Steam Chinese broccoli for 3 minutes. In a wok, stir-fry chopped fresh ginger for 30 seconds. Add broccoli, 1 tsp sugar, and 1 Tbsp chicken broth. Stir-fry for 1 minute more. Drizzle with oyster sauce and serve.

french peas & lettuce

Cut a head of butter lettuce into quarters. Sauté in butter with baby peas until lettuce wilts. Add ½ cup (4 fl oz/125 ml) chicken broth and cook until lettuce is tender. Season with salt and pepper, sprinkle with chopped mint, and serve.

brussels sprouts with capers & lemon

Sauté thinly sliced sprouts in oil until bright green. Add a generous splash of chicken broth and continue cooking until sprouts are tender-crisp. Mix in rinsed capers, some lemon zest, a squirt of lemon juice, salt, and pepper.

garlic spinach

Purée 2 garlic cloves with 1 cup (8 fl oz/250 ml) water. Cut Savoy or regular spinach, including tender stems, into wide strips and sauté in olive oil until wilted. Add garlic water. Cook until tender. Season with salt and pepper.

stir-fried calamari & pea shoots

1 lb (500 g) green pea shoots

¾ lb (375 g) cleaned squid bodies

4 Tbsp (2 fl oz/60 ml) peanut oil

2 Tbsp minced garlic

1 Tbsp minced fresh ginger

½ cup (1½ oz/45 g) chopped green (spring) onions, green part only

¼ cup (2 fl oz/60 ml) chicken broth

1 Tbsp low-sodium soy sauce

1 tsp Asian chile paste

1 tsp sugar

1 tsp Asian sesame oil

Steamed brown rice for serving

Rinse pea shoots, remove and discard tough parts, and dry thoroughly. Set aside. Cut squid into ¾-inch (2-cm) rings and set aside.

Heat 2 Tbsp peanut oil in a wok over medium-high heat. Add garlic and ginger and stir-fry until fragrant, about 30 seconds. Add pea shoots and green onions and stir-fry until volume is reduced by half, 3 minutes. Add broth, ½ tsp salt, and ⅛ tsp pepper and cook until shoots are tender-crisp, about 2 minutes. Remove to a plate with a slotted spoon.

Wipe out wok. In a small bowl, mix together soy sauce, chile paste, sugar, and sesame oil. Heat 2 Tbsp peanut oil in wok over medium-high heat. Add squid and stir-fry until opaque, about 2 minutes. Return pea shoots to wok, add soy sauce mixture, and stir-fry, tossing to combine and heat through, about 1 minute. Using a slotted spoon, remove greens and squid to serving platter. Serve hot over brown rice.

To prepare: 15 minutes

To cook: 9 minutes

4 servings

chicken with tomatillo sauce

1 Tbsp canola oil

2 shallots, chopped

2 green (spring) onions, white part only, chopped

1 serrano chile, seeded and minced

3 medium tomatillos, chopped

½ cup (½ oz/15 g) cilantro (fresh coriander) leaves

1 tsp dried oregano

½ cup (4 fl oz/125 ml) chicken broth

1 Tbsp lime juice

4 skinless, boneless chicken breast halves, 4 oz (125 g) each

Heat oil in a medium frying pan over medium-high heat. Sauté shallots until translucent, about 4 minutes. Add green onions and chile and cook for 1 minute. Add tomatillos, half the cilantro, and the oregano and sauté until tomatillos are soft, about 4 minutes. Add chicken broth and continue to cook until most of liquid has evaporated, about 5 minutes. Remove contents of pan to a blender, add lime juice, and process to a pulpy purée, making about 1 cup (8 fl oz/250 ml) sauce. Set aside.

Pound each breast between 2 sheets of plastic wrap, using a meat pounder, until ¼ inch (6 mm) thick. Season with salt and pepper. Heat a heavy nonstick frying pan over medium-high heat. Sear chicken in dry pan until opaque throughout, turning breasts once, 5 minutes total.

To serve, place chicken on warmed dinner plates and spoon sauce over. Garnish with remaining cilantro. Pass remaining sauce in a pitcher.

To prepare: 20 minutes

To cook: 20 minutes

4 servings

okra with yellow plum tomatoes

1 Tbsp olive oil

½ cup (2 oz/60 g) chopped onion

½ lb (250 g) okra, sliced crosswise ½ inch (12 mm) thick

3 yellow plum (Roma) tomatoes, halved lengthwise and sliced crosswise ½ inch (12 mm) thick

1 tsp dried oregano

¼ cup (2 fl oz/60 ml) low-sodium chicken or vegetable broth

Heat oil in a medium frying pan over medium-high heat. Add onion and sauté until it starts to soften, about 3 minutes. Stir in okra and sauté until it starts to soften, 3 minutes more.

Add tomatoes, oregano, and broth. Cook, stirring often, until tomatoes are warmed through but not breaking down, 1–2 minutes. Serve warm.

To prepare: 20 minutes

To cook: 7 minutes

4 side-dish servings

swiss chard with lemon & anchovy

1 large bunch Swiss chard (12–14 oz/375–440 g)

3 Tbsp olive oil

¾ cup (6 fl oz/180 ml) low-sodium vegetable or chicken broth

2 to 3 anchovy fillets, rinsed

2 Tbsp lemon juice

½ cup (2 oz/60 g) chopped onion

½ cup (3 oz/90 g) canned diced tomatoes or 2 plum (Roma) tomatoes, seeded and chopped

Separate stems from chard leaves by cutting along both sides of center vein. Stack leaves, roll up lengthwise, and cut crosswise into strips ¾ inch (2 cm) wide. Trim off tough bottoms from stems and cut crosswise into ½-inch (12-mm) pieces.

Heat 1 Tbsp oil in a frying pan over medium-high heat. Add stems and sauté for 5 minutes. Add one-third of broth and cook until stems are tender and pan is almost dry, almost 4 minutes. Off heat, push stems to one side and mash anchovies in pan until creamy, using back of a wooden spoon, then stir in stems and season with lemon juice and pepper. Arrange cooked stems on one side of a warmed serving platter.

To cook leaves, heat remaining 2 Tbsp oil in a clean pan over medium-high heat. Add onion and sauté until golden, 6–7 minutes. Stir in sliced leaves in 3 or 4 batches, until wilted. Add tomatoes and remaining broth and cook, stirring occasionally, until chard is tender, about 10 minutes. Spoon leaves next to stems. Serve warm.

To prepare: 15 minutes

To cook: 25 minutes

4 side-dish servings

green figs with almond custard

2 Tbsp sliced (flaked) almonds

1 cup (8 fl oz/250 ml) low-fat or whole milk

2 egg yolks

¼ cup (2 oz/60 g) sugar

2 or 3 drops almond extract (essence)

2 tsp butter

8 green figs, halved lengthwise

½ cup (4 fl oz/125 ml) unfiltered apple juice

Preheat oven to 350°F (180°C). Spread almonds in a single layer on a baking sheet. Toast for 3 minutes, stir, and continue toasting until golden, 3–4 minutes more. Spread nuts at once on a plate to cool. Set aside.

Pour milk into a heavy saucepan and place over medium heat until small bubbles ring edges of pan. In a bowl, beat together egg yolks and sugar until creamy. Pour about ¼ cup (2 fl oz/60 ml) hot milk into egg mixture while whisking constantly. Return milk-egg mixture to pan and stir constantly over medium heat with a wooden spoon until mixture thickens and lightly coats the back of the spoon, about 2 minutes. Do not allow to boil. An instant-read thermometer inserted into the custard should read 180°F (82°C). Remove from heat and stir in almond extract. Pour custard into a pitcher, place plastic wrap directly on the surface to prevent skin from forming, and refrigerate for 4 hours.

Just before serving, pour ¼ cup (2 fl oz/60 ml) custard onto the center of each of 4 chilled dessert plates and set aside.

In a medium nonstick frying pan, heat butter over medium-high heat. Add figs, cut side down, and sauté until pale gold, about 1 minute. Add apple juice and boil until syrupy, about 3 minutes.

Arrange 4 fig halves on the custard on each plate. Garnish with almonds and serve.

To prepare: 10 minutes, plus 4 hours to chill

To cook: 8 minutes

4 dessert servings

green apples baked
with dried cranberries

4 large green-skinned apples such as Granny Smith

½ cup (3½ oz/105 g) firmly packed light brown sugar

½ cup (2 oz/60 g) dried cranberries

2 Tbsp butter, cut into 4 bits

Heavy (double) cream for serving (optional)

Preheat oven to 350°F (180°C).

Using an apple corer, cut cores from apples in neat plugs. In a small bowl, combine sugar and cranberries. Divide mixture evenly among apples, stuffing into cavities. Top each stuffed apple with a bit of butter. Place apples in a deep baking dish just large enough to hold them. Pour in enough water to cover the bottom of the pan by ¼ inch (6 mm). Put pan in oven and bake until apples have turned golden brown, are slightly shrunken, and are easily pierced with a fork, about 1 hour.

Place apples onto dessert plates and drizzle each with cream, if desired. Serve hot or warm.

To prepare: 15 minutes

To cook: 1 hour

Serves 4

green pear &
grape clafoutis

1 firm but ripe green pear such as Bartlett (Williams')

2 eggs

½ cup (4 fl oz/125 ml) heavy (double) cream

1 cup (8 fl oz/250 ml) low-fat or whole milk

8 Tbsp (4 oz/125 g) sugar

⅔ cup (3½ oz/105 g) all-purpose (plain) flour

1 tsp butter

½ cup (3 oz/90 g) seedless green grapes

Preheat oven to 350°F (180°C). Halve and core pear and cut into ¼-inch (6-mm) dice. Set aside. Butter a baking dish just large enough to hold diced pear in a single layer.

In a bowl, using an electric mixer or a whisk, beat together eggs, cream, milk, and 5 Tbsp (2½ oz/75 g) sugar until well combined. Sprinkle in flour and beat until flour is incorporated and batter is smooth.

Cover bottom of prepared baking dish with diced pear, patting into a single layer. Layer grapes on top. Sprinkle with remaining 3 Tbsp sugar. Pour batter over. Bake until golden and puffed, about 45 minutes. Serve clafoutis hot or warm.

To prepare: 10 minutes

To cook: 45 minutes

4–6 dessert servings

cauliflower shallots mushrooms

WHITE AND TAN FRUITS AND VEGETABLES CONTAIN

white turnips tan figs bananas

ANTIOXIDANTS FOR HEALING AND PROTECTION • HELP

tan pears parsnips white corn

MAINTAIN A HEALTHY CHOLESTEROL LEVEL • PROMOTE

potatoes jerusalem artichokes

HEART HEALTH • BOOST THE IMMUNE SYSTEM • SLOW

ginger kohlrabi white asparagus

CHOLESTEROL ABSORPTION • WHITE AND TAN FRUITS

garlic white nectarines jicama

AND VEGETABLES OFFER ANTIOXIDANTS FOR HEALING

White & tan

Though subtle and understated in color, this group of white and tan foods is a varied market basket, ranging from familiar root vegetables to earthy mushrooms to smooth and satisfying tropical fruits. Together they offer a wonderful panoply of enticing flavors and valuable vitamins, minerals, and phytonutrients not available in more dramatically colored produce.

Vegetables and fruits in this group include members of the healthful Allium genus—garlic, onions, leeks, and shallots—along with meaty mushrooms, sugar-sweet nectarines, pungent ginger, and the ubiquitous banana.

We use alliums often for seasoning, but they are so beneficial that they deserve to be the center of the dinner plate. An entrée of pork chops smothered under a heap of sautéed onions and apples touched with Calvados (page 127) proves that the alliums can star in a dish with delicious results.

Sicilian cooks enliven nutrient-rich cauliflower by sautéing it with a mix of capers, anchovies, and nuts. Adding shrimp turns this traditional southern Italian side dish into an appealing main course (page 124).

Pan-searing mushrooms intensifies their taste (page 140), making them an ideal dish to serve with fish or fowl, fold into an omelet, or simply enjoy on their own.

SPRING	SUMMER	AUTUMN	WINTER
white asparagus	bananas & plantains	cauliflower	cauliflower
bananas & plantains	white corn	fennel	celery root
bok choy	white eggplant	tan figs	garlic
cauliflower	garlic	Jerusalem artichokes	ginger
garlic	ginger	kohlrabi	Jerusalem artichokes
ginger	kohlrabi	leeks	leeks
mushrooms	white nectarines	mushrooms	dried mushrooms
onions	onions	onions	onions
parsnips	white peaches	parsnips	parsnips
tan pears	tan pears	tan pears	tan pears
potatoes	plantains	potatoes	shallots
shallots	potatoes	shallots	turnips
turnips	shallots	turnips	water chestnuts

mushroom bruschetta

3 Tbsp olive oil, plus more for drizzling

2 Tbsp lemon juice

1 clove garlic, crushed

1 lb (500 g) portobello mushrooms, brushed clean and stemmed, cut into slices ¼ inch (6 mm) thick

8 slices country-style bread, cut on diagonal ½ inch (12 mm) thick

¼ cup (1 oz/30 g) crumbled feta cheese

2 Tbsp thinly sliced fresh basil leaves

In a bowl, stir together 3 Tbsp olive oil, lemon juice, garlic, ½ tsp salt, and several grindings of pepper. Add mushroom slices and turn to coat evenly. Let stand for 10 minutes–1 hour.

Build a fire in a charcoal grill for cooking over medium-high heat or preheat a gas grill to 375°F (190°C). Brush bread slices on both sides with olive oil and grill until lightly grill-marked, about 1 minute per side. You may need to press bread into grill to get nice grill marks. Remove to a platter, cover with foil, and place near grill to keep warm.

Arrange mushroom slices in a single layer in an oiled grill basket or on oiled heavy-duty aluminum foil. Place basket on or slide foil onto grill. Grill, turning once, until softened and richly browned, about 3 minutes per side. Divide mushrooms among grilled bread slices, drizzle with olive oil, and sprinkle with feta and basil. Serve at once.

To prepare: 10 minutes, plus 10 minutes to marinate

To cook: 8 minutes

4 starter servings

mustard-honey leeks

¼ cup (2 fl oz/60 ml) extra-virgin olive oil

2 Tbsp white wine vinegar

2 tsp Dijon mustard

1 tsp honey

1 lb (500 g) leeks, preferably no more than ½–¾ inch (12 mm–2 cm) thick

Build a fire in a charcoal grill for cooking over medium heat or preheat a gas grill to 350°F (180°C). Oil grill rack. Whisk olive oil, vinegar, mustard, honey, ½ tsp salt, and several grindings of pepper together in a bowl.

Bring a large sauté pan of lightly salted water to a boil. If using small leeks, trim tough green parts and root ends. If using slightly larger leeks, remove any tough or bruised outer leaves, trim, then cut down 2–3 inches (5–7.5 cm) through the length, without cutting into the white base. Rinse under cold running water to remove any grit, spreading leaves gently but keeping bulbs intact. Simmer leeks in boiling water to soften slightly, about 5 minutes. Drain thoroughly.

Brush leeks lightly with olive oil and sprinkle with salt and pepper. Grill, turning often, until lightly browned, 10–12 minutes. Remove to a serving platter. Pour dressing over and turn gently to coat thoroughly. Let stand for 30 minutes before serving.

To prepare: 15 minutes, plus 30 minutes to stand

To cook: 15 minutes

4 starter or side-dish servings

baked onion & white eggplant purée

1 large white globe eggplant (aubergine), quartered

1 tsp olive oil

2 yellow onions, quartered

4 cloves garlic, peeled but left whole

2 tsp minced fresh thyme

1 tsp lemon juice

Flat bread or crackers for serving

Preheat oven to 350°F (180°C). Lightly oil a small baking dish.

Rub eggplant quarters with olive oil. Arrange eggplant, onions, and garlic in prepared dish and cover tightly with foil. Roast until vegetables are very tender, about 1 hour. Let cool.

When eggplant is cool enough to handle, scoop flesh from skin into blender or food processor with a large spoon. (Discard skin.) Add other roasted vegetables, thyme, lemon juice, 1 tsp salt, and ½ tsp pepper and process until smooth. Taste and adjust seasoning. Serve with flat bread or crackers.

To prepare: 10 minutes, plus 20 minutes to cool

To cook: 1 hour

4 starter servings

mashed jerusalem artichokes with truffle oil

1½ lb (750 g) Jerusalem artichokes

1½ tsp olive oil

2 Tbsp heavy (double) cream

1 tsp white or black truffle oil (see Note)

Preheat oven to 350°F (180°C). Place Jerusalem artichokes in a baking dish and rub with olive oil. Roast until fork-tender, about 45 minutes. Remove from oven and set aside until cool enough to handle.

Peel Jerusalem artichokes with a paring knife or vegetable peeler and place in a bowl. Add cream, 1 tsp salt, and ½ tsp pepper and mash with a fork or potato masher to a smooth paste. Taste and adjust seasoning with salt and pepper. Scoop into a serving dish and drizzle with truffle oil. Serve at once, directly from dish.

Note: Use white truffle oil for a subtle earthy flavor, or black truffle oil for more pronounced taste.

To prepare: 5 minutes

To cook: 45 minutes

4 side-dish servings

white asparagus mimosa with browned butter

16 spears white asparagus, lower halves peeled

2 Tbsp butter

1 hard-boiled egg, whites finely chopped and yolk reserved

Steam asparagus or blanch in boiling water for 4 minutes. Chill in ice water, drain, and pat dry. (This step may be done up to 4 hours ahead.)

Melt butter in a frying pan over medium-high heat. Add asparagus and sauté until butter starts to brown, 2–3 minutes. Divide asparagus among 4 warmed salad plates and spoon on butter from pan. Spoon chopped egg whites on top of asparagus. Press some egg yolk through a fine-mesh sieve over egg whites and serve.

To prepare: 20 minutes

To cook: 6 minutes

4 side-dish servings

potato galettes with smoked salmon

2 medium russet potatoes, about ¾ lb (375 g) total, peeled

About 2 Tbsp canola or olive oil

3 oz (90 g) thinly sliced smoked salmon

1 Tbsp snipped fresh chives

1–2 Tbsp reduced-fat sour cream for garnish (optional)

Shred potatoes at an angle on largest holes of a box grater-shredder to make long shreds. A small handful at a time, squeeze potatoes dry.

Heat 2 tsp oil in a frying pan over medium-high heat. Put 1 heaping Tbsp potato in pan for each galette, making 4 at a time. With a spatula, firmly flatten potatoes into 3-inch (7.5-cm) pancakes, repeatedly pressing to compact potatoes and pushing in loose edges so they do not burn. Work spatula under potatoes to prevent sticking. Keep pressing and lifting galettes until tops look translucent, about 3 minutes. Turn and cook, continuing to press and lift, until galettes are well browned, about 3 minutes more. While still hot, season to taste with salt and pepper. Wipe out pan.

Add oil by the teaspoon, as needed, and repeat, cooking galettes in 2 more batches. As pan gets hotter, potatoes will cook more quickly. Lower heat if necessary so galettes cook through in center.

Serve galettes as they are cooked, topped with a 2-inch (5-cm) square of smoked salmon and a sprinkle of chives. Dot with sour cream, if desired.

To prepare: 10 minutes

To cook: 20 minutes

4 starter servings (12 galettes)

turkey sandwiches
with sweet onions

2 tsp ground cumin

½ tsp *each* ground smoked paprika, fennel, cardamom, ginger, cinnamon, and pepper

½ cup (4 fl oz/125 ml) reduced-fat or regular mayonnaise

2 Tbsp olive oil

2 cloves garlic, crushed

1 lb (500 g) turkey scaloppine, ¼ inch (6 mm) thick

2 large Vidalia or other sweet onions, sliced in rings ½ inch (12 mm) thick

4 sandwich rolls, split

Mixed salad greens, tomato slices, and avocado slices for garnish

Stir spices together. In a separate bowl, combine 1 tsp spice mixture and the mayonnaise, stir to mix well, and refrigerate. Stir together remaining spice mixture, olive oil, garlic, and 1 tsp salt. Pour over turkey in a shallow dish and turn to coat evenly. Cover and refrigerate for 30 minutes–4 hours. Remove from the refrigerator 15 minutes before grilling.

Build a fire in a charcoal grill for cooking over medium heat or preheat a gas grill to 350°F (180°C). Oil grill rack. Brush onion slices on both sides with olive oil. Grill until lightly browned, 4 minutes per side. Add turkey to grill and cook until browned, 2 minutes per side. Meanwhile, continue grilling onions, turning often, until golden and just caramelized, 5–7 minutes more. Remove onions and turkey to a platter.

Grill rolls until lightly browned and grill-marked, about 1 minute. Divide turkey among rolls. Top with grilled onions. Spread tops of rolls with flavored mayonnaise. Top sandwiches and serve with garnishes.

To prepare: 10 minutes, plus 30 minutes to marinate

To cook: 15 minutes

4 servings

grilled white corn salad

6 ears white corn, husked

2 Tbsp *each* olive oil and lime juice

2 cloves garlic, minced

1–2 green chiles, seeded and minced

1 tsp firmly packed light brown sugar

1 tsp ground cumin

½ tsp red pepper flakes

½ cup (½ oz/15 g) cilantro (fresh coriander) leaves

2 green (spring) onions, including tender green parts, thinly sliced

Build a fire in a charcoal grill for cooking over medium heat or preheat a gas grill to 350°F (180°C). Oil grill rack. Fill a bowl with cold water, add 1 tsp salt, and stir to dissolve. Add corn and let stand for 10 minutes.

Combine olive oil, lime juice, garlic, chile to taste, brown sugar, cumin, red pepper flakes, ½ tsp salt, and several grindings of black pepper. Stir to dissolve sugar and mix well. Set dressing aside.

Drain corn thoroughly, pat dry, and brush with olive oil. Grill, turning often, until lightly browned and tender, about 15 minutes. Let cool, then use a sharp, heavy knife to cut kernels from cobs. Put kernels in a mixing bowl. Add cilantro and green onions and toss gently to combine. Add dressing and again toss gently to coat thoroughly. Taste and adjust seasoning. Arrange on a platter and serve at room temperature.

To prepare: 10 minutes, plus 10 minutes to stand

To cook: 15 minutes

4–6 side-dish servings

grilled white corn with herb butter

Soak husked ears of white corn in lightly salted cold water for 10 minutes. Brush kernels lightly with oil. Grill over medium heat until lightly browned and tender. Spread with butter mixed with minced garlic, herbs, salt, and pepper.

grilled shallots

Grill whole unpeeled shallots over very low or indirect heat until collapsed and blackened, about 25 minutes. Let cool, then peel. Drizzle with a little olive oil and balsamic vinegar. Scatter with toasted pine nuts. Serve with grilled meats.

grilled parsnip chips with lemon & honey

Rinse and peel parsnips and slice lengthwise into long, thin chips. Toss with olive oil to coat and grill over medium heat, turning often, until lightly browned. Drizzle with a mixture of honey, lemon zest and juice, and chopped fresh herbs.

pesto portobellos

Brush portobello mushrooms clean and trim stems. Spoon a little pesto over gill sides. Sprinkle with lemon juice, salt, and pepper; dot with butter. Grill, gill side up, over medium-low heat until mushrooms are soft and pesto bubbles.

pork pot roast with parsnips, carrots & apples

1 boneless pork shoulder roast, about 2¾ lb (1.5 kg)

3 Tbsp olive oil

½ cup (2 oz/60 g) coarsely chopped yellow onion

3 cloves garlic, minced

1 cup (8 fl oz/250 ml) low-sodium chicken broth

3 Tbsp Dijon mustard

2 parsnips, peeled and sliced ¾ inch (2 cm) thick

2 carrots, peeled and sliced ¾ inch (2 cm) thick

2 firm, sweet apples such as Gala or Golden Delicious, cored and cut into ¾-inch (2-cm) pieces

Chopped parsley for garnish

Rub pork roast all over with 1 tsp salt and 1 tsp pepper.

In a Dutch oven or flameproof casserole with a lid, heat olive oil over medium-high heat. Add onion and sauté until just translucent, about 3 minutes. Add garlic and sauté until garlic is fragrant and golden, about 1 minute more. Using a slotted spoon, remove onion and garlic to a bowl.

Add pork to pot and sear until bottom is browned, about 3 minutes. Using tongs to turn pork, brown all other sides, 3–4 minutes per side. Return garlic and onion to pot and add chicken broth, stirring to scrape up browned bits from bottom of pan. Spread mustard over top of roast and tuck parsnips and carrots around it. Raise heat to high, bring liquid to a boil, and then cover and place in oven. Bake for 45 minutes, then remove from oven and add apples, tucking them beneath other vegetables and into juices. Re-cover and cook until an instant-read thermometer inserted into center of meat registers 145°–150°F (63°–65°C) and vegetables and apples are tender, 30 minutes more.

Remove roast to a cutting board and, using a slotted spoon, transfer vegetables and apples to a warmed platter. Cover both loosely with foil and let rest for 10 minutes.

To serve, cut pork into slices about ¼ inch (6 mm) thick and arrange overlapping on a warmed platter or on warmed individual plates. Spoon vegetables and apples alongside, sprinkle with parsley, and serve.

To prepare: 10 minutes

To cook: 1½ hours, plus 10 minutes to rest

4–6 servings

sicilian shrimp with cauliflower & almonds

½ cup (3 oz/90 g) golden raisins (sultanas)

¾ lb (375 g) small shrimp (prawns)

6 cups 1-inch (2.5-cm) cauliflower florets (about 12 oz/375 g)

2 Tbsp olive oil

1½ cups (6 oz/185 g) diced yellow onions

2 cloves garlic, finely chopped

1 cup (6 oz/185 g) chopped tomatoes

4 anchovy fillets, rinsed

½ cup (4 fl oz/125 ml) chicken broth

1 tsp dried basil

Pinch of red pepper flakes

Toasted sliced (flaked) almonds for garnish (see Note, page 84)

In small bowl, cover raisins with warm water and let stand until plumped, about 20 minutes. Meanwhile, peel shrimp. Drain raisins and set raisins and shrimp aside.

Steam cauliflower until fork-tender, about 5 minutes. Drain and set aside.

Heat oil in a sauté pan over medium-high heat. Add onions and sauté until lightly browned, 8–10 minutes. Add garlic and tomatoes and cook, stirring occasionally, until tomatoes start to break down, 5 minutes. Add shrimp and sauté until bright pink, about 3 minutes. Add anchovies, mashing them with back of a wooden spoon. Add cauliflower, raisins, broth, basil, and red pepper flakes. Lower heat to medium and cook until shrimp are opaque in center, about 3 minutes.

Remove from heat and stir in almonds. Serve on a warmed platter.

Note: Serve with steamed brown rice or cooked spaghetti.

To prepare: 25 minutes, plus 20 minutes to soak

To cook: 25 minutes

4 servings

potatoes with chorizo & parsley

1½ lb (750 g) large boiling potatoes, quartered

½ cup (2 oz/60 g) peeled, thinly sliced hot or sweet dry chorizo (see Note)

¼ cup (1 oz/30 g) finely chopped red onion

¼ cup (2 fl oz/60 ml) dry white wine such as Chablis or Soave

2 Tbsp chopped fresh parsley

Boil potatoes until fork-tender, about 20 minutes. Drain and keep warm.

Heat a nonstick medium frying pan over medium-high heat. Add chorizo and sauté to render most of its fat, about 2 minutes. Pour off fat and continue cooking chorizo until lightly browned, 1–2 minutes more. Add onion and sauté for 1 minute. Add potatoes and wine and cook until most of liquid has evaporated, about 1 minute. Remove to a shallow serving bowl and toss with parsley. Serve warm.

Note: To peel chorizo, lightly run a sharp knife down its length. With your fingers, peel skin away from sausage, as if unwrapping it.

To prepare: 12 minutes

To cook: 25 minutes

4 side-dish servings

turkey fricassee with kohlrabi, pears & mushrooms

¾ lb (375 g) boneless turkey breast

2 Tbsp canola oil

¾ cup (3 oz/90 g) chopped yellow onion

2 Tbsp chopped shallot

¼ cup (1½ oz/45 g) all-purpose (plain) flour

1 cup (8 fl oz/250 ml) hard apple cider

⅓ cup (3 oz/90 g) Dijon mustard

1 Tbsp ground coriander

1 Bosc pear, peeled, cored, and diced

2 medium kohlrabi, peeled and diced

½ lb (250 g) white mushrooms, stemmed and quartered

Cut turkey into bite-sized pieces. Heat oil in a large sauté pan over medium-high heat. Add turkey and cook, stirring occasionally, until white on all sides, 3–4 minutes; lower heat if necessary to avoid scorching. Using slotted spoon, remove to a plate.

Return pan to medium-high heat, add onion and shallot, and sauté until translucent, about 4 minutes. Lower heat, stir in flour, and cook for 1 minute, stirring constantly. Add cider, which will splatter, and stir to combine with flour. Add mustard, coriander, pear, kohlrabi, mushrooms, and turkey and stir well. Simmer, stirring occasionally, until turkey is opaque at the center and vegetables and pear are tender, about 20 minutes.

Remove to a warmed serving bowl and serve at once.

Note: Serve accompanied with green beans and steamed brown rice.

To prepare: 20 minutes

To cook: 30 minutes

4 servings

pork chops smothered in onions & apples

2 Tbsp canola oil

1 lb (500 g) onions, halved and thinly sliced crosswise

1 Crispin or Golden Delicious apple, halved, cored, and cut crosswise into slices ¼ inch (6 mm) thick

4 boneless pork chops, 4 oz (125 g) each

½ cup (4 fl oz/125 ml) low-sodium chicken broth

2 Tbsp Calvados

Heat 1 Tbsp oil in a medium sauté pan over medium-high heat. Add onions and sauté until wilted, about 5 minutes. Add apple and sauté for 2 minutes. Using slotted spoon, remove onions and apples to a plate.

Return pan to medium-high heat and add remaining 1 Tbsp oil. Season chops with salt and pepper. Sauté chops, turning once, until lightly browned on both sides, 4–5 minutes total. Spoon onion mixture over chops and cook until meat is barely pink in center, 4–5 minutes. Remove onion and apples to a warmed serving platter and arrange chops on top.

Add broth and Calvados to pan and stir to scrape up browned bits. Boil until liquid is reduced by half, about 4 minutes. Spoon sauce over meat and serve at once.

To prepare: 20 minutes

To cook: 22 minutes

4 servings

monkfish with roasted white corn salsa

2 ears white corn, husks and silk removed

3½ tsp corn oil

1 tsp mild paprika

1 avocado, pitted, peeled, and cut into small dice

4 tomatillos, husked, rinsed, and minced

2 Tbsp minced cilantro (fresh coriander)

2 serrano chiles, seeded and minced

3 Tbsp lime juice

¼ cup (1 oz/30 g) crumbled *queso fresco* or feta cheese

1⅓ lb (655 g) monkfish, membrane removed, cut into slices 1 inch (2.5 cm) thick

Preheat oven to 400°F (200°C). Rub corn with 2 tsp oil and season with paprika and salt and pepper to taste. Place in a baking dish and roast, turning occasionally, until kernels are lightly browned and beginning to wrinkle, 35–40 minutes. Remove from oven and set aside to cool. Raise oven temperature to 450°F (230°C). Lightly oil another baking dish just large enough to accommodate the fish medallions in a single layer.

When corn is cool enough to handle, use a heavy, sharp knife to cut kernels from cobs into a bowl. Add avocado, tomatillos, cilantro, chiles, and lime juice. Toss gently until ingredients are evenly distributed. Sprinkle with cheese. Set aside.

Season fish with salt and pepper and arrange in a single layer in prepared baking dish. Drizzle with 1½ tsp oil and turn to coat evenly. Roast until fish is opaque throughout and flakes easily with a fork, 15–20 minutes.

To serve, spoon some salsa onto each of 4 warmed plates, dividing evenly, and top with the fish medallions.

To prepare: 15 minutes

To cook: 1 hour

4 servings

roasted onions with balsamic & pepper

Peel and quarter several yellow onions. Arrange snugly in a small baking dish, drizzle with olive oil and balsamic vinegar, sprinkle with pepper, and turn to coat. Cover and roast at 350°F (180°C), turning occasionally, until tender, about 1 hour.

roasted mushrooms with sage butter

Mash butter with minced fresh sage, salt, and pepper. Arrange mushrooms snugly, stem side up, in a buttered baking dish. Dot with sage butter and scatter with a few sage leaves. Roast in a hot oven until tender and fragrant.

roasted garlic spread with thyme

Cut off top third of 3 garlic heads. Nestle in a baking dish, cut side up, and drizzle with olive oil. Roast at 325°F (165°C) until tender, about 1 hour. Squeeze garlic pulp into a bowl and mix in extra-virgin olive oil, cream, thyme, salt, and pepper.

tan pear crumble with lavender

Snugly arrange pear halves, cut side up, in a buttered baking dish. Top with a crumbly mix of cold butter, flour, sugar, and lavender blossoms. Cover and bake until tender, 40 minutes. Uncover and broil (grill) until golden. Serve with cream.

white eggplant
& green onion salad

2 Tbsp extra-virgin olive oil

2 Tbsp lemon juice

1 Tbsp tahini

2 cloves garlic, minced

4 Asian white eggplants (slender aubergines), about 1 lb (500 g), cut crosswise into slices ¼ inch (6 mm)

2 green (spring) onions, white parts only, finely chopped

2 Tbsp finely chopped fresh parsley

Build a fire in a charcoal grill for cooking over medium heat or preheat a gas grill to 350°F (180°C). Oil grill rack. Whisk oil, lemon juice, tahini, and garlic together in a bowl. Set dressing aside.

Brush eggplant slices on both sides with oil and sprinkle with salt and pepper. Grill, turning once, until golden and softened, 4–5 minutes per side. Remove from heat and place in a covered bowl to steam and cool (this softens them fully and makes them more tender).

Add green onions and parsley to bowl with eggplant. Pour dressing over and toss well. Taste and adjust seasoning. Let stand for 30 minutes to meld flavors. Serve at once, or cover and refrigerate for up to 8 hours and bring to room temperature before serving.

To prepare: 10 minutes, plus 30 minutes to stand

To cook: 10 minutes

4 starter servings

grilled fennel
with indian spices

2 medium or 4 small fennel bulbs, about 1 lb (500 g)

Boiling water as needed

3 Tbsp olive oil

2 tsp *each* mustard seeds and ground coriander

1¼ tsp ground cumin

½ tsp *each* ground cloves and cardamom

½ cup (4 oz/125 g) low-fat or whole plain yogurt

¼ cup (1 oz/30 g) shredded cucumber

1 Tbsp chopped fresh mint

Trim fennel and slice thinly lengthwise. Place fennel in a heatproof bowl, pour over boiling water to cover, and let stand for 2 minutes to soften slightly. Drain thoroughly, pat dry, and return to bowl. Add oil, mustard seeds, coriander, 1 tsp cumin, cloves, cardamom, ½ tsp salt, and several grindings of pepper and toss to mix well and coat evenly. (This step can be done up to 4 hours ahead of grilling.)

Combine yogurt, cucumber, mint, and remaining cumin and set aside.

Build a fire in a charcoal grill for cooking over medium heat or preheat a gas grill to 350°F (180°C). Oil grill rack. Grill fennel, turning occasionally, until softened and lightly browned, about 3 minutes per side. Serve at once, with flavored yogurt.

To prepare: 10 minutes

To cook: 6 minutes

4 side-dish servings

cuban-style pork & plantains

Marinade

2 Tbsp olive oil

Grated zest of ½ orange

Grated zest of ½ lime

2 Tbsp *each* orange juice and lime juice

1 Tbsp white wine vinegar

2 tsp maple syrup

2 cloves garlic, crushed

1 Tbsp chopped fresh oregano or 1 tsp dried oregano

1 tsp *each* ground cumin and allspice

½ tsp red pepper flakes (optional)

4 bone-in center-cut rib or loin pork chops, each about ¾ inch (2 cm) thick

4 pineapple slices, 1 inch (2.5 cm) thick, each cut into thirds (optional)

2 yellow plantains

For Marinade: In a glass measuring pitcher, whisk together olive oil, orange and lime zests, orange and lime juices, vinegar, maple syrup, garlic, oregano, cumin, allspice, red pepper flakes (if using), ¾ tsp salt, and ½ tsp black pepper.

Put pork and pineapple, if using, in a bowl. Add half of marinade; cover and refrigerate remainder until ready to serve. Turn pork and pineapple to coat evenly. Cover and marinate at room temperature for 20 minutes, or refrigerate for up to 2 hours. Bring to room temperature before grilling.

Build a fire in a charcoal grill for cooking over medium-high heat or preheat a gas grill to 375°F (190°C). Oil grill rack.

Meanwhile, cook plantains whole in their skins in a saucepan of boiling water for 5 minutes. Drain and let cool for about 10 minutes. When cool enough to handle, peel off the skins and cut the flesh crosswise into slices ¾ inch (2 cm) thick.

Remove pork chops and pineapple, if using, from marinade and discard marinade. Grill pork until golden on outside and just faintly pink in center (an instant-read thermometer inserted in thickest part, away from bone, should read 145°F/63°C), 2–3 minutes per side. Remove to a platter, tent with foil, and let rest for 5 minutes. Brush plantain slices with olive oil on both sides and sprinkle with salt and pepper. Grill plantains and pineapple, if using, turning once, until softened and lightly browned, 2–3 minutes per side.

Arrange pork and fruit on warmed plates, drizzle with reserved marinade, and serve at once.

To prepare: 15 minutes, plus 20 minutes to marinate

To cook: 15 minutes

6 servings

mu shu pork

¾ lb (375 g) lean pork such as boneless loin or sirloin cutlets

Eight 8-inch (20-cm) flour tortillas

2 Tbsp hoisin sauce

1 Tbsp low-sodium soy sauce

1 Tbsp sherry

2 Tbsp low-sodium chicken broth

2 tsp sugar

1 tsp Asian sesame oil

¼ cup (2 fl oz/60 ml) peanut or canola oil

1 Tbsp minced garlic

1 Tbsp minced fresh ginger

1 carrot, cut into thin strips

1 stalk celery, cut into thin strips

1 leek, white part only, cut into thin strips

¼ lb (125 g) fresh shiitake mushrooms, stemmed and cut into thin strips

¾ cup (5 oz/155 g) canned sliced water chestnuts, drained and cut into thin strips

Freeze meat for up to 1 hour to make it easier to slice. Thinly slice meat with the grain, then cut slices into thin strips. Set aside.

Preheat oven to 350°F (180°C). Wrap tortillas in foil and warm for 10 minutes in oven. Set aside.

In a small bowl, mix together hoisin and soy sauces, sherry, chicken broth, sugar, and sesame oil. Set aside.

Heat oil in a wok over medium-high heat until almost smoking. Add pork and stir-fry until color changes, then remove to a plate using a slotted spoon. Pour off all but 1 Tbsp peanut oil. Add garlic and ginger and stir-fry until fragrant, about 30 seconds. Add carrot, celery, leek, mushrooms, and water chestnuts and stir-fry until vegetables are just tender, about 1½ minutes. Add hoisin sauce mixture and return meat to wok. Cook until opaque in center, 1–2 minutes. Remove to a warmed platter and serve, accompanied with warmed tortillas.

To prepare: 35 minutes, plus 1 hour to freeze meat

To cook: 5 minutes

4 servings

spicy cauliflower gratin

1 medium head cauliflower

4 tsp butter

3½ Tbsp all-purpose (plain) flour

1½ cups (12 fl oz/375 ml) whole milk

⅓ cup (⅔ oz/20 g) fresh bread crumbs (see Notes, page 251)

1 Tbsp capers, rinsed and drained

1 tsp red pepper flakes

Preheat oven to 400°F (200°C). Butter a medium baking dish.

In a covered steamer over boiling water, cook cauliflower head whole until nearly fork-tender, 15–20 minutes. Remove to a cutting board. When cool enough to handle, cut lengthwise into 8 spearlike wedges and arrange in prepared baking dish.

In a saucepan over medium heat, melt 3 tsp butter. When it foams, remove from heat and whisk in flour. Return to medium heat and slowly add milk, whisking constantly. Reduce heat to low, add 1 tsp salt and ½ tsp black pepper, and cook, whisking occasionally, until taste of flour is gone and sauce is thickened and smooth, about 15 minutes.

Meanwhile, in a small frying pan over medium heat, melt remaining 1 tsp butter. When it foams, add bread crumbs and cook, stirring often, until golden, 3–4 minutes.

Stir capers and red pepper flakes into white sauce and pour over cauliflower. Sprinkle evenly with toasted crumbs.

Bake until sauce is bubbling and edges are golden, about 30 minutes. Serve hot, directly from baking dish.

To prepare: 10 minutes

To cook: 1 hour

4 servings

parsley portobellos

4 portobello mushrooms, brushed clean and stemmed

3 Tbsp olive oil, plus more if needed

6 cloves garlic, coarsely chopped

1½ cups (1½ oz/45 g) fresh parsley leaves, plus sprigs for garnish

Preheat oven to 375°F (190°C). Lightly oil a baking dish just large enough to hold mushrooms in a single layer. Rub caps of mushrooms with 1 Tbsp olive oil.

In a food processor, combine 2 Tbsp olive oil, garlic, parsley leaves, ½ tsp salt, and ½ tsp pepper and process until smooth to make *persillade*. If mixture seems too thick, add more olive oil a few drops at a time.

Arrange mushrooms, gill side up, in prepared baking dish. Spread *persillade* on each, dividing evenly and covering gills all the way to the edges. Roast until mushrooms are juicy and tender when pricked with a fork, about 20 minutes. Serve hot, garnished with parsley sprigs.

To prepare: 10 minutes

To cook: 20 minutes

4 side-dish servings

pan-seared mushrooms

Sauté thinly sliced white or cremini mushrooms in a dry skillet over medium-high heat until they release their liquid. Add minced garlic, salt, and pepper. Cook until mushrooms are dry and tender. Sprinkle with chopped parsley and serve.

garlic chips

Sauté thinly sliced garlic cloves in a generous amount of olive oil until pale gold on both sides, then drain on paper towels. The garlic turns crisp as it cools. Sprinkle on steamed vegetables and use to garnish soups.

hot & sour bok choy

Combine juice of ½ lime, 2 tsp sugar, red pepper flakes, and salt in a small bowl. Stir-fry 1-inch (2.5-cm) slices of white part of mature bok choy in peanut oil for a minute. Add lime sauce and stir-fry for a minute more. Serve hot or warm.

plantain with jalapeño

Sauté a thinly sliced jalapeño chile in coconut oil until fragrant. Set aside. Add a thinly sliced ripe plantain to pan. Cook until slices are golden on both sides. Drain on paper towels. Sprinkle jalapeño slices over plantain and serve at once.

roasted fennel
with fennel seed

1 tsp fennel seeds

3 medium fennel bulbs, with stems and fronds still attached, if possible

2 Tbsp olive oil

½ cup (4 fl oz/125 ml) dry white wine

¼ cup (2 fl oz/60 ml) low-sodium vegetable broth, chicken broth, or water

Preheat oven to 400°F (200°C). Put fennel seeds in a small sauté pan and toast over low heat, shaking pan frequently so seeds toast evenly, until fragrant, 2–3 minutes. Crush and grind seeds with a mortar and pestle, or chop finely using a sharp chef's knife.

Cut stalks from fennel bulbs, reserving a handful of green fronds. If fronds do not look fresh, discard; otherwise, lightly chop enough to measure about ¼ cup (⅓ oz/10 g). Remove any bruised outer leaves from fennel bulbs, then cut bulbs into 1½-inch (4-cm) wedges and arrange in a small, shallow baking dish. Drizzle olive oil and wine over fennel and sprinkle with salt to taste and fennel seeds. Add broth and sprinkle chopped fennel fronds over all, if using. Toss to coat evenly.

Cover dish with foil and place in oven. Cook for 30 minutes. Remove foil and continue roasting until fennel is golden, 15–20 minutes more. Fennel should be tender when pierced with a sharp knife. Serve warm.

To prepare: 15 minutes

To cook: 50 minutes

4 side-dish servings

celery root &
potato gratin

1 lb (500 g) celery root (celeriac), peeled and cut into 1-inch (2.5-cm) cubes

1 lb (500 g) russet potatoes, peeled and cut into 1-inch (2.5-cm) cubes

½ cup (4 fl oz/125 ml) heavy (double) cream

¼ cup (2 fl oz/60 ml) low-fat or whole milk

2 Tbsp butter

⅓ cup (1½ oz/45 g) grated Parmesan cheese

Preheat oven to 400°F (200°C). Butter a medium baking dish.

In a saucepan, combine celery root and potatoes with water to cover by 2 inches (5 cm). Add 1 tsp salt and bring to a boil over high heat. Cover and reduce heat to medium. Cook until very tender, 10–15 minutes.

Drain vegetables thoroughly in a colander and return to warm saucepan. Add cream, milk, butter, and 1 tsp pepper. Using a potato masher or an electric mixer, beat until smooth and creamy. Spread celery root mixture evenly in prepared baking dish and sprinkle with Parmesan. Bake until top is lightly browned, 15–20 minutes.

Serve hot, directly from baking dish.

To prepare: 10 minutes

To cook: 35 minutes

6 side-dish servings

turnips with peas & mushrooms

2 tsp grape seed or canola oil

4 small white turnips, about 1 lb (500 g) total, peeled and cut into ½-inch (12-mm) wedges

⅔ cup (5 fl oz/160 ml) low-sodium chicken broth

1 cup (5 oz/155 g) frozen peas

½ cup (3 oz/90 g) pan-seared mushrooms (page 140), warmed

Heat oil in a large nonstick frying pan over medium-high heat. Add turnips and stir to coat with oil. Sauté for 1 minute; do not let turnips take on color.

Add ½ cup (4 fl oz/125 ml) broth. When it boils, lower heat and cook turnips for 3 minutes, then turn with tongs. When pan is almost dry, add remaining broth and cook until turnips are fork-tender, 3 minutes more. Add peas and heat through. Spoon vegetables into a wide, shallow serving bowl, top with mushrooms, and serve.

To prepare: 15 minutes

To cook: 7 minutes

4 side-dish servings

chicken with caramelized shallots & wine

2 Tbsp butter

¾ lb (375 g) large shallots, cut into slices ¼ inch (6-mm) thick (1½ cups)

2 tsp sugar

1 tsp minced fresh rosemary

4 skinless, boneless chicken breast halves, 4–5 oz (125–155 g) each

½ cup (4 fl oz/125 ml) light red wine such as a fruity Pinot Noir

½ cup (4 fl oz/125 ml) low-sodium chicken broth

1 tsp red wine vinegar

2 Tbsp fresh chervil leaves or chopped fresh parsley for garnish

Melt 1 Tbsp butter in a medium frying pan over medium-high heat. Add shallots and sauté until translucent, about 8 minutes. Stir in sugar and rosemary and cook until shallots are limp and gold, 8 minutes, lowering heat if needed to avoid burning. Remove shallots to a plate and wipe out pan with paper towels.

Pound each breast half between 2 sheets of plastic wrap, using a mallet or rolling pin, until ½ inch (12 mm) thick. Heat 1 Tbsp butter in same pan over medium-high heat. Add chicken, season to taste with salt and pepper and sauté, turning often, until browned on both sides, about 12 minutes. Remove to a warmed serving platter and tent with foil.

Add shallots, wine, broth, and vinegar to pan, bring to a boil, and stir to scrape up browned bits. Cook until liquid is reduced by half, about 4 minutes. Remove from heat. Spoon sauce over chicken. Garnish with chervil and serve at once.

To prepare: 20 minutes

To cook: 32 minutes

4 servings

white nectarines
with raw sugar & rum

1 Tbsp butter

4 white nectarines, halved and pitted

8 tsp raw sugar

8 tsp dark rum

Preheat oven to 375°F (190°C). Butter a baking dish just large enough to hold nectarine halves in a single layer. Arrange nectarines, cut sides up, in prepared dish.

Put 1 tsp sugar and 1 tsp rum into the cavity of each nectarine half.

Bake until sugar has melted and nectarines are soft but not collapsed, 10–15 minutes. Serve hot or warm.

To prepare: 5 minutes

To cook: 15 minutes

4 dessert servings

baked bananas
& tapioca pudding

⅓ cup (3 oz) granulated sugar

3 Tbsp instant tapioca

2¾ cup (22 fl oz/680 ml) low-fat or whole milk

1 egg, well beaten

1 tsp vanilla extract (essence)

3 barely ripe bananas, still slightly green at the tips

1½ Tbsp lemon juice

1½ Tbsp firmly packed light brown sugar

1 Tbsp butter

Sliced (flaked) almonds, toasted, for garnish (optional; see Note page 84)

In a medium saucepan, combine granulated sugar, tapioca, milk, and egg and mix well. Let stand for 5 minutes. Place saucepan over medium heat and bring mixture to a full, rolling boil. Remove from heat and stir in vanilla. Let cool for 20 minutes, then stir and pour into individual pudding dishes. Refrigerate for up to 12 hours in advance of serving.

Preheat oven to 400°F (200°C). Peel bananas and cut into slices ½ inch (12 mm) thick. Butter a shallow baking dish just large enough to hold sliced bananas in a single layer.

Place bananas in a bowl and drizzle with lemon juice, turning several times. Place in prepared baking dish in a crowded or slightly overlapping single layer, sprinkle brown sugar over them, and dot with butter. Bake until sugar has melted and formed a syrup, 10–15 minutes.

To serve, spoon warm bananas and some of their syrup on top of tapioca puddings. Garnish with toasted almonds, if desired.

To prepare: 30 minutes

To cook: 30 minutes

5 or 6 servings

grapefruit   papayas   pineapples

YELLOW AND ORANGE FRUITS AND VEGETABLES HELP

apricots yellow pears pumpkins

PROMOTE HEART HEALTH • HELP REDUCE THE RISK OF

persimmons peaches kumquats

CERTAIN CANCERS • PROMOTE EYE HEALTH • CONTAIN

rutabagas golden beets carrots

ANTIOXIDANTS FOR HEALING AND PROTECTION • BOOST

yellow apples orange tomatoes

THE IMMUNE SYSTEM • YELLOW AND ORANGE FRUITS

mangoes sweet potatoes corn

AND VEGETABLES OFFER ANTIOXIDANTS FOR HEALING

Yellow & orange

Corn, oranges, sweet potatoes, pumpkins, apples, pears, lemons—this chapter offers a basketful of beloved vegetables and fruits that even picky eaters are happy to eat. These nutrient-rich members of the yellow and orange family get their eye-catching hues from carotenes, important antioxidants that give these fruits and vegetables their vibrant color and a healthy load of vitamin A.

These antioxidants turn peppers, potatoes, and berries usually associated with other color groups a glowing gold or orange. The color of yellow and orange bell peppers, yellow-fleshed potatoes, and golden raspberries let you know they offer different benefits from their more familiarly colored cousins.

Sautéing caramelizes the natural sugars in the orange-fleshed sweet potatoes often called yams, giving a crust to creamy hash made with sweet potatoes, smoky ham, and apples (page 184). Hard-shelled orange winter squashes and pumpkin can taste bland on their own, but coating thin slices with a dry spice rub adds

the aromatic and hot flavors of Indian curry (page 183). Rutabaga turns irresistibly sweet when cooked with golden beets until tender (page 183). And combining pineapple with preserved ginger results in an almost-instant dessert whose digestive benefits make it a perfect ending to a meal (page 180).

SPRING	SUMMER	AUTUMN	WINTER
carrots	apricots	yellow apples	yellow apples
grapefruit	yellow bell peppers	dried apricots	dried apricots
golden kiwifruit	corn	golden beets	golden beets
kumquats	mangoes	yellow bell peppers	carrots
lemons	nectarines	lemons	grapefruit
mangoes	Valencia oranges	navel & Mandarin oranges	lemons
navel & Mandarin oranges	passion fruit	yellow pears	navel & Mandarin oranges
papayas	papayas	persimmons	yellow pears
yellow-fleshed potatoes	peaches	yellow-fleshed potatoes	yellow-fleshed potatoes
orange-fleshed winter squash	pineapples	pumpkins	pumpkins
sweet potatoes	golden raspberries	rutabagas	rutabagas
	yellow summer squash	orange-fleshed winter squash	orange-fleshed winter squash
	yellow tomatoes	sweet potatoes	sweet potatoes

yellow tomatoes
with mint & pecorino

2 tsp firmly packed light brown sugar

1 tsp curry powder

6 large yellow tomatoes, cored and halved lengthwise

1½ oz (45 g) pecorino cheese, coarsely grated (⅓ cup)

14 mint leaves, finely chopped

2 green (spring) onions, including tender green parts, finely chopped

1 Tbsp extra-virgin olive oil

Preheat broiler (grill). Put sugar, curry powder, 1 tsp salt, and several grindings of pepper on a saucer and stir to combine. Press cut surfaces of tomatoes into spice mixture and then arrange, coated side up, on a baking sheet lined with foil.

Slide tomatoes under broiler (grill) 4–6 inches (10–15 cm) from heat and cook until topping bubbles and starts to caramelize, 10 minutes.

Meanwhile, combine pecorino, mint, green onions, and olive oil in a bowl and stir to mix well. Remove tomatoes to a platter. Sprinkle cheese mixture over tomatoes and serve hot.

To prepare: 10 minutes

To cook: 10 minutes

4–6 side-dish servings

grilled pumpkin with
pumpkin seed dressing

¼ cup (1 oz/30 g) hulled pumpkin seeds

½ cup (4 fl oz/125 ml) orange juice

1 Tbsp grape seed oil

1 small red chile, seeded and minced

1 Sugar Pie pumpkin, 12–16 oz (375–500 g), halved and seeded

2 Tbsp olive oil

2 green (spring) onions, including tender green parts, thinly sliced

2 Tbsp chopped cilantro (fresh coriander) (optional)

Build a fire in a charcoal grill for cooking over medium-low heat or preheat a gas grill to 300°F (150°C). Oil grill rack.

Place pumpkin seeds in a small, dry frying pan over medium heat and toast, stirring occasionally, until golden, 3–4 minutes. In a blender or food processor, combine pumpkin seeds, orange juice, grape seed oil, chile, ½ tsp salt, and several grindings of pepper and process to make a dressing that is almost smooth but retains some texture.

With a heavy knife, cut pumpkin into 3-inch (7.5-cm) wedges, then cut each wedge crosswise into slices ¼ inch (6 mm) thick. Put in a bowl and add olive oil and salt and pepper to taste. Turn to coat pumpkin evenly. Grill pumpkin, turning often, until lightly browned and nearly fork-tender, 8–10 minutes. Remove to a cutting board and let cool to touch. Put in a bowl. Pour dressing over and toss gently to combine, taking care not to break up pumpkin. Remove to a serving platter and sprinkle with green onions and cilantro, if using. Serve warm or at room temperature.

To prepare: 20 minutes

To cook: 10 minutes

4–6 side-dish servings

corn & crab quesadillas

½ tsp chili powder

2 ears yellow corn, husks and silk removed

1½ Tbsp corn or grape seed oil

4 burrito-sized flour tortillas

¼ lb (125 g) fresh lump crabmeat, picked over for bits of shell and cartilage

1 cup (4 oz/125 g) Monterey jack cheese, shredded

¼ cup (⅓ oz/10 g) chopped cilantro (fresh coriander), plus sprigs for garnish

Preheat oven to 375°F (190°C). Stir together chili powder, ½ tsp salt, and ½ tsp pepper. Rub each ear of corn with 1 tsp oil, then rub with spice blend. Put in a large baking dish and roast, turning occasionally, until kernels are lightly browned and beginning to wrinkle, about 35 minutes. Remove from oven, let cool, and then cut kernels from cobs. Divide corn among tortillas, mounding it on one-half of each tortilla. Top corn with equal amounts of crabmeat, cheese, and chopped cilantro, in that order. Fold filled tortillas in half.

Heat remaining 2½ tsp oil in a large frying pan over medium-high heat. When oil is hot, add filled tortillas and cook until golden on first side, 3–4 minutes. Turn carefully and cook until second side is golden and cheese is melted, 2–3 minutes more. Cook in batches, if needed. Serve hot, whole or cut into wedges, garnished with cilantro sprigs.

To prepare: 10 minutes

To cook: 45 minutes

4 servings

scallops with golden beets

4 or 5 golden beets, about 1½ lb (750 g) total, greens trimmed to 2 inches (5 cm)

1 Tbsp plus 2 tsp olive oil

12 sea scallops

2 Tbsp cider vinegar

½ cup (½ oz/15 g) packed baby arugula (rocket) leaves

Preheat oven to 350°F (180°C). Rub beets with 1 Tbsp olive oil, ¾ tsp salt, and ¾ tsp pepper. Arrange in a baking dish and roast, turning once or twice, until easily pierced with a sharp knife, about 1¼ hours. Remove from oven and let cool. Trim and peel beets and cut into slices about ¼ inch (6 mm) thick. Make a bed of beet slices on each of 4 plates.

Pat scallops dry with paper towels and season with salt and pepper. Heat 2 tsp olive oil in a large frying pan over medium-high heat. When oil is hot, swirl pan to coat bottom. Add scallops and sear until golden on first side, about 1½ minutes. Turn and cook until golden on second side and nearly opaque throughout, about 45 seconds more. Add 1 Tbsp cider vinegar and stir to scrape up browned bits from bottom of pan, about 30 seconds. Turn scallops once or twice in the pan juices to give them a light mahogany color.

Arrange 3 scallops on each bed of beets. Top each portion with a little arugula. Stir 1 Tbsp cider vinegar into pan juices, then drizzle juices over scallops and arugula and serve at once.

To prepare: 10 minutes

To cook: 1 hour 20 minutes

4 servings

spanish tortilla with golden potatoes

5 Tbsp (3 fl oz/80 ml) olive oil

1½ lb (750 g) Yukon gold potatoes, peeled and cut into slices ⅛ inch (3 mm) thick

1 leek, white and pale green part, thinly sliced

3 extra-large eggs

3 extra-large egg whites

Heat 2 Tbsp oil in a light-colored, heavy frying pan over medium-high heat. Cover bottom of pan with one-fourth of potatoes, arranged in overlapping rings. Add one-third of leeks and 1 Tbsp oil. Repeat, finishing with potato layer. Cook for 5 minutes, working spatula under potatoes to prevent sticking. As potatoes on bottom brown, bring them to the top to let the others brown. Continue to stir occasionally for even cooking. When potatoes are almost soft, after about 20 minutes, turn them into a colander set over a bowl to drain. Reserve oil. Wipe out pan.

Beat eggs, egg whites, and 1 tsp salt together in a large mixing bowl. Gently stir in potatoes and leeks.

Heat 2 Tbsp reserved oil in pan over medium-high heat. Add potato-egg mixture. Cook until set, about 5 minutes, lowering heat as needed to prevent scorching. Loosen tortilla by working spatula under and cook, shaking pan occasionally, until bottom is well browned, about 5 minutes more.

Slide tortilla onto a large plate. Invert pan over it. Holding plate and pan firmly in place, flip them, dropping uncooked side of tortilla into pan. Cook until browned on second side, about 5 minutes.

Slide tortilla onto a serving platter and let stand for at least 10 minutes, or until cool. Cut into wedges and serve.

To prepare: 25 minutes

To cook: 40 minutes

8 starter servings or 4 main-course servings

grilled salmon, yellow potato & corn salad

4 salmon fillets, skin on, about 5 oz (155 g) each

1 cup (2 oz/60 g) tightly packed fresh basil leaves

½ cup (4 fl oz/125 ml) extra-virgin olive oil

4 ears corn, husks and silk removed

½ lemon

½ lb (250 g) yellow potatoes such as Yukon Gold or Yellow Finn, boiled until tender and diced

2 Tbsp finely chopped sweet onion such as Vidalia or Maui

1 cup (6 oz/185 g) yellow cherry tomatoes, halved

Put salmon fillets, flesh side up, in a shallow dish. Combine basil, olive oil, ¼ cup (2 fl oz/60 ml) water, ½ tsp salt, and several grindings of pepper in a blender or food processor and process until smooth. Set aside half the basil mixture for dressing. Brush other half over flesh sides of salmon. Cover and refrigerate for 30 minutes–6 hours. Remove from the refrigerator 15 minutes before grilling.

Build a fire in a charcoal grill for cooking over medium heat or preheat a gas grill to 350°F (180°C). Oil grill rack.

Fill a large bowl with cold water, add 1 tsp salt, and stir to dissolve. Add corn and let stand for 10 minutes.

Drain corn thoroughly, pat dry, and brush with olive oil. Grill, turning often, until lightly browned and tender-crisp, about 15 minutes. Remove to a platter and let cool.

If using a charcoal grill, let coals burn down to medium-low. If using a gas grill, reduce heat to 300°F (158°C). Arrange fish in an oiled grill basket or place on oiled heavy-duty aluminum foil, fish skin side down. Place basket on or slide foil onto grill. Cover grill and cook until white droplets start to appear on surface of fish, about 8 minutes. Turn carefully and grill just until flesh sides are nicely sealed, about 2 minutes more. Remove to a platter, squeeze half lemon over, tent with foil, and let stand for 5 minutes.

Use a sharp, heavy knife to cut kernels from cobs and put in a large bowl. Add potatoes, onion, tomatoes, and reserved basil mixture. Toss gently to distribute and coat evenly. Remove and discard skin and any stray bones from salmon and flake in large chunks into bowl. Toss again gently, taking care not to break up salmon. Taste and adjust seasoning. Serve at room temperature.

Note: This salad is also excellent prepared with grilled chicken in place of the salmon.

To prepare: 10 minutes, plus 30 minutes to marinate

To cook: 10 minutes

4 servings

moroccan carrot salad

Shred carrots with a vegetable peeler
and mix with olive oil, a pinch of cumin, a
splash of rosewater, and salt and pepper.
Toss with chopped unsalted pistachios
and cilantro (fresh coriander). Serve with
grilled lamb or beef.

orange gazpacho

Purée the flesh of 2 grilled and peeled
yellow or orange bell peppers (capsicums)
with 2 cups (16 fl oz/500 ml) *each* chilled
tomato juice and beef broth. Season with
salt, pepper, and sherry vinegar to taste.
Chill and serve.

grilled pineapple

In a shallow dish, sprinkle pineapple slices with brown sugar, a little rum, and a grating of fresh ginger. Let stand for 30 minutes–3 hours. Grill over medium heat on both sides until golden. Serve drizzled with juices from dish.

broiled pomelo

Cut pomelo in half crosswise. Using a sharp knife cut around circumference of each half, then cut between segments to release flesh. Drizzle with maple syrup and dust with ground star anise and ginger. Broil (grill) until golden.

grilled duck breast with papaya

½ cup (4 fl oz/125 ml) orange juice

Zest of 1 lime, plus 3 Tbsp lime juice

2 Tbsp Thai sweet chile sauce

2 tsp minced fresh ginger

1 tsp fish sauce

¼ tsp Chinese five-spice powder

4 skinless, boneless duck breast halves

Olive oil for brushing

4 cups (4 oz/125 g) mâche

1 firm yet ripe papaya, peeled, seeded, and cut into thin wedges

2 green (spring) onions, including tender green parts, thinly sliced

In a glass measuring pitcher, stir together orange juice, lime zest and juice, chile sauce, ginger, fish sauce, five-spice powder, ½ tsp salt, and several grindings of pepper. Pour half of orange juice mixture into a bowl to use as marinade; cover and refrigerate remainder for dressing. Add duck to bowl with marinade and turn to coat evenly. Cover and refrigerate for 30 minutes–6 hours. Bring to room temperature before grilling.

Build a fire in a charcoal grill for cooking over high heat or preheat a gas grill to 400°F (200°C). Oil grill rack.

Remove duck breast halves from marinade, pat dry, and brush with olive oil. (Discard marinade.) Grill, turning once, until golden brown, 3–4 minutes per side, depending on size. Cover grill and cook until duck is still slightly pink in the center and has a little give when pressed in thickest part (an instant-read thermometer should read 135°F/54°C), 3–4 minutes more. Remove to a cutting board, tent with foil, and let rest for 5 minutes.

Arrange a bed of mâche and papaya on each of 4 plates and sprinkle with green onions. Cut duck on diagonal into slices and put in a bowl. Add reserved orange juice mixture and toss to coat. Taste and adjust the seasoning if needed. Arrange duck on greens and drizzle with dressing collected in bowl. Serve at once.

To prepare: 10 minutes, plus 30 minutes to marinate

To cook: 10 minutes

4 servings

grilled snapper & mandarin salad

4 snapper fillets, 6 oz (185 g) each

2 Tbsp chopped cilantro (coriander)

1 Tbsp olive oil

Zest of ½ mandarin orange, plus
4 peeled and segmented mandarins

1 small head romaine (cos) lettuce,
cored and cut into slices

2 green (spring) onions, including
tender green parts, thinly sliced

2 stalks celery, thinly sliced

8–10 caper berries

2 Tbsp lemon juice

Pinch of sugar

Put fish in a shallow dish. Stir together cilantro, olive oil, mandarin zest, ½ tsp salt, and several grindings of pepper. Brush fish on both sides with cilantro mixture. Cover and refrigerate for 15 minutes–4 hours.

In a bowl, combine lettuce, mandarin segments, green onions, celery, and caper berries and toss to mix. Cover and refrigerate.

Build a fire in a charcoal grill for cooking over high heat or preheat a gas grill to 400°F (200°C). Arrange fillets in an oiled grill basket and place on grill. Grill fillets, turning once, until lightly browned and opaque throughout, about 3 minutes per side.

Add lemon juice and sugar to salad, season with salt and pepper, and toss to mix. Taste and adjust seasoning if needed. Divide salad among plates, top each with a fillet, and serve at once.

To prepare: 10 minutes,
plus 15 minutes to marinate

To cook: 6 minutes

4 servings

mahimahi & mango salsa

4 mahimahi steaks, each about
6 oz (185 g) and 1 inch (2.5 cm) thick

2 tsp grated fresh ginger

1 Tbsp oyster sauce

1 Tbsp grape seed or canola oil

1 large, just-ripe mango, peeled,
pitted, and finely chopped

1 small red chile, seeded and minced

2 Tbsp chopped cilantro
(fresh coriander)

2 Tbsp lime juice

Put fish steaks in a shallow dish. Stir together ginger, oyster sauce, and oil. Pour over fish and turn to coat. Cover and refrigerate for 1–4 hours.

In a small bowl, combine mango, chile, cilantro, lime juice, a pinch of salt, and several grindings of pepper and stir to mix well. Cover and refrigerate until ready to serve (it will keep for up to 8 hours). Remove from refrigerator 20 minutes before serving. Taste and adjust seasoning.

Build a fire in a charcoal grill for cooking over medium heat or preheat a gas grill to 350°F (180°C). Arrange fish in an oiled grill basket and place on grill. Grill fish, turning once, until seared and browned but still slightly translucent in the center, 3–4 minutes per side. Do not overcook. Remove to a platter, tent with foil, and let rest for 5 minutes. To serve, place a fish steak on each plate and mound salsa alongside.

To prepare: 10 minutes,
plus 1 hour to marinate

To cook: 10 minutes

4 servings

halibut with roasted nectarine chutney

5 yellow nectarines, halved, pitted, and coarsely chopped

1 Tbsp olive oil

¼ cup (1½ oz/45 g) golden raisins (sultanas)

2 Tbsp minced onion

1 tsp lemon juice

1 tsp firmly packed light brown sugar

1 tsp grated fresh ginger

4 halibut steaks, each about 5 oz (155 g) and ¾ inch (2 cm) thick

1 Tbsp butter, cut into 4 pieces

Preheat oven to 400°F (200°C). In a small baking dish, combine nectarines, olive oil, raisins, and onion. Turn to coat, then spread evenly in dish. Roast, stirring occasionally, until nectarines are tender, about 15 minutes. Remove from oven. Add lemon juice, brown sugar, and ginger and stir to mix well. Taste and adjust seasoning with salt and pepper. Set chutney aside and cover to keep warm.

Lightly oil a baking dish just large enough to hold halibut steaks in a single layer. Season fish on both sides with 1½ tsp salt and 1 tsp pepper, place in prepared dish, and top each steak with a piece of butter. Roast until fish is opaque throughout and flakes easily with a fork, 15–20 minutes.

To serve, place a fish steak on each warmed plate and top each with a dollop of chutney. Serve at once and pass remaining chutney at the table.

To prepare: 10 minutes

To cook: 35 minutes

4 servings

roasted sea bass with carrot purée

4 carrots, peeled and cut into 1-inch (2.5-cm) pieces

2 Tbsp low-sodium chicken broth

2 Tbsp heavy (double) cream

3 tsp minced fresh tarragon

4 black sea bass steaks, each about 6 oz (185 g) and 1 inch (2.5 cm) thick

1 Tbsp butter, cut into 4 pieces

Preheat oven to 400°F (200°C). Butter a baking dish just large enough to hold sea bass steaks in a single layer.

In a saucepan, combine carrots with plenty of water to cover and 1 tsp salt. Bring to a boil over high heat, cover, and reduce heat to medium. Cook until carrots are tender, 15–20 minutes. Drain carrots and remove to a blender or food processor. Add chicken broth, cream, and 1 tsp tarragon and process to a smooth purée. Taste and adjust seasoning.

Spread purée on bottom of prepared baking dish and arrange fish on top. Top each fish steak with a piece of butter and season with salt and pepper. Roast until fish is opaque throughout, 15–20 minutes. Place a fish steak and a scoop of purée on each plate and sprinkle with remaining tarragon. Serve at once.

To prepare: 10 minutes

To cook: 40 minutes

4 servings

rack of lamb with orange bell pepper relish

1 rack of lamb, about 1¾ lb (875 g)

1 Tbsp olive oil

1 orange bell pepper (capsicum), seeded and finely chopped

2 Tbsp minced onion

1-inch (2.5-cm) piece fresh ginger, minced

3 Tbsp minced cilantro (fresh coriander)

1 mandarin orange, peeled and chopped

Preheat oven to 475°F (245°C). Rub lamb all over with 1 tsp salt and 1 tsp pepper. Heat olive oil in a large, nonstick frying pan over medium heat. When hot, add rack of lamb, fat side down, and sear until browned, 1–2 minutes. Using tongs to turn and hold the lamb, brown both ends, about 1 minute per end. Finally, sear bone side for 1–2 minutes.

Remove browned rack of lamb to a carving board and cover exposed bones with foil. Place rack, bone side down, in a roasting pan. Roast until an instant-read thermometer inserted into thickest part of meat (but not touching bone) registers 130°–140°F (54°–60°C) for medium-rare, 13–15 minutes. Remove to a carving board, tent loosely with foil, and let rest for 10 minutes.

In a bowl, combine bell pepper, onion, ginger, cilantro, orange, and ¼ tsp salt and stir to mix well. Taste and adjust seasoning.

Serve on a warmed platter, accompanied with relish.

To prepare: 10 minutes

To cook: 30 minutes, plus 10 minutes to rest

4 servings

baked sweet potato & rutabaga mash

1 lb (500 g) orange-fleshed sweet potatoes, peeled and cut into slices 1 inch (2.5 cm) thick

½ lb (250 g) rutabaga, peeled and cut into slices 1 inch (2.5 cm) thick

¼ cup (2 fl oz/60 ml) chicken broth

1 tsp minced fresh thyme

2 Tbsp butter

2 Tbsp heavy (double) cream (optional)

Preheat oven to 350°F (180°C).

In a baking dish, combine sweet potatoes, rutabaga, and chicken broth. Sprinkle with thyme, ½ tsp salt, and ½ tsp pepper and turn to mix well. Cover tightly with aluminum foil and bake until vegetables are very tender, about 1¼ hours.

Remove contents of baking dish to a large bowl and add butter. Using a potato masher or electric mixer, mash or beat until fluffy, adding cream, if using. Taste and adjust seasoning. Remove to a warmed serving bowl and serve hot.

To prepare: 10 minutes

To cook: 1¼ hours

4 side-dish servings

wild rice with apricots

Sauté cooked wild rice in butter and oil with chopped walnuts, celery, and onion until onion is translucent. Mix in chopped dried apricots and season to taste. Scoop into a buttered baking dish, cover, and bake in a hot oven for about 30 minutes.

grapefruit baked with brown sugar

Cut grapefruits in half and seed. Using a grapefruit knife, cut around edge of fruit and between sections. Sprinkle each half with 1 Tbsp light brown sugar and bake at 400°F (200°C) until sugar has melted and grapefruit is heated through.

roasted pumpkin purée

Place a small Sugar Pie pumpkin on a
baking sheet and bake at 350°F (180°C)
until flesh pulls away from skin, about
1 hour. Cut pumpkin in half, seed, and
scoop out flesh. Purée and season with
cinnamon, cloves, nutmeg, and salt.

baked golden raspberries

Pour a mixture of brandy, brown sugar,
honey, and vanilla over golden raspberries
in a baking dish and dot with butter. Bake,
uncovered, at 350°F (180°C) until juices
are bubbling, about 20 minutes. Stir gently
before serving.

spaghetti squash aglio e olio

1 spaghetti squash, about 2 lb (1 kg)

1 Tbsp extra-virgin olive oil

¼ tsp minced garlic

¼ cup (1 oz/30 g) finely grated Parmesan cheese

1 tsp minced fresh oregano

Preheat oven to 350°F (180°C). Using a sharp, heavy knife or cleaver, trim stem end from squash, then cut in half lengthwise. Scoop out seeds and discard. Place, cut side down, in a baking dish and add ⅓ cup (3 fl oz/80 ml) water. Bake until tender, about 1 hour.

Remove squash to a cutting board. When cool enough to handle, use a fork to scrape out flesh in noodlelike strands, scraping all the way to skin. Place squash in a serving bowl and add olive oil, garlic, ½ tsp salt, and ½ tsp pepper. Stir gently to mix well. Sprinkle with Parmesan and toss to combine. Taste and adjust seasoning. Sprinkle with oregano and serve hot.

To prepare: 10 minutes

To cook: 1 hour, plus 10 minutes to cool

3 or 4 side-dish servings

turban squash with honey butter

1 turban squash, about 2½ lb (1.25 kg)

2 Tbsp butter

3 Tbsp mild honey such as wildflower or orange blossom

Preheat oven to 375°F (190°C). Place whole squash in a baking dish or on a baking sheet and roast until skin begins to look hard and shiny and pulls away from flesh and squash is easily pieced with a sharp knife, about 2¼ hours.

Just before squash is ready, in a saucepan over medium-high heat, combine butter and honey. Cook, stirring, until butter has melted and honey is incorporated, about 3 minutes. Keep hot.

Remove squash to a cutting board. When cool enough to handle, cut in half and scoop out and discard seeds and coarse strings. Sprinkle flesh with ½ tsp salt and ½ tsp pepper, then scoop it out and spread in a warmed serving dish, breaking up any chunks. Pour honey butter over squash and serve hot.

To prepare: 5 minutes

To cook: 2¼ hours, plus 10 minutes to cool

4 side-dish servings

baked stew of curried root vegetables

3 Tbsp butter

½ cup (2 oz/60 g) chopped yellow onion

2 carrots, peeled and cut crosswise into rounds ½ inch (12 mm) thick

1 parsnip, peeled and cut into 1-inch (2.5-cm) cubes

1 large yellow-fleshed sweet potato, peeled and sliced crosswise 1 inch (2.5 cm) thick, then cut in half

½ head cauliflower, cut into florets

1½ Tbsp all-purpose (plain) flour

1½ tsp coriander seeds, crushed

1½ tsp fennel seeds, crushed

1½ tsp ground turmeric

1½ tsp chili powder

1 tsp ground cumin

¼ cup (2 fl oz/60 ml) low-sodium chicken broth

1 can (14 fl oz/430 ml) coconut milk

Steamed brown or white rice for serving (optional)

Chopped cilantro (fresh coriander) for garnish

Preheat oven to 400°F (200°C).

In a Dutch oven, melt butter over medium-high heat. When it foams, add onion and sauté until translucent, about 2 minutes. Add carrots, parsnip, sweet potato, and cauliflower and sauté until vegetables begin to soften, about 10 minutes.

In a small bowl, stir together flour, coriander and fennel seeds, turmeric, chili powder, cumin, 1 tsp salt, and 1 tsp pepper. Sprinkle mixture over vegetables and continue to cook, stirring occasionally, until flour mixture begins to stick to bottom of pot and brown, 3–4 minutes.

Add chicken broth and stir to scrape up browned bits from bottom of pot, then stir in coconut milk. Raise heat to high and bring to a boil, stirring occasionally. Cover, place in oven, and bake until vegetables are tender, about 25 minutes.

Remove to a serving bowl and serve hot, spooned over rice, if desired. Garnish with cilantro and freshly ground pepper.

To prepare: 20 minutes

To cook: 40 minutes

4–6 servings

chicken with yellow peppers & passion fruit

1 lb (500 g) skinless, boneless chicken breasts

2 yellow bell peppers (capsicums)

1 Cubanelle frying pepper or small green bell pepper (capsicum)

2 Tbsp grape seed oil

1 yellow onion, chopped

1 large clove garlic, minced

1 tsp dried oregano

¼ cup (2 fl oz/60 ml) fresh passion fruit juice (see Note)

1 Tbsp champagne vinegar

Steamed brown, basmati, or jasmine rice for serving

Slice chicken into ½-inch (12-mm) strips. Season to taste with salt and pepper. Stem, seed and slice bell peppers lengthwise into ½-inch (12-mm) strips; stem, seed and cut frying pepper into ⅛-inch (3-mm) strips.

In a large nonstick skillet, heat 1 Tbsp oil over medium-high heat. Cook chicken until white on all sides, 4 minutes total, and remove to a plate.

Heat remaining 1 Tbsp oil in pan. Sauté onion, yellow and green peppers, and garlic until onion is translucent, 4 minutes. Return chicken and any accumulated juices to pan. Add oregano and cook until chicken is white in center, about 3 minutes. Stir in passion fruit juice and vinegar and cook 1 minute more. Serve with rice.

Note: To make passion fruit juice, scrape pulp and seeds from 2 fresh passion fruits into a blender or mini-food processor. Whirl with ½ cup water and strain through a fine-mesh sieve.

To prepare: 15 minutes

To cook: 13 minutes

4 servings

stuffed squash blossoms

1 cup (8 oz/250 g) part-skim ricotta cheese

½ cup (2 oz/60 g) finely diced mozzarella cheese

¼ cup (1 oz/30 g) freshly grated Parmesan cheese

2 Tbsp chopped fresh parsley

12 large squash blossoms

¾ cup (4 oz/125 g) all-purpose (plain) flour

½ cup (4 fl oz/125 ml) olive oil

Drain ricotta in a strainer lined with cheesecloth for 2 hours in refrigerator. Combine ricotta, mozzarella, and Parmesan cheeses with parsley, ½ tsp salt, and several grindings of pepper in a bowl.

Rinse blossoms and remove stamens. Gently spoon 1 generous Tbsp cheese mixture into each blossom and press and twist ends closed.

In a small bowl, whisk flour with cold water, starting with ⅓ cup (3 fl oz/80 ml), until it has consistency of cream. Let batter rest for 30 minutes.

Heat oil in a small frying pan over medium-high heat. Holding each end, dip 3 blossoms in batter and let excess drip back into bowl. Add blossoms to hot oil and pan-fry, turning once with tongs, until golden and crisp, 3–4 minutes. Using a slotted spoon, remove blossoms, shake, and place on a brown paper bag to drain. Season to taste with salt and serve.

To prepare: 25 minutes, plus 2½ hours to stand

To cook: 12 minutes

Makes 4 side-dish servings (12 blossoms)

shrimp with papaya & coconut

¾ lb (375 g) medium shrimp (prawns)

1 can (15 oz/470 g) mandarin oranges

2 Tbsp unsweetened flaked coconut

1 Tbsp peanut oil

2 Tbsp finely chopped shallots

1 tsp grated fresh ginger

1 cup (5 oz/155 g) cubed papaya

½ cup (2½ oz/75 g) cubed jicama

1 tsp curry powder

Cilantro (coriander) leaves for garnish

Peel and devein shrimp. Drain oranges. Set shrimp and oranges aside.

Toast coconut in a small, dry frying pan over medium heat, shaking pan constantly, until flakes are golden, about 4 minutes. Remove at once to small bowl and set aside.

Heat oil in a nonstick frying pan over medium-high heat. Add shallots and ginger and sauté just until fragrant, about 30 seconds. Add shrimp and cook, turning once, until bright pink on both sides, about 4 minutes total. Add papaya and jicama and sauté until shrimp are browned in places on outside and opaque in center, 3–4 minutes. Stir in curry powder and ¼ tsp pepper, and then oranges. Remove to a warmed serving platter, garnish with coconut and cilantro, and serve.

To prepare: 15 minutes

To cook: 12 minutes

4 servings

apricot-stuffed chicken breasts

12 dried apricot halves

6 pitted prunes

⅓ cup (1 oz/30 g) dried apples

¼ cup (1½ oz/45 g) dried currants

⅛ tsp ground cardamom

2 cinnamon sticks

1 cup (8 fl oz/250 ml) apple juice

½ cup (4 fl oz/125 ml) brandy

¼ cup (2 fl oz/60 ml) brewed coffee

4 skinless, boneless chicken breast halves, 6 oz (185 g) each

2 Tbsp butter

Combine dried fruit, cardamom, cinnamon, apple juice, brandy, and coffee in a saucepan. Bring to a boil, cover, lower heat to a simmer, and cook for 10 minutes. Set aside to soak until fruit is soft, about 30 minutes. Strain, discarding cinnamon but reserving cooking liquid. If less than 1 cup, add more juice. Cool and chop apricots, prunes, and apples.

Slit a deep pocket in each chicken breast, cutting in from thickest side to within ½ inch (12 mm) of edge on 3 sides. Pack each breast with dried fruit. Reserve leftover fruit for another use.

Melt butter in a medium sauté pan over medium heat. Brown breasts well on both sides, turning them every 2 minutes, about 8 minutes total. Add reserved liquid and simmer, turning chicken once, about 10 minutes. Remove chicken to a warmed platter. Boil liquid down to ⅓ cup (3 fl oz/ 80 ml), 4 minutes. Strain, spoon over chicken, and serve.

To prepare: 20 minutes,
plus 30 minutes to soak

To cook: 32 minutes

4 servings

peppered yellow pears with honey

Sauté quartered cored pears in butter and lemon juice, turning to coat. When warmed through, transfer to plates and add 3 Tbsp lavender honey and coarse black pepper to the pan. Spoon syrup on pears and serve with fresh goat cheese.

pineapple with preserved ginger

Sear fresh, sliced pineapple rings in a dry nonstick frying pan until golden on both sides. Place on plates and sprinkle generously with brown sugar. Top with minced preserved ginger in a syrup or rinsed crystallized ginger.

sautéed summer squash with corn

Sauté thinly sliced rounds of yellow summer squash and fresh corn kernels in butter. Add a splash of chicken broth and chopped green (spring) onions. Cook, stirring often, until pan is almost dry. Garnish with fresh basil threads.

savory sautéed persimmons

Melt butter in a large pan over medium heat. Add zest and juice of ½ orange, 1 Tbsp Worcestershire sauce, and thin crosswise slices of Fuyu persimmon. Cook, stirring, until sauce thickens slightly. Serve with pork or chicken.

rutabaga & golden beets
with pomegranate seeds

1 medium unwaxed rutabaga, ¾ lb (375 g), peeled and halved lengthwise

1 large golden beet, 8 oz (250 g), peeled and halved lengthwise

1 Tbsp olive oil

1 tsp sugar

¾ cup (6 fl oz/180 ml) low-sodium chicken or vegetable broth

½ cup (4 oz/125 g) pomegranate seeds

Cut rutabaga halves crosswise into slices ⅛ inch (3 mm) thick. Stack 3 or 4 slices at a time and cut into ⅛-inch (3-mm) matchsticks, making 4 cups. Cut beets in the same fashion, making about 3 cups.

Heat oil in a medium sauté pan over medium-high heat. Add rutabaga and sauté for 3 minutes. Add beets and sauté for 3 minutes more, lowering heat to prevent vegetables from browning.

When vegetables deepen in color, add sugar and broth and cook until vegetables are fork-tender, about 5 minutes more. Using a slotted spoon, remove vegetables to a warmed serving bowl. Sprinkle on pomegranate seeds, season to taste with salt and pepper, toss, and serve.

To prepare: 25 minutes

To cook: 12 minutes

4 to 6 side-dish servings

indian-spiced squash
with cashews

½ tsp ground cumin

½ tsp sweet paprika

¼ tsp ground turmeric

Pinch of cayenne pepper

¾ lb (375 g) calabaza squash or pumpkin, halved, seeded, peeled, and cut into slices ¼ inch (6 mm) thick (see Notes)

1 Tbsp ghee or clarified butter (see Notes)

2 Tbsp unsweetened shredded coconut

2 Tbsp roasted cashews, coarsely chopped

Combine spices and ½ tsp salt in a small bowl. Arrange squash on a plate and sprinkle with spice mixture, coating slices on both sides. Let stand for 30 minutes.

Heat ghee in a large nonstick frying pan over medium-high heat. Add squash to pan in a single layer. Cook, turning once, until squash is fork-tender, about 6 minutes total. Using tongs, remove to a serving platter. Wipe out pan with paper towels.

Return pan to medium-high heat and add coconut and cashews. Toast, stirring, until coconut is golden and nuts are warm, 1–2 minutes. Sprinkle them over the squash, and then sprinkle with ½ tsp salt. Serve warm or at room temperature.

Notes: Ghee, the clarified butter used in Indian cooking, is sold in natural food stores and Indian markets. For more on clarified butter, see Note, page 208. To aid in peeling squash, microwave for 1 minute to soften skin.

To prepare: 15 minutes, plus 30 minutes to stand

To cook: 8 minutes

6 side-dish servings

ham & sweet
potato hash

2 medium orange-fleshed sweet
potatoes (yams), ¾ lb (375 g) total,
peeled and cut into slices
¾ inch (2 cm) thick

4 tsp canola oil

1 cup (5 oz/155 g) finely chopped
red onion

½ cup (2½ oz/75 g) finely diced
Granny Smith apple

3 oz (90 g) sliced Black Forest or
Westphalian ham, chopped

2 tsp fresh thyme leaves or
1 tsp dried thyme

¼ tsp sweet paprika

1 Tbsp white vinegar

6 eggs

Steam sweet potato slices until center just resists light pressure, about
8 minutes. Let cool to room temperature or refrigerate for up to 24 hours.

Heat 2 tsp oil in a medium nonstick frying pan over medium-high heat.
Add onion and apple and sauté over medium-high heat until onion is
browned, about 10 minutes. Remove to a mixing bowl and wipe out pan.

Dice sweet potatoes and add them to bowl with onion and apple. Stir
in ham, thyme, and paprika, using a fork to mash potatoes coarsely.

Heat 2 tsp oil in same pan over medium-high heat. Add hash mixture
in ½-cup (3 oz/90 g) mounds, flattening them with a spatula into patties
¾ inch (2 cm) thick. Brown well on both sides, turning after 4–5 minutes.
If they break apart, pat back into shape. Place the patties on plates.

While hash cooks, poach eggs. Fill a deep sauté pan with cold water. Add
vinegar and 1 tsp salt and set pan over medium heat. When water begins
to simmer, break eggs, one at a time, into a cup and slip each one gently
into the water. Cook for 1 minute, slide spatula under eggs to avoid
sticking, and poach to desired doneness, 3–5 minutes. Using a slotted
spoon, remove eggs and place on hash. Serve at once.

To prepare: 15 minutes

To cook: 30 minutes

6 servings

butternut squash &
pears with rosemary

¾ lb (375 g) butternut squash

1 Bosc pear

1 Tbsp grape seed or canola oil

1 Tbsp finely chopped fresh rosemary

Pinch of cayenne pepper

½ cup (4 fl oz/125 ml) apple juice

Peel squash, halve lengthwise, remove seeds and strings, and cut
lengthwise into thin slices. Halve and core pear and slice thinly.

Heat oil in a frying pan over medium-high heat. Add squash and season
with 1 tsp salt. Sauté until squash begins to soften, about 5 minutes,
lowering heat if needed so squash does not color. Add pear, rosemary,
cayenne, and apple juice and cook until liquid evaporates and squash
is tender, 6–8 minutes. Serve hot, warm, or at room temperature.

To prepare: 20 minutes

To cook: 12 minutes

4 side-dish servings

grilled apricots with sabayon

2 Tbsp orange juice

2 tsp honey

12 apricots, halved and pitted

4 egg yolks

5 Tbsp (2½ oz/75 g) superfine (caster) sugar

⅔ cup (5 fl oz/160 ml) unsweetened apple juice

Finely grated zest of ½ orange

1–2 tsp orange liqueur such as Cointreau (optional; see Note)

Grape seed or canola oil for brushing

Combine orange juice and honey in a small saucepan or in a microwave-safe cup and heat on high for 1–2 minutes on stove top over medium heat or in microwave on high for 30 seconds. Stir to dissolve honey. Pour into a shallow dish and arrange apricot halves, cut side down, in warm syrup. Let stand at room temperature for 30 minutes–4 hours.

Build a fire in a charcoal grill for cooking over medium heat or preheat a gas grill to 350°F (180°C). Oil grill rack.

Drain apricots in a colander set over a stainless-steel bowl to catch their syrup. Set apricots aside. Add egg yolks, sugar, apple juice, orange zest, and liqueur, if using, to syrup and whisk to combine. Nest bowl in a saucepan over (but not touching) simmering water. Whisk until mixture has thickened but is fluffy and light and has tripled in volume, 2–3 minutes; there should be no liquid left at bottom of bowl. When you lift whisk, mixture should fall in thick ribbons that hold their shape. Remove from heat.

Brush apricots on both sides with oil and grill until lightly browned and tender, about 3 minutes per side. Serve at once with warm sabayon.

Note: You can substitute rum or Drambuie for the Cointreau.

To prepare: 5 minutes, plus 30 minutes to marinate

To cook: 10 minutes

4 dessert servings

pumpkin flan

1 cup (8 oz/250 g) sugar

2 cups (16 fl oz/500 ml) half-and-half (half cream)

1 cup (8 fl oz/250 ml) whole milk

6 eggs

¼ tsp salt

1 tsp vanilla extract (essence)

¾ cup (6 oz/185 g) canned or homemade pumpkin purée (page 171)

Preheat oven to 325°F (165°C).

Put ½ cup (4 oz/125 g) sugar in an 8-inch (20-cm) metal pie pan and place on stove top over medium-low heat. Holding edge of pan with an oven mitt, tilt it from side to side until sugar is melted and turns a rich brown color, about 5 minutes. Remove from heat and set aside.

In a saucepan, combine half-and-half and milk and warm over medium heat until bubbles form around edges, about 5 minutes. At the same time, bring a teakettle of water to a boil.

In a bowl, whisk eggs lightly, then add remaining ½ cup (4 oz/125 g) sugar, the salt, and the vanilla and whisk until sugar dissolves. Slowly pour hot cream mixture into egg mixture, stirring constantly. Stir in pumpkin purée.

Place pie pan with caramel in a roasting pan and pour custard into pie pan. Pour boiling water into roasting pan to come halfway up sides of pie pan. Bake until a knife inserted into middle of flan comes out clean, about 40 minutes.

Remove flan to a wire rack and let cool. Serve at room temperature, or cover and refrigerate for up to several hours. To unmold flan for serving, slide a knife or icing spatula around edges. Invert a serving plate over pie pan. Holding pan and serving plate firmly together, flip them, then gently lift off pie pan. Cut into wedges and serve on dessert plates.

To prepare: 20 minutes

To cook: 50 minutes

6 dessert servings

winter peach shortcake

Shortcakes

1 cup (15 oz/155 g) plus 2 Tbsp (plain) all-purpose flour

2 Tbsp plus ½ tsp sugar

1 Tbsp baking powder

1 tsp ground cinnamon

¼ tsp salt

5 Tbsp cold butter, cut into small pieces

½ cup (4 fl oz/125 ml) low-fat or regular buttermilk

½ tsp pure vanilla extract (essence)

2 Tbsp unsalted butter

1 bag (1 lb/500 g) frozen sliced peaches, thawed, (4 cups)

⅓ cup (3 fl oz/80 ml) orange juice

¼ cup (3 oz/90 g) maple syrup

Sweetened whipped cream for serving

For Shortcakes: Preheat oven to 400°F (200°C). Have ready an ungreased baking sheet.

In a bowl, whisk together flour, 2 Tbsp sugar, baking powder, cinnamon, and salt until well blended. Using a pastry blender, cut in 5 Tbsp butter until mixture resembles coarse crumbs. Add buttermilk and vanilla and gently toss with fork or rubber spatula until flour is just moistened and ingredients are blended.

Turn dough out onto lightly floured work surface. Gently press dough into a thick 4-inch (10-cm) square. Trim edges even with large sharp knife, then cut into 4 equal squares.

Place squares on baking sheet, spacing them well apart. Sprinkle remaining ½ tsp sugar over tops. Bake until puffed and golden, 15–18 minutes. Remove to wire rack to cool completely.

Meanwhile, melt 2 Tbsp butter in a large nonstick frying pan over medium-high heat. Add peaches in a single layer and cook, turning once with tongs, until warmed through, about 2 minutes total. Add orange juice and simmer until peaches are fork-tender, about 4 minutes more. Add maple syrup and simmer until peaches are glazed and some syrup remains in pan, 1–2 minutes. Set aside to cool to lukewarm.

To serve, split or cut shortcakes in half horizontally and place bottom halves, cut side up, on dessert plates. Spoon some of the peaches, including syrup, over each half and top with a dollop of whipped cream. Top with remaining shortcake halves, cut side down. Serve at once.

To prepare: 25 minutes

To cook: 25 minutes

4 dessert servings

rhubarb cranberries red onions

RED FRUITS AND VEGETABLES PROVIDE ANTIOXIDANTS

ruby grapefruit radishes beets

FOR PROTECTION AND HEALING • PROMOTE HEART

cherries watermelon red plums

HEALTH • PROMOTE URINARY TRACT HEALTH • HELP

tomatoes red pears raspberries

REDUCE THE RISK OF CERTAIN CANCERS • IMPROVE

pomegranates red bell peppers

MEMORY FUNCTION • RED FRUITS AND VEGETABLES

radicchio strawberries quinces

OFFER ANTIOXIDANTS FOR PROTECTION AND HEALING

Red

Many red fruits and vegetables—sweet bell peppers (capsicums) and tomatoes, red onions and hot chiles, red apples and red grapes—work well in savory dishes like sautés and stir-fries, while others—cherries and cranberries—complement meats, fish, and poultry. All of them are good for you, and some, including strawberries and raspberries, boast the highest concentration of antioxidants.

Red fruits are frequently served with game, but they complement ordinary poultry, meat, and fish as well. A cranberry-orange relish widely enjoyed at Thanksgiving can be enhanced with red onion and apple and served with turkey tenderloin for a delicious combination at any time of year (page 215).

For a flavor and color revelation, try spaghetti cooked in red wine in place of water and served topped with red pepper (capsicum), onion, and broccoli (page 202). Sautéed trout sauced with red wine and grapes is a bold update of a French classic that provides all the health benefits found in red grapes (page 208).

Traditional duck with orange sauce gains a new color profile when thinly sliced duck breast is served on a bed of watercress leaves and drizzled with a simple reduction of blood orange juice, a nuanced sauce whose flavor balances bittersweet caramelized sugar with the mildly acidic scarlet red juice (page 215).

SPRING	SUMMER	AUTUMN	WINTER
beets	cherries	red apples	red apples
pink or red grapefruit	red bell peppers	beets	beets
red onions	red chiles	red bell peppers	cranberries
blood oranges	red currants	red chiles	pink or red grapefruit
red potatoes	red onions	cranberries	red grapes
radicchio	red plums	red grapes	blood oranges
radishes	radishes	red pears	pomegranates
rhubarb	raspberries	red plums	red potatoes
strawberries	rhubarb	pomegranates	quinces
	strawberries	red potatoes	radicchio
	tomatoes	quinces	radishes
	watermelon	raspberries	

grilled radicchio

4 Tbsp (2 fl oz/60 ml) extra-virgin olive oil

1 Tbsp lemon juice

1 tsp sugar

2 firm heads radicchio, cores intact, cut into 1-inch (2.5-cm) wedges

½ cup (4 fl oz/125 ml) balsamic vinegar

2 oz (60 g) Parmesan cheese, grated or shaved

Combine 2 Tbsp olive oil, lemon juice, sugar, and a pinch each of salt and pepper. Add radicchio and turn to coat. Let stand for up to 4 hours.

Build a fire in a charcoal grill for cooking over medium heat or preheat a gas grill to 350°F (180°C). Oil grill rack.

Put vinegar in a small saucepan and bring to a boil over medium heat. Reduce heat to medium-low and simmer until reduced by half and the consistency of thick syrup, 10 minutes. Remove from heat and set aside.

Grill radicchio, turning often, until softened, 5–6 minutes; cores should be translucent and edges lightly browned. Remove to a serving platter. Pour balsamic glaze over radicchio, scatter with Parmesan, and drizzle with remaining 2 Tbsp olive oil. Serve radicchio at once.

To prepare: 10 minutes, plus 30 minutes to marinate

To cook: 25 minutes

4–6 side-dish servings

liver & onion bruschetta

2 Tbsp olive oil

¼ cup (2 fl oz/60 ml) red wine

2 cloves garlic, crushed

1 tsp *each* chopped fresh thyme and rosemary

2 bay leaves

½ lb (250 g) calf's liver, trimmed of membrane and cut into strips ½ inch (12 mm) wide

2 red onions, sliced into thin rounds

4 strips bacon

6–8 slices country-style bread, cut on diagonal, 1 inch (2.5 cm) thick

¼ cup (2 oz/60 g) light sour cream

1½ Tbsp lemon juice

2 tsp Dijon mustard

In a glass measuring pitcher, whisk together olive oil, wine, garlic, thyme, rosemary, and bay leaves, and ½ tsp each salt and pepper. Put liver in a dish and pour mixture over, turning to coat evenly. Cover and marinate at room temperature for 20 minutes, or refrigerate for up to 2 hours.

Build a fire in a charcoal grill for cooking over medium heat or preheat a gas grill to 350°F (180°C). Oil grill rack. Arrange onions and bacon strips on grill and cook until onions are browned and softened and bacon is crisp. Remove from grill and set aside. When cool enough to handle, crumble bacon and combine with onions. Oil the grill rack again. Arrange liver on grill and cook until lightly browned on first side, 1½–2 minutes. Turn and cook on second side until browned but still pink in center, about 2 minutes more. Do not overcook. Remove to a plate. Grill bread slices until lightly browned and grill-marked, about 1 minute per side.

To serve, stir together sour cream, lemon juice, and mustard. Divide onions and bacon over toasted bread slices, top with liver, and garnish with a spoonful of sour cream mixture. Serve at once.

To prepare: 5 minutes, plus 20 minutes to marinate

To cook: 15 minutes

4 starter servings

grilled calamari

1 recipe Romesco Sauce (below)

1¼ lb (625 g) cleaned medium squid, bodies and tentacles separated, rinsed

2 Tbsp olive oil

Zest and juice of 1 lemon

2 grilled or roasted red bell peppers (capsicums), peeled, seeded, and thinly sliced (optional; page 205)

2 cups (4 oz/125 g) arugula (rocket) leaves, tightly packed

Follow recipe below to make *romesco* sauce, and set aside.

Place squid in a bowl. Add olive oil, lemon zest, ½ tsp salt, and several grindings of pepper. Turn squid to coat evenly. Cover and refrigerate for at least 30 minutes or up to 4 hours.

Build a fire in a charcoal grill for cooking over high heat or preheat a gas grill to 400°F (200°C). Oil grill rack.

Grill squid in 2 or 3 batches, turning bodies after 1½–2 minutes and tentacles often. Do not crowd grill. Cook just until flesh turns white and is lightly charred, about 1½ minutes more. (The squid bodies will roll up). Remove to a cutting board and let cool slightly.

Drizzle lemon juice over squid and cut each rolled squid body diagonally into 3 or 4 slices. If using roasted peppers, combine in a bowl with squid and toss to mix. To serve, divide arugula among plates, arrange squid on top, and spoon warm romesco sauce on the side. Serve at once.

To prepare: 15 minutes, plus 30 minutes to marinate

To cook: 15 minutes

4 servings

romesco sauce

2 thick slices country-style bread, crusts removed

4 tomatoes, cored

2 red bell peppers (capsicums), seeded and quartered

3 cloves garlic, peeled but left whole

½ cup (2½ oz/75 g) unsalted roasted almonds

1 small red chile, halved and seeded

1 tablespoon sherry vinegar or red wine vinegar

1 tsp sugar

Build a fire in a charcoal grill for cooking over medium heat or preheat a gas grill to 350°F (180°C). Oil grill rack.

Grill bread slices until lightly browned and grill-marked, about 1 minute per side. Set aside. Arrange tomatoes, bell peppers, and garlic in oiled grill basket or on oiled heavy-duty aluminum foil. Place basket on or slide foil onto grill. Grill, shaking or turning often, until lightly browned and starting to soften, 10–12 minutes. (Remove tomatoes from heat before they start releasing juices; peppers may take another minute or two.) Combine tomatoes, peppers, and garlic in a food processor or blender and process until combined. Tear up bread slices and add them along with almonds, chile, vinegar, and sugar. Process to a coarse purée; do not let sauce get too smooth. Season with ½ tsp salt and plenty of ground pepper. Pour into a jug or spoon into bowls to serve.

To prepare: 10 minutes

To cook: 12 minutes

3 cups (24 fl oz/750 ml)

roasted tomato tart

2 oz (60 g) soft fresh goat cheese

3 Tbsp low-fat or whole milk

1½ Tbsp minced shallot

1½ tsp fine sea salt

2 Tbsp extra-virgin olive oil

12 plum (Roma) tomatoes, halved lengthwise

1 tsp herbes de Provence

1 partially baked 9-inch (23-cm) Tart Shell (below)

Preheat oven to 250°F (120°C). In a bowl, mash cheese with milk, shallot, and ½ tsp sea salt to make a spreadable paste. Set aside.

Drizzle about half the olive oil onto a baking sheet and arrange tomatoes on sheet, cut sides up. Drizzle with remaining olive oil and sprinkle with herbes de Provence, 1 tsp sea salt, and ½ tsp pepper. Roast until tomatoes are soft and have partially collapsed, 1½–2 hours. Remove from oven.

Raise the oven temperature to 375°F (190°C). Spread partially baked tart shell with cheese mixture and top with roasted tomatoes, cut sides up. Return tart to oven and bake until pastry edges are golden, about 15 minutes. Remove and let stand for 20 minutes. Serve warm.

To prepare: 20 minutes, plus 20 minutes to cool

To cook: 2 hours 20 minutes

6–8 servings

tart shell

¾ cup (6 oz/185 g) butter, softened

½ cup (3½ oz/105 g) superfine (caster) sugar

2 eggs, lightly beaten

2–3 Tbsp low-fat or whole milk

2½ cups (12½ oz/390 g) all-purpose (plain) flour

1 tsp baking powder

⅔ cup (3 oz/90 g) cornstarch (cornflour)

Canola oil cooking spray

Cream butter and sugar until fluffy. Beat in eggs and milk to blend. Stir in dry ingredients until mixture comes together in a soft ball. Turn out onto a lightly floured work surface and knead lightly. For a 9-inch (23-cm) shell, divide into thirds. Press each piece into a disk and wrap in plastic. (Refrigerate extra dough for up to 1 week or freeze for up to 6 months.)

Roll out a dough disk between 2 sheets plastic wrap to form a round 2 inches (5 cm) larger in diameter than tart pan. Remove plastic from the top and carefully invert dough into tart pan. With other plastic still attached, press dough firmly and evenly into pan. Remove plastic and run rolling pin over top to trim. Chill for 10–15 minutes.

Preheat oven to 325°F (165°C). Cover dough with oiled parchment (baking) paper or foil. Press evenly into corners of dough and fill with pie weights or dried beans. For a partially baked shell, bake for 15 minutes. If paper sticks to pastry, bake for a few more minutes; it should come off easily. Remove paper and weights. For a fully baked shell, after removing paper and weights, bake until a pale golden color, 15–20 minutes more. Let cool in pan on a wire rack.

To prepare: 30 minutes, plus 10 minutes to chill

To cook: 30 minutes

Three 9-inch (23-cm) pastry shells

warm tomato & olive bruschetta

1 Tbsp olive oil

2 cups (12 oz/370 g) chopped fresh plum (Roma) tomatoes (4 medium)

3 Tbsp green olives, chopped lengthwise

2 tsp chopped fresh oregano or ½ tsp dried oregano

1 Tbsp capers, rinsed and chopped

4 slices rustic Italian whole-wheat (wholemeal) bread

2 cloves garlic, halved

Heat oil in a frying pan over medium-high heat. Add tomatoes, olives, and oregano and sauté until tomatoes start to soften, about 1 minute. Remove from heat and stir in capers and a few grindings of black pepper. Set aside.

Grill or toast bread. Rub warm bread generously on one side with cut side of the garlic halves. Top with warm tomato mixture and serve.

To prepare: 10 minutes

To cook: 5 minutes

4 starter servings

red wine spaghetti with red bell pepper & onion

¾ lb (375 g) whole-wheat (wholemeal) spaghetti

1 bottle (750 ml) medium- to full-bodied red wine such as Merlot

2 Tbsp olive oil

2 Tbsp chopped garlic

4 cups (8 oz/250 g) 1-inch (2.5-cm) broccoli florets

1 large red bell pepper (capsicum), seeded and sliced

1 red onion, diced

¼ lb (125 g) shiitake mushrooms, stemmed and quartered

¼ cup (1 oz/30 g) crumbled ricotta salata or feta cheese

Cook pasta in salted boiling water for about 8 minutes. It will still be quite hard. Drain and return pasta to pot. Add wine and cook until pasta is just under al dente, 2–3 minutes. Drain spaghetti in colander set over a bowl, reserving the wine.

Meanwhile, heat oil in a medium sauté pan over medium-high heat. Add garlic and sauté for 1 minute. Add broccoli, bell pepper, onion, and mushrooms and cook until broccoli is tender-crisp, about 5 minutes. Add pasta and reserved wine and cook, stirring a few times, until three-quarters of the liquid has evaporated. Divide among warmed wide, shallow bowls, sprinkle with cheese, and serve at once.

To prepare: 10 minutes

To cook: 20 minutes

4 servings

grilled chile sauce

Grill 1 red chile and 1 red bell pepper (capsicum) until blackened, then peel and seed. Boil ¾ cup (6 fl oz/180 ml) rice vinegar with ½ cup (4 oz/125 g) sugar for 5 minutes. Purée peppers with syrup. Use as dipping sauce for chicken or pork.

sweet & sour beets

Cut peeled beets into large matchsticks and toss with olive oil to coat. Arrange in a basket and grill until tender, shaking often. Season with a little sugar and sherry vinegar, salt, and pepper. Toss with oregano leaves and garnish with feta.

grilled red bell peppers

Grill whole bell peppers (capsicums) over high heat, turning until charred all over. Cover and let cool, then peel. Slice flesh into strips, discarding seeds, and season. Combine equal parts pesto and extra-virgin olive oil and drizzle over peppers.

red onions with fennel

Cut red onions into thick rounds. Brush with olive oil and grill over medium heat until browned and softened, 8–10 minutes. Drizzle with honey and sprinkle with red wine vinegar and toasted fennel seeds. Serve with grilled meats.

shrimp with watermelon, feta & mint

1 lb (16 oz/500 g) large shrimp (prawns), peeled and deveined, tail intact

1 Tbsp grape seed or canola oil

1 tsp red pepper flakes

1 clove garlic, crushed

2 Tbsp lime zest

½ tsp garam masala

1½ lb (750 g) watermelon

3 Tbsp lime juice

4 fresh mint leaves, thinly sliced

4 iceberg lettuce leaves

4 oz (125 g) feta cheese, cut into ½-inch (12-mm) cubes

2 Tbsp pine nuts, toasted (see Note, page 37)

Put shrimp in a bowl. Add oil, red pepper flakes, garlic, lime zest, garam masala, ½ tsp salt, and several grindings of black pepper. Turn to coat shrimp evenly. Cover and refrigerate for 30 minutes–4 hours.

Peel and seed watermelon; cut into 1-inch (2.5 cm) chunks. You should have about 3 cups. Combine watermelon, 2 Tbsp lime juice, and mint in a bowl. Toss to coat watermelon evenly. Cover and refrigerate until ready to serve; it will keep for up to 3 hours.

Build a fire in a charcoal grill for cooking over high heat or preheat a gas grill to 400°F (200°C). Oil grill rack. Drain shrimp and grill, turning often, until opaque throughout, 3–4 minutes. Remove to a platter and drizzle with remaining 1 Tbsp lime juice.

Line bowls with lettuce leaves. Divide watermelon salad among bowls, scatter feta and pine nuts over, and pile on the hot shrimp and serve.

To prepare: 15 minutes, plus 30 minutes to marinate

To cook: 3 minutes

4 servings

grilled cherry tomatoes

2½ cups (15 oz/470 g) cherry tomatoes

3 tsp extra-virgin olive oil

½ tsp sugar

½ cup (½ oz/15 g) loosely packed basil leaves, torn

12 fresh mint leaves, thinly sliced

1 tsp balsamic vinegar

Build a fire in a charcoal grill for cooking over medium-high heat or preheat a gas grill to 375°F (190°C).

Put tomatoes in a bowl. Add 1 tsp olive oil, sugar, ½ tsp salt, and several grindings of pepper and toss to coat evenly.

Put tomatoes in an oiled grill basket and place basket on grill. Grill, shaking often, until tomatoes are softened and lightly browned and skins are starting to split, about 3 minutes. Do not cook until fully collapsed. Return tomatoes to bowl and toss with herbs, vinegar, and remaining 2 tsp olive oil. Serve warm or at room temperature.

To prepare: 5 minutes

To cook: 3 minutes

4–6 side-dish servings

sautéed trout with red grape sauce

2 cups (16 fl oz/500 ml) light, fruity red wine, such as a Beaujolais

⅓ cup (2 oz/60 g) finely chopped carrots

¼ cup (1½ oz/45 g) finely chopped celery

¼ cup (1 oz/30 g) finely chopped onion

2 sprigs fresh thyme

1 small bay leaf

⅛ tsp whole peppercorns

4 skin-on trout fillets, 6 oz (185 g) each

¼ cup (1½ oz/45 g) all-purpose (plain) flour

2 Tbsp clarified butter or olive oil (see Note)

⅔ cup (4 oz/125 g) halved seedless red grapes

2 tsp cold butter, diced

Boil wine, carrot, celery, onion, thyme, bay leaf, and peppercorns in a saucepan until reduced to ½ cup (4 fl oz/125 ml), about 12 minutes. Strain through a fine-mesh sieve into a bowl, pressing on vegetables with the back of a wooden spoon. Discard vegetables and set wine aside for up to 4 hours.

Pat fish dry with paper towels. Season to taste with salt and pepper. Dredge fillets in flour and shake off excess. Heat clarified butter in a frying pan just large enough to hold fish. While shaking pan, add trout, skin side up, and continue shaking for 1 minute to prevent sticking. Cook until fish is golden brown, 2–3 minutes. Using a wide spatula, turn trout and cook, again shaking pan for 30 seconds to prevent sticking. Cook until fish is just opaque when tested in the center at thickest point, 1–2 minutes. Place fillets on a warmed plate and tent loosely with foil. Wash out the pan and dry thoroughly.

Add reduced wine and grapes to pan over medium heat and simmer until grapes are heated through, 1 minute. Off heat, swirl in cold butter. Place fillets on warmed plates. Spoon sauce over fish and serve.

Note: Clarified butter, which is butter with the milk solids removed, does not burn at the high temperatures used for sautéing. It can be purchased jarred in specialty-food shops. To prepare your own, slowly melt unsalted butter in saucepan over medium-low heat. When white solids sink to bottom, pour off clear yellow liquid through a fine-mesh strainer into a heatproof container. Cover tightly and refrigerate up to 1 month.

To prepare: 15 minutes

To cook: 20 minutes

4 servings

mahimahi with red potato, red bell pepper & rosemary

¾ lb (375 g) medium-sized red potatoes, scrubbed

4 Tbsp (2 fl oz/60 ml) olive oil

1 large red bell pepper (capsicum), seeded and coarsely chopped

½ red onion, coarsely chopped

2 tsp minced fresh rosemary, plus sprigs for garnish

3 Tbsp dry white wine

1 lb (500 g) mahimahi fillets

Preheat oven to 450°F (230°C). Cut potatoes into slices a generous ¼ inch (6 mm) thick, then cut slices in half.

In a large, ovenproof frying pan, heat 3 Tbsp olive oil over medium-high heat. Add potatoes, bell pepper, and onion and sprinkle with ½ tsp salt, ½ tsp pepper, and 1 tsp minced rosemary. Sauté until potatoes are golden on first side, about 6 minutes. Turn and cook until potatoes are golden on second side and peppers and onions are soft, 6–7 minutes more. Add wine and stir to scrape up browned bits from bottom of pan.

Place fish on top of potatoes and vegetables and sprinkle with ½ tsp salt, ½ tsp pepper, and remaining 1 tsp minced rosemary. Drizzle remaining 1 Tbsp olive oil over all. Roast until fish is opaque throughout and flakes easily with a fork, 10–12 minutes. Remove to a platter, garnish with rosemary sprigs, and serve at once.

To prepare: 15 minutes

To cook: 25 minutes

4 servings

baked mackerel with red currants

4 mackerel fillets, about 1½ pounds (750 g) total

1 tsp fresh thyme leaves

1 Tbsp plus ½ teaspoon butter

2 Tbsp raspberry vinegar

4 oz (125 g) fresh red currants or small grapes

Preheat oven to 400°F (200°C). Butter a baking dish just large enough to hold mackerel fillets in a single layer and arrange fillets in dish. Sprinkle with 1 tsp salt, 1 tsp pepper, and thyme. Cut butter into small pieces. Dot fillets with butter and pour vinegar over them. Sprinkle with red currants.

Bake until fish is opaque and flakes easily with a fork, 15–20 minutes. Serve hot with pan juices and currants.

To prepare: 10 minutes

To cook: 20 minutes

4 servings

game hens with pears

2 Cornish game hens

1½ tsp dried lavender blossoms, crushed

1 tsp fresh thyme leaves, plus 2 sprigs

2 Tbsp melted butter, if needed for basting

2 firm but ripe red pears such as red Bartlett (Williams') or Anjou, halved, cored, and thinly sliced

3 Tbsp lavender honey

Preheat oven to 350°F (180°C). Pat hens dry inside and out with paper towels, then rub inside and out with lavender, thyme leaves, 2 tsp salt, and 1½ tsp pepper. Tuck a thyme sprig into cavity of each hen.

Place hens on a rack in a roasting pan and roast, uncovered, basting once or twice with pan juices or melted butter, until juices run clear when the thigh is pierced with a sharp knife, about 45 minutes.

Remove pan from oven. Add pear slices to pan juices, spreading evenly. Using a pastry brush, glaze hens with 1 Tbsp honey and return to oven. Roast until honey has melted, about 5 minutes. Repeat glazing process twice with remaining honey, roasting for 5 minutes more each time. Remove hens to a cutting board, tent loosely with foil, and let rest for 10 minutes. Cover roasting pan with foil to keep pears warm.

To serve, cut each hen in half along backbone with kitchen scissors. Make a bed of pear slices on each warmed plate, dividing evenly, and top each with a half game hen.

To prepare: 20 minutes

To cook: 1 hour, plus 10 minutes to rest

4 servings

roasted chicken & red onion

1 roasting chicken, 3–3½ lb (1.5–1.75 kg)

2 tsp olive oil

2 tsp minced fresh thyme, plus sprigs for garnish

2 large red onions, quartered

1 Tbsp butter, cut into 8 pieces

Preheat oven to 350°F (180°C). Rub chicken inside and out with olive oil, then with 1 tsp thyme, 1 tsp salt, and ¾ tsp pepper.

Put chicken in a roasting pan and surround with onion quarters. Sprinkle onions with remaining 1 tsp minced thyme, ½ tsp salt, and ¼ tsp pepper and top each quarter with a piece of butter.

Roast, basting chicken and onions with pan juices after 30 minutes and then occasionally thereafter, until chicken skin is golden brown and juices run clear when a thigh joint is pierced with a sharp knife, 1¼–1½ hours depending on size of chicken. Remove to a carving board, tent loosely with foil, and let rest for 10 minutes.

Carve chicken into serving pieces and arrange on plates with 2 onion quarters alongside each portion. Garnish with thyme and serve at once.

To prepare: 10 minutes

To cook: 1¼–1½ hours, plus 10 minutes to rest

4 servings

duck with blood orange sauce

⅓ cup (3 oz/90 g) sugar

1¼ cups (10 fl oz/310 ml) blood orange juice (from about 6 oranges), plus 2 blood oranges, peeled and sectioned

4 Pekin duck breast halves, 6 oz (185 g) each, fat trimmed

1 bunch watercress, stemmed

3 Tbsp pomegranate seeds for garnish (optional)

Put sugar and 1 Tbsp water in a heavy saucepan, tilting pan to wet sugar. Boil over medium-high heat, swirling occasionally, until mixture turns golden, 3 minutes. Off heat, carefully pour in orange juice. Return to heat and boil until frothy bubbles rise, 10–13 minutes. Set aside.

Place duck, skin side down, in a large nonstick frying pan over medium heat. Sprinkle with salt and pepper. Cook until skin is light gold, about 8 minutes, then pour off fat. Lower heat and cook until skin is dark brown, 10 minutes more. Turn and cook for 4 minutes for medium-rare, or 5 minutes for medium. Remove to a plate and let rest for 5 minutes.

Divide watercress among warmed plates. Slice the duck thinly, with the grain. Arrange slices of duck and oranges on plates. Spoon 2 Tbsp sauce over duck. Sprinkle with pomegranate seeds, if using, and serve.

To prepare: 25 minutes

To cook: 35 minutes

4 servings

turkey tenderloin with cranberry compote

2 cups (8 oz/250 g) cranberries

1 Honeycrisp or Jonagold apple, peeled, cored, and chopped

1 small red onion, diced

1 wide strip orange zest

1 Tbsp canola oil

1 lb (500 g) turkey tenderloin, cut lengthwise into ¾ inch (2 cm) strips

½ cup (4 fl oz/125 ml) chicken broth

1 Tbsp sugar

½ tsp stuffing seasoning (see Note)

Pulse cranberries, apple, onion, and orange zest in a food processor until coarsely chopped. Set aside.

Heat oil in a medium nonstick frying pan over medium-high heat. Add turkey and sauté until browned on all sides and opaque in center, about 8 minutes total. Remove to a plate and tent with foil.

Add broth to pan and stir, scraping up browned bits. Add cranberry mixture, sugar, and stuffing seasoning to pan. Cook over medium heat, stirring occasionally, until mixture resembles thick applesauce, about 10 minutes. Spoon warm compote beside tenderloin and serve.

Note: You can substitute ½ tsp ground thyme, ¼ tsp ground ginger, and pinch of ground pepper for stuffing seasoning.

To prepare: 15 minutes

To cook: 20 minutes

4 servings

tomatoes stuffed with sausage

Cut off top third of medium tomatoes. Scoop out flesh and pulp and mix with ground sausage, bread crumbs, minced onion, beaten egg, parsley, salt, and pepper. Stuff tomatoes and bake until sausage is browned, about 40 minutes.

cranberry & blood orange sauce

Bake fresh or frozen cranberries with water and sugar until they begin to soften and are easily mashed, about 20 minutes. Purée with blood orange juice and a little zest. Taste and adjust for sweetness. Serve with meat.

red bell peppers baked with anchovies

Cut bell peppers into strips 1 inch (2.5 cm) wide. Place in an oiled baking dish, skin side down. Place an anchovy fillet on each; season with salt, pepper, and thyme; and drizzle with olive oil. Bake in a hot oven until soft, 25 minutes.

roasted beet salad with eggs

Rub beets with olive oil and roast at 350°F (180°C) until tender, about 1½–2 hours, depending on size. Cut off stems, peel, and cut beets into wedges. Toss with vinaigrette, then arrange on lettuce and sprinkle with chopped hard-boiled egg.

pork tenderloin with sour cherry sauce

¼ cup (1½ oz/45 g) dried sour cherries

½ cup (4 fl oz/125 ml) unsweetened cherry juice

1 Tbsp canola oil

¾–1 lb (375–500 g) pork tenderloin, cut into slices ½ inch (12 mm) thick

¼ cup (2 fl oz/60 ml) ruby port

¼ cup (1 oz/30 g) finely chopped red onion

¼ tsp ground coriander

1 oz (30 g) bittersweet chocolate, finely chopped

Soak cherries in juice until plumped, about 20 minutes. Drain, reserving the soaking liquid.

Heat oil in a medium sauté pan over medium-high heat. Season pork to taste with salt and pepper. Add pork and cook, turning once and reducing heat so meat does not brown, about 3 minutes total. Arrange meat in 2 rows on a warmed serving platter, overlapping the slices. Tent with foil and set aside.

Add reserved cherry juice, plumped cherries, port, onion, and coriander to pan. Bring to a boil, scraping up any browned bits, and cook until liquid is reduced by one-third, 4–5 minutes. Off heat, stir in chocolate until sauce thickens slightly, about 1 minute.

Spoon sauce over each row of pork medallions and serve.

To prepare: 10 minutes, plus 20 minutes to plump

To cook: 9 minutes

4 servings

red-hot hash browns

¾ lb (375 g) walnut-sized red new potatoes

1 Tbsp canola oil

½ cup (2 oz/60 g) finely chopped yellow onion

⅓ cup (2 oz/60 g) finely chopped red bell pepper (capsicum)

½ tsp sweet paprika

1 fresh red chile, thinly sliced

Place potatoes in a saucepan of cold water and bring to a boil. Boil until fork-tender, about 12 minutes. Drain and cool in cold water or let stand until cooled to room temperature. Using a sharp knife, halve potatoes.

Heat oil over medium-high heat in a frying pan large enough to hold potatoes in a single layer. Add onions and pepper and sauté until onion is translucent, about 4 minutes. Stir in paprika. Add potatoes, cut side down, and cook until browned and crusty on first side, 4–5 minutes. Add chile and 1 tsp salt. Cook, stirring, until some of the onions are deeply browned, about 1 minute more. Serve potatoes in a shallow bowl.

Note: If you prefer a milder dish, omit the chile, or seed the chile and use less. Leftover boiled or roasted potatoes, cut into 1½-inch (4-cm) pieces, can also be used in this recipe.

To prepare: 10 minutes

To cook: 25 minutes

4 side-dish servings

lamb kebabs with blood orange salad

1 lb (500 g) boneless lamb steaks or fillets, cut into 1-inch (2.5-cm) cubes

1 Tbsp olive oil

Zest of 1 blood orange

1½ tsp ground cumin

1 tsp ground coriander

½ tsp red pepper flakes

1 tsp dried oregano

4 blood oranges, peeled and sliced crosswise into thin rounds

4-inch (10-cm) piece cucumber, thinly sliced

2 avocados, pitted, peeled, and cut into ½-inch (12-mm) chunks

2 green (spring) onions, including tender green parts, thinly sliced

2 Tbsp lime juice

2 Tbsp chopped cilantro (fresh coriander)

Put lamb in a bowl. Add olive oil, orange zest, 1 tsp cumin, ground coriander, red pepper flakes, oregano, ½ tsp salt, and several grindings of black pepper. Turn lamb to coat evenly. Cover and marinate at room temperature for at least 30 minutes, or refrigerate for up to 4 hours. Remove from refrigerator 20 minutes before cooking.

Soak 8 wooden skewers in water to cover for 30 minutes. Build a fire in a charcoal grill for cooking over medium-high heat or preheat a gas grill to 375°F (190°C). Oil grill rack.

Layer oranges, cucumber, avocados, and green onions on a serving platter. Drizzle with lime juice, sprinkle with remaining ½ tsp cumin, and season with salt and pepper.

Thread lamb onto skewers. Grill, turning often, until lightly browned and tender, about 5 minutes. Remove to a platter, tent with foil, and let rest for 5 minutes.

To serve, divide salad among plates and top each with 2 lamb skewers. Sprinkle with cilantro and serve at once.

To prepare: 15 minutes, plus 30 minutes to marinate

To cook: 5 minutes

4 servings

veal with red plum sauce

2 Tbsp olive oil

1½ Tbsp fruit vinegar such as plum or raspberry

2 shallots, minced

2 tsp *each* finely chopped fresh thyme, oregano, and rosemary

4 veal loin chops, about 10 oz (310 g) each

4 large, firm red plums, pitted and finely diced

2 tsp sugar

Stir together oil, vinegar, shallots, herbs, 1 tsp salt, and several grindings of pepper. Brush veal on both sides with half of herb mixture; put remainder in a small saucepan. Cover veal and let sit for 30 minutes, or refrigerate for up to 6 hours. Bring to room temperature before grilling.

Build a fire in a charcoal grill for cooking over medium-high heat or preheat a gas grill to 375°F (190°C). Oil grill rack. Grill veal until nicely browned on the first side, about 3½ minutes. Turn and cook other side for 1½–2 minutes more for medium-rare (an instant-read thermometer inserted in thickest part, away from bone, should read 135°F/54°C). Remove to a platter, tent with foil, and let rest for 5 minutes.

While veal is resting, add plums and sugar to saucepan with remaining herb mixture and bring to a boil, stirring, just to soften plums. Put a veal chop on each plate and spoon warm plum sauce over. Serve at once.

To prepare: 10 minutes, plus 30 minutes to marinate

To cook: 6 minutes

4 servings

chicken with cherry salsa

4 skinless, boneless chicken breast halves, 5 oz (150 g) each

4 Tbsp balsamic vinegar

2 tsp light brown sugar

1½ tsp finely grated fresh ginger

6 whole fresh mint leaves, plus 5 leaves torn into small pieces

½ lb (250 g) cherries, pitted and finely chopped

1 Tbsp grape seed or canola oil

1 tsp sugar

Place chicken between 2 pieces of plastic wrap. Using a meat pounder, pound to an even thickness. Sprinkle with 3 Tbsp vinegar, brown sugar, 1 tsp ginger, whole mint leaves, ½ tsp salt, and several grindings of fresh pepper. Turn to coat evenly, cover, and refrigerate for 30 minutes–4 hours. Remove from refrigerator 15 minutes before cooking.

Combine cherries, oil, remaining 1 Tbsp vinegar, torn mint, sugar, and remaining ½ tsp ginger in a bowl and toss to make a salsa. Let stand for at least 30 minutes, or cover and refrigerate for up to 4 hours. Bring to room temperature before serving. Taste and adjust seasoning.

Build a fire in a charcoal grill for cooking over medium heat or preheat a gas grill to 350°F (180°C). Oil grill rack. Grill chicken, more attractive side down, until golden, about 8 minutes. Turn, cover grill, and cook until chicken feels springy to the touch and juices run clear when pierced in the thickest part, about 5 minutes more. Remove to a platter, tent with foil, and let rest for 10 minutes. Serve warm with the salsa.

To prepare: 15 minutes, plus 30 minutes to marinate

To cook: 10 minutes, plus 10 minutes to rest

4 servings

baked pasta with radicchio & blue cheese

¾ lb (375 g) rigatoni

1½ Tbsp olive oil

1 head radicchio, cored and coarsely chopped

2 cloves garlic, minced

4 oz (125 g) blue cheese such as Maytag, crumbled (1 cup)

¼ cup (2 fl oz/60 ml) heavy (double) cream

Preheat oven to 400°F (200°C). Lightly oil a medium flameproof baking dish.

Bring a large pot of salted water to a boil over high heat. Add rigatoni and reduce heat to medium, stirring once or twice. Cook until barely al dente, 12–15 minutes.

Drain thoroughly and place in prepared baking dish. Add ½ Tbsp olive oil and stir to coat evenly.

In a large frying pan, heat 1 Tbsp olive oil over medium-high heat. Add radicchio and garlic and sauté until radicchio wilts and is lightly browned, 7–8 minutes. Stir in 1 tsp salt and pepper to taste, spoon contents of pan into dish with pasta, and mix well.

In a small bowl, mash cheese together with cream until smooth. Add cheese mixture to pasta and radicchio and toss and stir until ingredients are evenly distributed.

Cover with foil and bake until cheese has melted, about 20 minutes. Remove from oven and remove foil.

Preheat broiler (grill). Slide dish under broiler about 4 inches (10 cm) from heat source and broil (grill) until top is lightly browned, about 4 minutes. Serve hot, directly from baking dish.

To prepare: 10 minutes

To cook: 50 minutes

4 servings

prosciutto grapes

Wrap whole seedless red grapes with thin strips of prosciutto, overlapping it and pressing firmly. Sauté grapes in a lightly oiled pan, shaking constantly, until grapes and prosciutto are golden. Season with pepper. Serve warm, on toothpicks.

warm ruby grapefruit salad

Sauté thinly sliced red onion and jalapeño in a pan coated with cooking oil spray for 1 minute. Gently mix in sliced avocado and ruby grapefruit sections until warmed. Serve on tender lettuce, sprinkled with cilantro (fresh coriander).

hungarian red peppers

Sauté red bell pepper (capsicum) and red onion strips in some canola oil until soft, about 10 minutes. Mix in 2 tsp sweet paprika. Off heat, stir in ½ cup (4 oz/125 g) sour cream. Serve warm with sautéed pork, chicken, or tofu.

herbed cherry tomatoes

Heat cherry tomatoes in a pan with olive oil, shaking to toss for a minute. Add chopped rosemary and garlic, salt, and pepper. Continue rolling the tomatoes in the pan until wilted and soft to the touch, 2–4 minutes. Scoop into a serving bowl.

rib-eye steaks
with baked plums

5 red plums, halved, pitted, and coarsely chopped

2 tsp olive oil

4 rib-eye steaks, about 5 oz (155 g) each

1 Tbsp butter

Preheat oven to 400°F (200°C). Place plums in a baking dish. Coat with olive oil and season with ½ tsp salt.

Put dish in oven and bake until plums are tender and just starting to collapse, 10–15 minutes. Remove to a wire rack and tent loosely with foil to keep warm.

Season steaks generously on both sides with salt and pepper. In a large frying pan, melt butter over medium-high heat. When it foams, add steaks and sear until a deep brown on first side, about 4 minutes. Turn to sear second side and cook to desired doneness, about 4 minutes more for medium-rare.

Remove steaks to warmed plates and spoon warm plums alongside. Serve at once.

To prepare: 10 minutes

To cook: 25 minutes

4 servings

roasted beets
with indian spices

1 tsp ground cumin

1 tsp ground coriander

½ tsp ground turmeric

½ tsp ground cloves

6 medium red beets, stems trimmed to ½ inch (12 mm)

2 Tbsp olive oil

Preheat oven to 350°F (180°C). In a small bowl, combine cumin, coriander, turmeric, cloves, 1 tsp salt, and 1 tsp pepper and mix well.

Arrange beets in a shallow baking dish just large enough to hold them in a single layer. Rub with olive oil, then rub with spice mixture, coating evenly. Roast, turning occasionally, until beets are easily pierced with a sharp knife and skins are slightly wrinkled, about 1¼ hours. Let cool slightly, then cut off stems and peel.

Cut lengthwise into wedges and serve warm or at room temperature.

To prepare: 10 minutes

To cook: 1¼ hours

4 side-dish servings

berry gratin

2 large eggs, separated

3 Tbsp sugar

1 Tbsp crème de cassis

2 cups (8 oz/250 g) red raspberries

2 cups (8 oz/250 g) strawberries, hulled and halved lengthwise

Preheat broiler (grill). In a bowl, using an electric mixer or a whisk, beat egg whites until soft peaks form when beater is lifted. Set aside.

In top pan of a double boiler or a heatproof bowl set over (but not touching) simmering water, combine 2 Tbsp sugar and egg yolks and beat with electric mixer or whisk until frothy and thickened, about 10 minutes, scraping down sides of pan or bowl occasionally with a rubber spatula. Remove from heat and stir in crème de cassis. Fold 1 Tbsp of yolk mixture into egg whites, then fold in remaining yolk mixture just until evenly blended.

Divide berries among four 1-cup (8–fl oz/250-ml) gratin dishes or ramekins and pour egg mixture over them, filling to top. Sprinkle with remaining 1 Tbsp sugar. Place on a baking sheet and slide under broiler about 4 inches (10 cm) from heat source. Broil (grill) until tops are golden, about 4 minutes. Serve hot or warm.

To prepare: 10 minutes

To cook: 15 minutes

4 dessert servings

deep-dish cherry pie

4 cups (1 lb/500 g) Bing or other sweet red cherries, stemmed and pitted

1¼ cups (6½ oz/200 g) all-purpose (plain) flour

1 cup (8 oz/250 g) sugar

1 tsp baking powder

¼ tsp salt

3 Tbsp cold butter, cut into ½-inch (12-mm) cubes

⅓ cup (3 fl oz/80 ml) low-fat or whole milk

Preheat oven to 425°F (220°C). Place cherries in a deep-dish pie dish.

In a bowl, stir together ¼ cup (1½ oz/45 g) flour and sugar. Sprinkle sugar mixture over cherries. In a second bowl, whisk together remaining 1 cup (5 oz/155 g) flour, baking powder, and salt. Add butter and cut in with a pastry blender or 2 knives until mixture resembles coarse crumbs. Add milk and stir just until dough holds together, about 30 seconds. Turn out onto a lightly floured work surface and knead several times. Roll out to a ¼-inch (6-mm) thickness and lay over cherries; it is not necessary to seal edges or for the cherries to be covered completely.

Bake until crust is golden brown, 15–20 minutes. Reduce oven temperature to 325°F (165°C) and continue baking until cherries are soft and juices are bubbling, 10–15 minutes more. Remove to a wire rack and let cool slightly, then serve warm.

To prepare: 20 minutes

To cook: 35 minutes

6 dessert servings

caramelized red pears with cinnamon

1 cup (8 fl oz/250 ml) red wine

½ cup (6 fl oz/185 ml) honey

1 tsp cinnamon

1 tsp finely grated fresh ginger

4 just-ripe red pears, quartered and cored, each quarter cut in half lengthwise

1 tsp butter

Combine wine, honey, cinnamon, and ginger in a saucepan and bring to a boil over medium-high heat. Boil for 5 minutes. Remove from heat and add sliced pears, turning to coat evenly. Let macerate at room temperature, turning occasionally, for 30 minutes.

Build a fire in a charcoal grill for cooking over medium heat or preheat a gas grill to 350°F (180°C). Oil grill rack.

Use a slotted spoon to lift pears from liquid and pour the liquid into a small pot. Bring the liquid to a boil over high heat, skimming any foam that may form on surface. Add butter and boil, stirring occasionally, until mixture starts to form large bubbles, is reduced by half, and is thick and syrupy, about 5 minutes.

Grill pears until they are lightly caramelized, about 2 minutes per side.

Divide pears among serving plates, allowing 1 whole pear (8 slices) per serving. Drizzle with reduced syrup and serve.

To prepare: 10 minutes, plus 30 minutes to macerate

To cook: 9 minutes

4 dessert servings

broiled grapes in yogurt & sour cream

2 cups (12 oz/375 g) seedless red grapes

¾ cup (6 oz/185 g) light sour cream

⅓ cup (2½ oz/75 g) plain low-fat or whole yogurt

1 tsp vanilla extract (essence)

Zest of ½ orange

½ cup (3½ oz/105 g) firmly packed light brown sugar

Arrange grapes in a single layer in a shallow flameproof baking or gratin dish; they should fit tightly. Stir sour cream, yogurt, vanilla, and orange zest together in a small bowl. Spread sour cream mixture evenly over grapes and sprinkle brown sugar on top. Refrigerate for 30 minutes–4 hours.

Preheat broiler (grill).

Slide grapes in baking dish under broiler about 4 inches (10 cm) from heat source and broil (grill) until mixture bubbles and sugar starts to caramelize, about 5 minutes. Serve hot.

To prepare: 5 minutes, plus 30 minutes to macerate

To cook: 5 minutes

4 dessert servings

strawberries
in red wine

1 pint (16 fl oz/500 ml) premium
vanilla ice cream

1 Tbsp butter

¾ lb (375 g) fresh strawberries,
hulled, larger ones halved lengthwise

2 Tbsp Demerara sugar or light
brown sugar

½ cup fruity but structured red wine,
such as a light Cabernet Sauvignon
or Merlot

4 mint sprigs (optional)

Scoop ice cream into four 2-ounce (60-g) balls and arrange on a plate. Freeze until ice cream is hard, about 1 hour. (Cover with foil if holding ice cream longer.) Save remaining ice cream for another use.

Melt butter in medium frying pan over medium-high heat. Sauté berries for 1 minute. Add sugar, wine, and 7 or 8 grindings of pepper. When liquid boils, reduce heat, and simmer fruit for 1 minute more, until sugar is dissolved and smaller berries are soft on the outside but still firm in the center. Let berries stand for 15 minutes to cool.

While berries cool, remove ice cream from freezer and let stand at room temperature to soften slightly. It should still be firm, so that it melts slowly into the warm fruit rather than all at once.

Divide strawberries and wine among 4 dessert bowls or large wine goblets. Top each with a scoop of ice cream and garnish with mint, if using. Serve at once.

To prepare: 12 minutes,
plus 1 hour to freeze

To cook: 2 minutes, plus
15 minutes to cool

4 dessert servings

cherries & pound cake

1 cup (8 fl oz/250 ml) unsweetened
cherry juice

⅓ cup (3 oz/90 g) sugar

¼ cup (2 fl oz/60 ml) Cointreau

2 strips lemon zest, each 2 x 1 inches
(5 x 2.5 cm)

½ tsp coriander seeds

¼ tsp peppercorns

1 lb (500 g) sweet cherries, pitted,
or 1½ cups (9 oz/280 g) frozen
cherries, thawed

4 thick slices pound cake

Combine cherry juice, sugar, liqueur, lemon zest, coriander, and peppercorns in a saucepan. Bring to a boil, lower heat, and simmer for 5 minutes. Remove from heat, cover, and steep for 1 hour. Strain, discarding spices. Return liquid to pan, add cherries, and simmer until cherries are tender. If not using at once, cover and set aside for up to 8 hours at room temperature, then reheat before serving.

Heat a nonstick frying pan over medium heat. Add cake slices and dry-sauté until browned on both sides, turning once and wiping out pan as needed when cake sticks to surface, 30–60 seconds total.

To serve, place cake slices on dessert plates. Spoon warm fruit and syrup over cake.

To prepare: 5 minutes,
plus 1 hour to steep

To cook: 6 minutes

4 dessert servings

soybeans brown rice garbanzos

WHOLE GRAINS, LEGUMES, SEEDS, AND NUTS PROMOTE

pecans chestnuts bulgur wheat

ARTERY AND HEART HEALTH • HELP REDUCE THE RISK

flaxseed sesame seeds polenta

OF DIABETES • REDUCE HIGH BLOOD PRESSURE • OFFER

pumpkin seeds cashews quinoa

ANTIOXIDANTS FOR PROTECTION AND HEALING • HELP

kasha macadamia nuts walnuts

REDUCE THE RISK OF STROKE • MAY REDUCE THE RISK

hazelnuts oats couscous millet

OF CANCERS OF THE BREAST, PROSTATE, AND COLON

Brown

This chapter adds another color band to the healthy eating rainbow to accommodate grains, legumes, seeds, and nuts. Their colors may range from the red of kidney beans to the yellow of split peas, but you can think of them as brown foods as a convenient way to group them to serve and to remember the importance of bringing whole, unrefined foods into your daily diet.

Most unrefined grains are brown, because their bran has not been removed. It is this coating, along with the oil- and nutrient-rich germ, that makes whole grains so important in the diet. Whole grains, from buckwheat to quinoa, deserve the spotlight because of the satisfying flavors and textures they offer.

Our modern diet has come to typically exclude whole grains, but the recipes in this chapter will help you to bring them back to your table, with simple and tempting dishes like Chicken, Mushroom & Barley Casserole (page 246) and Bulgur Salad with Zucchini, Asparagus & Green Onions (page 259). Legumes, which include peas, beans, and peanuts, are high in both protein and fiber and are represented here in dishes such as Lima Beans Baked with Ham (page 263).

Nuts and seeds also play a starring role here, in dishes such as Cashew Chicken Stir-Fry (page 255) and Popped Amaranth (page 266).

GRAINS	LEGUMES	SEEDS	NUTS
barley	black beans	amaranth	almonds
bulgur wheat	cannellini beans	flaxseed	brazil nuts
couscous (wheat pasta)	cranberry (borlotti) beans	pumpkin seeds	cashews
kasha (buckwheat groats)	chickpeas	sesame seeds	chestnuts
millet	kidney beans	sunflower seeds	hazelnuts
oats	lima beans		macadamia nuts
polenta (ground corn)	navy beans		pecans
quinoa	soy beans		pine nuts
brown rice	black-eyed peas		pistachios
whole wheat	split peas		walnuts
	lentils		
	peanuts		

broiled polenta with mushroom ragout

1 cup (7 oz/220 g) instant polenta

4 oz (125 g) blue cheese, crumbled (1 cup)

Zest of ½ lemon

3 Tbsp butter

1½ lb (750 g) cremini mushrooms, brushed clean, stemmed, and thinly sliced

2 cloves garlic, crushed

3 Tbsp chopped fresh basil

2 Tbsp lemon juice

½ cup (4 fl oz/125 ml) chicken stock

1 tsp cornstarch

½ cup (2 oz/60 g) walnut pieces, chopped

To prepare: 10 minutes, plus 70 minutes to cool and chill

To cook: 25 minutes

5–6 servings

Line a 12-inch (21.5-cm) baking pan with parchment (baking) paper.

Bring 5 cups (40 fl oz/1.25 l) water, 2 tsp salt, and several grindings of pepper to boil in a saucepan over medium-high heat. Add polenta in a thin stream, stirring constantly. Cover and cook until grains are tender and mixture starts to pull away from sides of pan, 3–5 minutes. Remove from heat, add cheese and lemon zest, and stir until cheese is melted. Pour into prepared pan, spread evenly with a rubber spatula, and let cool for about 40 minutes, and then refrigerate until firm, 30–40 minutes more.

Preheat broiler (grill) and butter a baking sheet. Melt butter in a frying pan over medium heat. Add mushrooms and garlic and cook until mushrooms are softened and starting to release their liquids, about 5 minutes. Add basil, lemon juice, stock mixed with cornstarch, ½ tsp salt, and several grindings of pepper and cook until mushrooms are tender and sauce is lightly thickened, 3–4 minutes more.

Toast walnuts in a small, dry frying pan over medium heat, shaking occasionally, until they start to brown and become fragrant, 3–4 minutes. Remove from heat.

Cut polenta into 4-inch (10-cm) rounds and arrange on prepared baking sheet. Slide under broiler (grill) 4–6 inches (10–15 cm) from heat source and broil (grill) until lightly browned, about 5 minutes. Divide polenta rounds among warmed plates. Spoon mushroom mixture on top and scatter with walnuts to garnish. Serve at once.

Note: Cover and refrigerate the cooked polenta for up to 3 days.

chicken thighs with lima bean purée

1½ lb (750 g) boneless chicken thighs

Zest and juice of 1 lemon

2 tsp olive oil

1 tsp dried oregano

¼ tsp red pepper flakes

Lima Bean Purée

2 Tbsp olive oil

1 clove garlic, minced

Zest of ½ lemon, plus zest for garnish

2 cans (13 oz/410 g each) lima beans or butter beans, rinsed and drained

4 oz (125 g) feta cheese, crumbled (¾ cup)

2 tsp chopped fresh marjoram, plus sprigs for garnish

Put chicken in a bowl. Add lemon zest and juice, olive oil, oregano, red pepper flakes, 1 tsp salt, and several grindings of black pepper. Turn chicken to coat evenly. Cover and refrigerate for 30 minutes–12 hours. Remove from refrigerator 30 minutes before grilling.

For Bean Purée: Combine olive oil, garlic, and lemon zest in a medium saucepan and place over medium heat until they sizzle. Add beans and ⅓ cup (3 fl oz/80 ml) water and cook for 3–4 minutes to infuse flavors, reducing heat if necessary to avoid scorching. Alternatively, combine olive oil, garlic and lemon zest in a heatproof bowl and microwave on high for 30 seconds. Stir in beans and water. Cover and return to microwave for 4 minutes. Remove from heat or microwave, add feta and chopped marjoram, and purée until smooth in a food mill or food processor. Spoon back into a saucepan or microwave-safe bowl and set aside.

Build a fire in a charcoal grill for cooking over medium-low heat or preheat a gas grill to 300°F (150°C). Oil grill rack. Grill chicken, skin side down, turning once, until browned on both sides and opaque throughout, about 12 minutes. Remove to a platter, tent with foil, and let stand for 5 minutes. While chicken is resting, gently reheat bean purée in saucepan on stove top for 3–4 minutes, or in microwave in microwave-safe bowl, 1–2 minutes.

To serve, spoon bean purée into warmed shallow bowls and top with chicken. Garnish with marjoram sprigs and a little lemon zest.

To prepare: 15 minutes, plus 30 minutes to marinate

To cook: 20 minutes

4 servings

broiled tuna with cannellini bean salad

4 tuna steaks, each about 6 oz (185 g) and 1 inch (2.5 cm) thick

Zest of ½ lemon

1 tsp finely chopped fresh rosemary

Cannellini Bean Salad

4 oil-packed sun-dried tomatoes, drained and thinly sliced

3 Tbsp extra-virgin olive oil

2 Tbsp lemon juice

2 small cloves garlic, minced

2 Tbsp tiny nonpareil capers, rinsed and drained

2 cans (13 oz/410 g each) cannellini beans, rinsed and drained

1¼ cups (8 oz/250 g) cherry tomatoes, halved

½ cup (2½ oz/75 g) oil-cured black olives such as Niçoise, pitted if desired

2 Tbsp torn fresh basil leaves or chopped fresh parsley

Arrange tuna in a single layer in a shallow dish and brush both sides with olive oil. Sprinkle with lemon zest, rosemary, ½ tsp salt, and several grindings of pepper. Cover and refrigerate for 1–4 hours. Remove from the refrigerator 15 minutes before cooking.

For Bean Salad: In a saucepan or heatproof bowl, combine sun-dried tomatoes, olive oil, lemon juice, garlic, and capers. Mix in beans, cover, and heat over medium-low heat for several minutes until liquid is absorbed. Alternatively, microwave on high in a heatproof bowl for 3–4 minutes. Let cool, then add cherry tomatoes, olives, and basil and toss to distribute evenly. Season with salt and pepper.

Preheat the broiler (grill). Place fish on an aluminum foil-lined baking sheet and slide under the broiler 4 inches (10 cm) from heat source. Broil (grill), turning once, until fish is browned but still pink in the center, 2–3 minutes per side. Do not overcook. Remove to a platter, tent with foil, and let rest for 5 minutes.

To serve, divide bean salad among individual plates and top each portion with a tuna steak.

To prepare: 10 minutes, plus 1 hour to marinate

To cook: 5 minutes

4 servings

chicken, mushroom & barley casserole

½ cup (3½ oz/105 g) hulled barley

1 Tbsp olive oil

4 skin-on, bone-in chicken thighs

1 Tbsp chopped fresh rosemary

1 stalk celery, chopped

2 Tbsp chopped yellow onion

1 clove garlic, minced

¼ cup (1 oz/30 g) pine nuts

½ lb (250 g) brown mushrooms, brushed clean and thinly sliced

¼ cup (2 fl oz/60 ml) low-sodium chicken broth

2 green (spring) onions, including tender green parts, chopped

Preheat oven to 400°F (200°C).

Bring a large pot of water to a boil over high heat. Add barley and ½ tsp salt to the pot. Reduce heat to low, cover, and simmer until barley is tender and most of water is absorbed, about 45 minutes. Drain in a coarse-mesh sieve to remove any excess water and set aside.

While barley is cooking, in a deep, ovenproof sauté pan or a Dutch oven, heat olive oil over medium-high heat. When oil is hot, add chicken thighs, skin side down, and sprinkle with rosemary, ½ tsp salt, and ½ tsp pepper. Cook until first side is golden brown, 4–5 minutes. Turn and cook until second side is golden brown, 4–5 minutes more. Pour off all but 1 Tbsp fat from pan and add celery, yellow onion, garlic, and pine nuts. Sauté until vegetables are soft, about 2 minutes.

Stir in barley, mushrooms, and chicken broth. Taste and adjust seasoning with salt.

Bake, uncovered, until mushrooms are tender and chicken meat slips easily from bones, 15–20 minutes. During last 5 minutes of baking, sprinkle green onions over top.

Serve hot, directly from pan or in a warmed serving bowl.

To prepare: 15 minutes

To cook: 1 hour 5 minutes

4 servings

shrimp, beans & tomatoes

Toss shrimp with salt, pepper, olive oil, and minced chile and garlic. Grill over medium heat until pink. Toss with rinsed canned navy beans, chopped tomatoes, and green (spring) onions. Dress with a garlicky herbed lemon juice vinaigrette.

grilled rice patties with asian flavors

Coarsely purée 1 cup (5 oz/155 g) cooked brown rice with 1 egg, grated ginger, and soy sauce. Stir in sliced green (spring) onion and grated carrot. Form into small patties and cook on a lightly oiled pan on a grill until set and lightly browned.

red kidney bean quesadillas

Spread a flour tortilla with chile sauce. Top with rinsed canned kidney beans and sprinkle with shredded mozzarella, chopped cilantro (fresh coriander), salt, and pepper. Top with a tortilla and grill on both sides until golden and melted.

chickpeas with baby spinach

In a baking dish, toss 3½ cups (24 oz/750 g) rinsed canned chickpeas (garbanzo beans) and 2 thinly sliced tomatoes with 2 Tbsp olive oil, salt, and pepper. Broil (grill) until top is browned. Toss while still warm with baby spinach and lemon juice.

duck sausage, tomato & cranberry bean casserole

2 tsp olive oil

4 duck or pork sausages

3 Tbsp butter

1 onion, thinly sliced

1 can (12 oz/375 g) chopped tomatoes, with juices

2 cans (15 oz/470 g each) cranberry (borlotti) beans, rinsed and drained

2 tsp minced fresh thyme

1 Tbsp fresh winter savory leaves or 1 tsp dried

½ cup (1 oz/30 g) fresh bread crumbs (see Notes)

Preheat oven to 350°F (180°C). In a frying pan over medium heat, heat olive oil. Add sausages and cook, turning occasionally, until well browned on all sides, 10–12 minutes. Remove to a cutting board and let cool.

Melt 1 Tbsp butter in same pan over medium heat, add onion, and sauté until onion is very soft and lightly golden, about 15 minutes. Stir in tomatoes and their juices, ½ tsp salt, and ½ tsp pepper and cook until tomatoes are heated through, about 5 minutes more. Set aside.

Cut sausage into 1-inch (2.5-cm) pieces. In a small saucepan, melt remaining 2 Tbsp butter over medium heat. Set aside.

In a baking dish, combine the sausage, beans, thyme, winter savory, ½ tsp salt, and ½ tsp pepper and stir to mix well. Pour tomato mixture over beans and sausage and stir until ingredients are evenly distributed. Top with bread crumbs and drizzle with melted butter. Bake until topping is golden and juices are bubbling around edges, 15–20 minutes. Serve hot, directly from dish.

Notes: If desired, place the casserole under a broiler (grill) for 2–3 minutes to brown the top further. To make fresh bread crumbs, lay country-style bread slices flat on countertop and leave overnight to dry out, or use any type a few days past its peak of freshness. Remove crusts, tear bread into large pieces, and process to crumbs in a blender or food processor. Each bread slice yields ½ cup (1 oz/30 g) fresh crumbs.

To prepare: 10 minutes

To cook: 50 minutes

4–6 servings

turkey with red mole

Mole

1 dried ancho chile, seeded

1–2 dried guajillo or ancho chiles, seeded

2 Tbsp raisins

Boiling water as needed

2 cloves garlic

1 small yellow onion, quartered

3 large tomatillos, husked and rinsed

2 Tbsp sliced (flaked) almonds

1 Tbsp unsweetened cocoa powder

⅛ tsp ground cloves

⅓ cup (3 fl oz/80 ml) low-sodium chicken broth

One 6-inch (15-cm) corn tortilla, torn into 1-inch (2.5-cm) pieces

1 Tbsp canola oil

3 or 4 turkey tenderloins, about 1 lb (500 g)

⅔ cup (5 fl oz/160 ml) low-sodium chicken broth

To prepare: 30 minutes, plus 20 minutes to soak

To cook: 35 minutes

4 servings

For Mole: Heat a cast-iron frying pan over medium-high heat. One at a time, rinse chiles and roast in dry pan, pressing with a heatproof spatula and turning them until softened and fragrant, about 2 minutes. Wearing latex gloves, tear chiles into 1-inch (2.5-cm) pieces and place in a heatproof bowl. Add raisins and boiling water to cover. Let soak until chiles are soft, about 20 minutes. Drain chiles and raisins and place in a blender.

Heat a dry sauté pan over medium-high heat, add garlic and onion, and pan-roast, turning often with tongs, until browned and blistered on all sides, 4–5 minutes. Remove to a cutting board. Add tomatillos to pan and dry-roast in same manner until browned and blistered on all sides, about 5 minutes. Remove to cutting board. Coarsely chop vegetables and transfer to a blender. Let pan cool and wipe out.

Add almonds, cocoa powder, 1 tsp salt, ¼ tsp pepper, cloves, and ⅓ cup (3 fl oz/80 ml) chicken broth to blender. Blend to make a coarse purée. Add tortilla and blend until purée is smooth.

Heat oil in same cast-iron frying pan over medium-high heat. Season turkey to taste with salt and pepper. Cook turkey until lightly browned on all sides, about 6 minutes total. Add mole and ⅔ cup (5 fl oz/160 ml) chicken broth. Bring to a boil, lower heat, and simmer until turkey is opaque in center at its thickest point, about 15 minutes.

Remove turkey from pan and let rest on a cutting board for 5 minutes. Slice turkey and arrange on a warmed serving platter, overlapping slices. Spoon mole over the top. Serve at once. (See Note).

Note: Serve with steamed spinach or kale or steamed brown rice.

cashew chicken stir-fry

1 medium head iceberg lettuce, quartered

2 Tbsp hoisin sauce

1 Tbsp low-sodium soy sauce

1 tsp rice vinegar

¼ cup (2 fl oz/60 ml) low-sodium chicken broth

1 Tbsp cornstarch (cornflour)

¼ tsp Asian sesame oil

2 Tbsp peanut oil

¾ lb (375 g) skinless, boneless chicken breasts, cut into ½-inch (12-mm) cubes

1 Tbsp minced garlic

4 green (spring) onions, white and tender green parts, cut into slices ½ inch (12 mm) thick

1 medium green bell pepper (capsicum), seeded and diced

1 large red bell pepper (capsicum), seeded and diced

1 fresh green chile, thinly sliced

½ cup (2 oz/60 g) coarsely chopped raw cashews

With your fingers, separate 3 layers from each of the lettuce quarters, making 4 lettuce cups. Place lettuce cups on a plate, cover with moist paper towels, and refrigerate.

In a small bowl, mix together hoisin sauce, soy sauce, vinegar, chicken broth, and cornstarch. Stir in sesame oil and set aside.

In a wok, heat peanut oil over medium-high heat until almost smoking. Add chicken and stir-fry until it changes color, 1–2 minutes. Using a slotted spoon, remove chicken to a plate. Add garlic, green onions, bell peppers, and chile and stir-fry until tender-crisp, about 2 minutes. Return chicken to wok and add nuts. Stir seasoning sauce again, add to wok, and stir-fry until chicken is cooked through, 2–3 minutes.

Divide stir-fry among chilled lettuce cups and serve at once.

To prepare: 30 minutes

To cook: 7 minutes

4 servings

baked potatoes with flaxseed & cheddar

Rub russet potatoes with olive oil and roast at 350°F (180°C) until tender. Slit lengthwise about halfway through and spread open. Stuff with shredded Cheddar and sprinkle with flaxseed. Broil (grill) just until cheese is melted.

roasted pine nuts & raisin sauce

Roast pine nuts on a baking sheet, stirring occasionally, until lightly golden. Cook raisins in a little water with lemon juice and sugar until raisins are soft and syrup is thickened, about 15 minutes. Stir in pine nuts. Serve with seared tuna.

roasted chestnuts
with savoy cabbage

Cut an X through the skin on the flat side
of chestnuts and roast at 500°F (260°C)
until cut edges curl, 15–20 minutes. Peel
and chop. Toss with shredded Savoy
cabbage and sauté mixture in butter with
thinly sliced onion. Season to taste.

pumpkin seed
crust for fish

Finely chop unsalted hulled pumpkin
seeds. Brush fish fillets with beaten egg,
then roll in chopped seeds. Place on a
baking sheet and roast at 350°F (180°C)
until fish is opaque throughout, about
20 minutes, depending on thickness.

bulgur salad with zucchini, asparagus & green onions

8–10 spears asparagus, tough ends snapped off

2 zucchini (courgettes), cut on diagonal into slices ¼ inch (6 mm) thick

Boiling water as needed

1 tsp extra-virgin olive oil

1½ cups (9 oz/280 g) bulgur wheat

Dressing

3 Tbsp extra-virgin olive oil

2 tsp lemon zest

2 Tbsp lemon juice

2 tsp ground cumin

½ tsp turmeric

½ tsp cardamom seeds, crushed

1 cup (7 oz/220 g) drained cooked or canned chickpeas (garbanzo beans)

2 green (spring) onions, including tender green parts, thinly sliced

30 fresh mint leaves, minced

2 Tbsp minced fresh parsley

Build a fire in a charcoal grill for cooking over medium heat or preheat a gas grill to 350°F (180°C). Oil grill rack.

Put asparagus and zucchini in a heatproof bowl, pour boiling water over them to cover, and let stand for 2 minutes to soften slightly. Drain, let cool, and toss with 1 tsp olive oil.

When grill is ready, put bulgur in a heatproof bowl and add boiling water to cover by 2 inches (5 cm). Let stand for 10 minutes. Meanwhile, grill asparagus and zucchini, placing them perpendicular to grill rack and turning often, until lightly browned and tender-crisp, 4–5 minutes. Remove to a platter and let cool slightly. Cut asparagus spears on diagonal into thirds.

For Dressing: In a medium bowl, whisk together 3 Tbsp olive oil, lemon zest and juice, cumin, turmeric, cardamom, 1 tsp salt, and several grindings of pepper.

Stir chickpeas into bowl with dressing and then microwave on high in a microwave-safe bowl for 1 minute to meld flavors. Alternatively, heat chickpeas with dressing in a saucepan over medium heat for a couple of minutes, stirring occasionally. Drain bulgur. Combine grilled vegetables, bulgur, green onions, mint, parsley, and chickpeas with dressing in a serving bowl and toss to distribute and coat evenly. Serve warm or at room temperature.

To prepare: 20 minutes

To cook: 5 minutes

6 side-dish servings

pork, quinoa & chile casserole

Ingredients

2 tsp canola or grape seed oil

½ cup (3 oz/90 g) quinoa, rinsed (see Note)

1 Tbsp olive oil

1 lb (500 g) boneless pork loin, cut into 1-inch (2.5-cm) cubes

2–5 serrano chiles, seeded and chopped

¼ cup (1 oz/30 g) chopped onion

2 cloves garlic, minced

½–1 tsp chili powder

½ tsp ground cumin

½ cup (4 fl oz/125 ml) low-sodium chicken broth

¼ cup (1 oz/30 g) shredded Monterey jack or manchego cheese

12 pitted oil-cured black olives

Preheat oven to 375°F (190°C).

In a saucepan, heat canola oil over medium-high heat. Add quinoa and sauté until grains separate and become opaque, 3–4 minutes. Add 1 cup (8 fl oz/250 ml) water and ½ tsp salt and bring to a boil. Reduce heat to low, cover, and simmer until quinoa is tender, about 12 minutes. Drain in a fine-mesh sieve to remove any excess water and set aside.

In a Dutch oven or deep sauté pan, heat olive oil over medium-high heat. When oil is hot, add pork. Sear pork, turning as needed, until lightly browned on all sides, 4–5 minutes. Stir in chiles, onion, and garlic, and sprinkle with chili powder, cumin, and ½ tsp salt. Cook until onion is soft, about 2 minutes.

Add chicken broth and stir to scrape up browned bits from bottom of pan. Remove from heat, add quinoa, and toss and stir until ingredients are evenly distributed. Remove to a casserole dish, if desired. Sprinkle with cheese and dot with olives. Bake, uncovered, until cheese is melted and pork is opaque throughout, about 15 minutes.

Serve hot, directly from baking dish or pot.

Note: Rinse quinoa to remove any soapy-flavored saponin residue from the seeds. Most of this natural coating is removed by commercial processing, but some can remain. Put the quinoa in a sieve and rinse well as you gently rub the grains between your fingers.

To prepare: 15 minutes

To cook: 40 minutes

4 servings

lima beans baked with ham

1½ cups (10½ oz/330 g) dried large lima beans, picked over and rinsed

1 lb (500 g) ham steak cut into ½-inch (12 mm) cubes

1 tsp minced fresh thyme

In a large saucepan over high heat, mix together lima beans, 4 cups (32 fl oz/1 l) water, and 1 tsp salt and bring to a boil. Reduce heat to low, cover, and simmer until beans are tender, about 1½ hours.

Preheat oven to 400°F (200°C). Ladle beans and their cooking liquid into a medium baking dish. Stir ham into beans with thyme. Cover with aluminum foil and bake until ham is heated through and has released some of its juices, about 20 minutes. To serve, ladle beans, broth, and ham into warmed bowls, making sure each portion gets an equal amount of ham.

To prepare: 5 minutes

To cook: 2 hours

4 servings

tamarind shrimp with peanuts

2 Tbsp peanut oil

¼ cup (1½ oz/45 g) unsalted peanuts

1 cup (4 oz/125 g) chopped shallots

2 Tbsp minced garlic

2 Tbsp minced fresh ginger

2 Tbsp minced lemongrass, white part only (see Notes)

1–2 fresh red chiles, thinly sliced

¾ lb (375 g) medium shrimp (prawns), peeled and deveined

¼ cup (2 fl oz/60 ml) tamarind water (see Notes)

2 Tbsp Asian fish sauce

Have ready a small plate lined with paper towels. Heat oil in a wok over medium-high heat until almost smoking. Add peanuts and stir-fry briefly, until just taking on color. Remove wok from heat and, using a slotted spoon, remove peanuts to paper towels to drain. Reserve oil.

Return wok to burner and reheat oil until almost smoking. Add shallots, garlic, ginger, lemongrass, and chiles and stir-fry until fragrant, about 30 seconds. Add shrimp and stir-fry until bright pink, about 2 minutes.

Add tamarind water, fish sauce, sugar, and ⅛ tsp pepper and stir-fry until shrimp are opaque in center, 1–2 minutes. Stir in pineapple and heat through. Serve at once, garnished with fried peanuts.

Notes: For lemongrass, cut off and discard green top. Peel off dry outer layers. Using a sharp knife, thinly slice base crosswise. For tamarind water, dissolve 1 Tbsp tamarind concentrate (available at Indian and Southeast Asian groceries) in 3 Tbsp warm water. Serve this dish over brown rice.

To prepare: 20 minutes

To cook: 5 minutes

4 servings

ginger couscous
with dried fruit

1 Tbsp olive oil

¼ cup (1 oz/30 g) pine nuts

½ tsp ground ginger

**⅔ cup (4 oz/125 g) instant
semolina couscous**

¼ cup (1½ oz/45 g) dried currants

**¼ cup (1½ oz/45 g) chopped
dried peach (about 1 large half)**

**¼ cup (1½ oz/45 g) chopped
dried pear (about 1 large half)**

2 Tbsp chopped crystallized ginger

Heat 2 tsp oil in a frying pan over medium heat. Add pine nuts and sauté, stirring constantly, until golden, 1–2 minutes. Using a slotted spoon, remove nuts to a plate. Lightly wipe out pan.

Add 1⅓ cups (11 fl oz/330 ml) water, the ground ginger, 1 tsp salt, and remaining 1 tsp oil to pan. Bring to a boil over medium-high heat. Stir in couscous, currants, peaches, pears, and crystallized ginger. Remove from heat, cover, and let stand for 5 minutes. Fluff couscous with a fork, stir in pine nuts, and serve hot or warm.

Note: Serve with stir-fried dark greens or grilled chicken.

To prepare: 5 minutes

To cook: 7 minutes

4 servings

split peas with
yogurt & mint

1 cup (7 oz/220 g) green split peas

1 bay leaf

2 tsp extra-virgin olive oil

**1 cup (8 fl oz/250 ml) low-fat or
whole plain yogurt**

**2 Tbsp chopped fresh mint, plus
sprigs for garnish**

Rinse peas. In a saucepan over medium-high heat, combine peas and bay leaf with 2 cups (16 fl oz/500 ml) water and 1½ tsp salt. Bring to a boil, then reduce heat to low and simmer until peas are tender and most of the water is absorbed, about 40 minutes. Drain any excess water.

Preheat oven to 400°F (200°C).

Add ½ tsp pepper to the peas and, using a fork or spoon, mash peas. Taste and season with salt and pepper.

Lightly oil an 8-inch (20-cm) square baking dish and spoon the mashed peas into it, smoothing the top. Drizzle with the remaining olive oil and bake until a light crust forms, about 5 minutes. In a small bowl, stir together yogurt and chopped mint. Garnish peas with mint sprigs and serve at once with the yogurt mixture.

To prepare: 10 minutes

To cook: 30 minutes

4 side-dish servings

white beans with tomato & bacon

Fry 2 slices bacon until crisp, then sauté a chopped small onion in the bacon fat. Stir in rinsed and drained canned white beans, chopped plum (Roma) tomato, chopped rosemary, and pepper. When heated through, crumble the bacon over.

popped amaranth

Add 3 Tbsp amaranth seeds to a dry, hot wok, vigorously shaking pan until they stop popping (some will brown and not pop). In a bowl, combine amaranth with a few drops grape seed oil, chili powder, and sea salt, mixing with your fingers.

crunchy breakfast topping

Toast 1 Tbsp *each* wheat germ and sunflower and sesame seeds in a sauce-pan over medium heat until fragrant and lightly colored. Combine with 1 Tbsp *each* ground flaxseed and brown sugar. Sprinkle on yogurt or over cereal.

peanut sambal

Combine 2 Tbsp *each* coconut milk, peanut butter, and lime juice with red pepper flakes and 1 Tbsp fish sauce. Stir-fry cubed firm tofu with chopped garlic and ginger in oil until aromatic. Add sauce and stir-fry until thick. Season with salt.

black bean & white corn salad

2 tsp canola oil

⅔ cup (2½ oz/75 g) chopped red bell pepper (capsicum)

⅔ cup (3 oz/90 g) chopped red onion

1 cup (7 oz/220 g) drained cooked or canned black beans

1 cup (6 oz/185 g) fresh or frozen white corn kernels

1 tsp chili powder

2 Tbsp lime juice

Romaine (cos) lettuce leaves for serving (optional)

⅓ cup (½ oz/15 g) chopped cilantro (fresh coriander)

Heat oil in a medium frying pan over medium-high heat. Add bell pepper and onion and sauté until juice from bell pepper moistens bottom of pan, about 3 minutes.

Stir in beans, corn, and chili powder. Cook until beans and corn are heated through, about 3 minutes. Corn and peppers will be tender-crisp. Remove pan from heat and stir in lime juice. Toss well and season to taste with salt and pepper.

Line a platter with lettuce leaves, if using, and spoon beans and corn on top. Or, spoon beans and corn into a warmed serving bowl. Garnish with cilantro and serve.

To prepare: 10 minutes

To cook: 6 minutes

4 side-dish servings

lentils with shallots & serrano ham

¾ cup (5 oz/155 g) pardina, Umbrian, or brown lentils, rinsed

1 Tbsp olive oil

¾ cup (4 oz/125 g) finely chopped celery

¼ cup (½ oz/45 g) finely chopped shallots

2 Tbsp sherry vinegar

2 oz (60 g) serrano ham, finely diced (¼ cup)

Butter (Boston) lettuce leaves for serving

Combine lentils and 3 cups (24 fl oz/750 ml) water in a deep saucepan and bring to a boil over medium-high heat. Reduce heat to a simmer, cover, and cook until tender, about 35 minutes. Drain lentils, reserving ¼ cup (2 fl oz/ 60 ml) cooking liquid.

Heat oil in a medium frying pan over medium-high heat. Add celery and shallots and sauté until golden, about 8 minutes. Add contents of pan to lentils. Add vinegar and reserved lentil-cooking liquid to pan, bring to a boil, and reduce liquid by half, 3 minutes. Add hot liquid to lentils and stir in ham. Season to taste with salt and pepper.

Line a serving bowl or platter with lettuce leaves, mound lentils on top, and serve.

To prepare: 30 minutes

To cook: 45 minutes

4 servings

mango chicken
with toasted quinoa

⅔ cup (4 oz/125 g) quinoa, rinsed and drained (see Note, page 260)

3 Tbsp low-fat or whole plain yogurt

1 tsp grated fresh ginger

1 tsp honey

1 Tbsp lemon juice

2 cups (10 oz/315 g) diced mango

¾ cup (4 oz/125 g) diced seeded Kirby cucumber

4 skinless, boneless chicken breast halves, 6 oz (185 g) each

1 Tbsp canola oil

Toast wet quinoa in a dry nonstick sauté pan over medium heat, stirring with a wooden spatula, until grains are dry, 2–3 minutes. Raise heat to medium-high and stir constantly until grains start popping. When quinoa is lightly browned, after about 6 minutes, remove from heat and pour in 2 cups (16 fl oz/500 ml) water; be careful, as it will splatter. Cover and simmer over medium-low heat until tender, about 15 minutes.

Meanwhile, whisk together yogurt, ginger, honey, and ¼ tsp salt in a mixing bowl. Stir in lemon juice, mango, and cucumber. Set aside.

Pound breasts to an even thickness between 2 sheets of plastic wrap, using a mallet or rolling pin. Rub chicken on both sides with ½ tsp salt and ¼ tsp pepper. Heat oil in a large nonstick frying pan over medium-high heat. Add chicken and sauté until browned, 3–4 minutes per side. Reduce heat and cook until chicken is opaque in center, about 3 minutes more. To serve, fluff quinoa with a fork and divide among warmed dinner plates. Top with chicken and mango mixture.

To prepare: 20 minutes

To cook: 35 minutes

4 servings

kasha with walnuts & pasta

2 Tbsp canola oil

½ cup (4 oz/125 g) kasha (toasted buckwheat groats)

1½ cups (12 fl oz/375 ml) low-sodium vegetable broth

¾ cup (3 oz/90 g) bow-tie pasta

1½ cups (6 oz/185 g) diced onion

⅓ cup (1½ oz/45 g) chopped walnuts

Heat 1 Tbsp oil in a saucepan. Add kasha and cook, stirring constantly, until grains darken, about 3 minutes. Pour in broth; be careful, as it will splatter. Lower heat, cover, and cook until kasha is soft, about 10 minutes. Off heat, let stand, covered, for 5 minutes. Fluff grains with a fork, season to taste with salt and pepper, and cover to keep warm.

While kasha cooks, cook pasta in salted boiling water until al dente, about 12 minutes. Drain and set aside.

Meanwhile, heat remaining 1 Tbsp oil in a medium frying pan over medium-high heat. Add onion and sauté until golden, about 8 minutes. Mix in cooked kasha, pasta, and ⅛ tsp pepper and stir until kasha is heated through. Sprinkle with walnuts and serve.

To prepare: 5 minutes

To cook: 25 minutes

4 servings

maple panna cotta
with candied walnuts

Cooking oil spray for greasing

2 cups (16 fl oz/500 ml) reduced-fat (2 percent) milk

4 tsp unflavored gelatin

½ cup (3½ oz/105 g) maple sugar

1 cup (8 fl oz/250 ml) heavy (double) cream

1 cup (4 oz/125 g) coarsely chopped walnuts

2 Tbsp sugar

Pinch of Chinese five-spice powder

1 cup (8 fl oz/250 ml) peanut or canola oil

To prepare: 25 minutes, plus 3 hours to chill

To cook: 15 minutes

6 dessert servings

Coat six ¾-cup (6–fl oz/180-ml) individual custard cups or ramekins with cooking oil spray and set on a small baking sheet.

Pour ½ cup (4 fl oz/125 ml) milk into a saucepan and sprinkle on the gelatin. Let gelatin soften, about 5 minutes. Add remaining 1½ cups (12 fl oz/375 ml) milk and the maple sugar and cook over medium heat, stirring constantly, until sugar and gelatin are dissolved, about 5 minutes. Do not let liquid boil. Pour mixture into a mixing bowl. Set bowl into a larger bowl filled with ice water. Whisk until mixture starts to thicken and registers 65°F (18°C) on an instant-read thermometer, about 10 minutes. Gently stir in cream. Divide mixture evenly among prepared dishes, cover with plastic wrap, and refrigerate until firm, at least 3 hours.

Cover another baking sheet with heavy-duty foil and a third sheet with paper towels. Set both aside. Bring 4 cups (32 fl oz/1 l) water to a boil in a saucepan. Add nuts. When water returns to a boil, drain nuts and place in a bowl. Sprinkle hot nuts with sugar and five-spice and mix with a rubber spatula until sugar completely dissolves and nuts look shiny.

Heat oil in a wok over medium-high heat until it registers 375°F (190°C) on a candy thermometer. Carefully add the nuts. Let them cook for 30 seconds, then stir-fry gently until evenly browned. Quickly remove nuts using a slotted spoon and let drain on foil-lined pan. When cool, remove to a paper towel–lined pan and blot off excess oil with more towels. Break nuts into pieces.

About 30 minutes before serving, remove ramekins from refrigerator and dip carefully in hot water to loosen custards. Invert and unmold custards onto dessert plates. Just before serving, sprinkle each panna cotta with walnuts. Place extra nuts in a little dish and set on the table for diners to nibble.

Note: Candied walnuts will keep for 2 days in an airtight container at room temperature.

pear, cranberry & walnut crisp

4 Bosc pears, cored and cut lengthwise into 6 or 8 slices, depending on size

1 cup (4 oz/125 g) fresh or frozen cranberries

¾ cup (4 oz/125 g) all-purpose (plain) flour

⅔ cup (5 oz/155 g) sugar

¼ tsp salt

½ cup (4 oz/125 g) cold butter, cut into ½-inch (12-mm) cubes

½ cup (2 oz/60 g) chopped walnuts

Preheat oven to 375°F (190°C). Put pears and cranberries in a medium baking dish about 2 inches (5 cm) deep and toss to mix.

Combine flour, sugar, and salt in a bowl and whisk to mix well. Using a pastry blender or 2 knives, cut in butter until mixture resembles coarse crumbs. Stir in walnuts. Sprinkle topping evenly over fruit.

Bake until topping is golden brown, fruit is tender, and juices are bubbling, 45–50 minutes. Serve hot, warm, or at room temperature, directly from baking dish.

To prepare: 15 minutes

To cook: 50 minutes

4–6 dessert servings

oatmeal & dried peach muffins

2½ cups (12½ oz/390 g) all-purpose (plain) flour

¾ cup (6 oz/185 g) granulated sugar

2 Tbsp firmly packed brown sugar

1 Tbsp baking powder

1 tsp cinnamon

½ tsp salt

¾ cup (6 fl oz/180 ml) whole milk

½ cup (4 fl oz/125 ml) canola oil

2 eggs

½ cup quick-cooking rolled oats

½ cup (3 oz/95 g) chopped dried peaches

Preheat oven to 350°F (180°C). Grease a muffin pan or line with paper muffin liners.

In a bowl, combine flour, sugars, baking powder, cinnamon, and salt and whisk together. In another, larger bowl, combine milk, oil, and eggs, whisking together until well blended. Stir flour mixture into milk mixture, stirring just enough to blend all ingredients. Gently stir in oats and peaches.

Spoon batter into prepared muffin cups, filling each about three-quarters full. Bake until muffins are risen and golden brown and a toothpick inserted in the middle comes out clean, 25–30 minutes. Let muffins stand for 10 minutes. Turn out onto a wire rack and let cool to desired temperature. Serve warm or at room temperature.

To prepare: 20 minutes

To cook: 30 minutes

Makes 18 muffins

Nutrients at work

Humans need more than forty nutrients to support life. Many foods are good sources of these various nutrients, but no single food provides everything. Eating a variety of foods, preferably in their whole form, is the best way to get all the nutrients your body needs. Some nutrients require others for optimal absorption, but excessive amounts may result in health problems.

Until recently, nutritionists believed that the distribution of carbohydrates, protein, and fat in a healthy diet to be 55 percent of calories from carbohydrates, 15 percent of calories from protein, and 30 percent of calories from fat. As we have learned more about individual health needs and differences in our metabolism, we have become more flexible in determining what will constitute a well-balanced diet. The table below shows macronutrient ranges recommended in September 2002 by the Institute of Medicine, part of the U.S. National Academies. These ranges are more likely to accommodate everyone's health needs. To help you evaluate and balance your diet as you prepare the recipes in this book, turn to pages 280–89 for nutritional analyses of each recipe.

Nutrition experts have also determined guidelines for vitamins and minerals. For more information, see pages 278–79.

CARBOHYDRATES, PROTEIN, AND FATS

NUTRIENTS AND FOOD SOURCES	FUNCTIONS	RECOMMENDED % OF DAILY CALORIES AND GUIDANCE
Carbohydrates COMPLEX CARBOHYDRATES • Grains, breads, cereals, pastas • Dried beans and peas, lentils • Starchy vegetables (potatoes, corn, green peas)	• Main source of energy for the body • Particularly important for the brain and nervous system • Fiber aids normal digestion	45–65% • Favor complex carbohydrates, especially legumes, vegetables, and whole grains (brown rice; whole-grain bread, pasta, and cereal). • Many foods high in complex carbohydrates are also good fiber sources. Among the best are bran cereals, canned and dried beans, dried fruit, and rolled oats. Recommended daily intake of fiber for adults under age 50 is 25 g for women and 38 g for men. For women over age 50, intake is 21 g; for men, 30 g.
SIMPLE CARBOHYDRATES • Naturally occurring sugars in fruits, vegetables, and milk • Added refined sugars in soft drinks, candy, baked goods, jams and jellies, etc.	• Provide energy	• Fruit and vegetables have naturally occurring sugars but also have vitamins, minerals, and phytochemicals. Refined sugar, on the other hand, has little to offer in the way of nutrition, so limit your intake to get the most from your daily calories.

Source: Institute of Medicine. Dietary Reference Intakes for Energy, Carbohydrates, Fiber, Fat, Protein, and Amino Acids (Macronutrients).

CARBOHYDRATES, PROTEIN, AND FATS

NUTRIENTS AND FOOD SOURCES	FUNCTIONS	RECOMMENDED % OF DAILY CALORIES AND GUIDANCE
Protein • Foods from animal sources • Dried beans and peas, nuts • Grain products	• Builds and repairs cells • Regulates body processes by providing components for enzymes, hormones, fluid balance, nerve transmission	10–35% • Choose lean sources such as dried beans, fish, poultry, lean cuts of meat, soy, and low-fat dairy products most of the time. • Egg yolks are rich in many nutrients but also high in cholesterol; limit to 5 per week.
Fats All fats are mixtures of saturated and unsaturated (polyunsaturated and monounsaturated) types. Polyunsaturated and especially monounsaturated types are more desirable because they promote cardiovascular health.	• Supply essential fatty acids needed for various body processes and to build cell membranes, particularly of the brain and nervous system • Transport certain vitamins	20–35% • Experts disagree about the ideal amount of total fat in the diet. Some say more is fine if it is heart-healthy fat; others recommend limiting total fat. Virtually all experts agree that saturated fat, trans fats, and cholesterol, all of which can raise "bad" (LDL) cholesterol, should be limited.
PRIMARILY SATURATED • Foods from animal sources (meat fat, butter, cheese, cream) • Coconut, palm, palm kernel oils	• Raises blood levels of "bad" (LDL) cholesterol	• Limit saturated fat.
PRIMARILY POLYUNSATURATED (PUFA) • Omega-3 fatty acids: herring, salmon, mackerel, lake trout, sardines, swordfish, nuts, flaxseed, canola oil, soybean oil, tofu • Omega-6: vegetable oils such as corn, soybean, and safflower (abundant in the American diet.)	• Reduces inflammation; influences blood clotting and blood vessel activity to improve blood flow	• Eat fish at least twice a week. • Substitute PUFA for saturated fat or trans fat when possible.
PRIMARILY MONOUNSATURATED (MUFA) Olive oil, canola oil, sesame oil, avocados, almonds, chicken fat	• Raises blood levels of "good" (HDL) cholesterol	• Substitute MUFA for saturated fat or trans fat when possible.
DIETARY CHOLESTEROL Foods from animal sources (egg yolks, organ meats, cheese, fish roe, meat)	• A structural component of cell membranes and some hormones	• The body makes cholesterol, and some foods contain dietary cholesterol. U.S. food labels list cholesterol values.
TRANS FAT Processed foods, purchased baked goods, margarine and shortening	• Raises blood levels of "bad" (LDL) cholesterol	• U.S. food labels list trans fats.

VITAMINS

FAT-SOLUBLE VITAMINS AND FOOD SOURCES	FUNCTIONS	DAILY RECOMMENDED INTAKES FOR ADULTS*
Vitamin A Dairy products, deep yellow-orange fruits and vegetables, dark green leafy vegetables, liver, fish, fortified milk, cheese, butter	• Promotes growth and healthy skin and hair • Helps build strong bones and teeth • Works as an antioxidant that may reduce the risk of some cancers and other diseases • Helps night vision • Increases immunity	700 mcg for women 900 mcg for men
Vitamin D Fortified milk, salmon, sardines, herring, butter, liver, fortified cereals, fortified margarine	• Builds bones and teeth • Enhances calcium and phosphorus absorption and regulates blood levels of these nutrients	5–10 mcg
Vitamin E Nuts and seeds, vegetable and seed oils (corn, soybean, sunflower), whole-grain breads and cereals, dark green leafy vegetables, dried beans and peas	• Helps form red blood cells • Improves immunity • Prevents oxidation of "bad" LDL cholesterol • Works as an antioxidant that may reduce the risk of some cancers	15 mg
Vitamin K Dark green leafy vegetables, carrots, asparagus, cauliflower, cabbage, liver, wheat bran, wheat germ, eggs	• Needed for normal blood clotting • Promotes protein synthesis for bone, plasma, and organs	90 mcg for women 120 mcg for men

WATER-SOLUBLE VITAMINS

B vitamins Grain products, dried beans and peas, dark green leafy vegetables, dairy products, meat, poultry, fish, eggs, organ meats, milk, brewer's yeast, wheat germ, seeds	• Helps the body use carbohydrates (biotin, B_{12}, niacin, pantothenic acid) • Regulate metabolism of cells and energy production (niacin, pantothenic acid) • Keep the nerves and muscles healthy (thiamin) • Protect against spinal birth defects (folate) • Protect against heart disease (B_6, folate)	• B_6: 1.3–1.5 mg • B_{12}: 2.4 mcg • Biotin: 30 mcg • Niacin: 14 mg niacin equivalents for women; 16 mg for men • Pantothenic acid: 5 mg • Riboflavin: 1.1 mg for women; 1.3 mg for men • Thiamin: 1.1 mg for women; 1.2 mg for men • Folate: 400 mcg
Vitamin C Many fruits and vegetables, especially citrus fruits, broccoli, tomatoes, bell peppers (capsicums), melons, strawberries, potatoes, papayas	• Helps build body tissues • Fights infection and helps heal wounds • Helps body absorb iron and folate • Helps keep gums healthy • Works as an antioxidant	75 mg for women 90 mg for men

Sources: Institute of Medicine reports, 1999–2001

*mcg=micrograms; mg=milligrams

VITAMINS

MINERALS** AND FOOD SOURCES	FUNCTIONS	DAILY RECOMMENDED INTAKES FOR ADULTS*
Calcium Dairy products (especially hard cheese, yogurt, and milk), fortified juices, sardines and canned fish eaten with bones, shellfish, tofu (if processed with calcium), dark green leafy vegetables	• Helps build bones and teeth and keep them strong • Helps heart, muscles, and nerves work properly	1,000–1,200 mg
Iron Meat, fish, shellfish, egg yolks, dark green leafy vegetables, dried beans and peas, grain products, dried fruits	• Helps red blood cells carry oxygen • Component of enzymes • Strengthens immune system	18 mg for women 8 mg for men
Magnesium Nuts and seeds, whole-grain products, dark green leafy vegetables, dried beans and peas	• Helps build bones and teeth • Helps nerves and muscles work properly • Necessary for DNA and RNA • Necessary for carbohydrate metabolism	310–320 mg for women 400–420 mg for men
Phosphorus Seeds and nuts, meat, poultry, fish, dried beans and peas, dairy products, whole-grain products, eggs, brewer's yeast	• Helps build strong bones and teeth • Has many metabolic functions • Helps body get energy from food	700 mg
Potassium Fruit, vegetables, dried beans and peas, meat, poultry, fish, dairy products, whole grains	• Helps body maintain water and mineral balance • Regulates heartbeat and blood pressure	2,000 mg suggested; no official recommended intake
Selenium Mushrooms, seafood, chicken, organ meats, brown rice, whole-wheat (wholemeal) bread, peanuts, onions	• Works as an antioxidant with vitamin E to protect cells from damage • Boosts immune function	55 mg
Zinc Oysters, meat, poultry, fish, soybeans, nuts, whole grains, wheat germ	• Helps body metabolize proteins, carbohydrates, and alcohol • Helps wounds heal • Needed for growth, immune response, and reproduction	8 mg for women 11 mg for men

** The following minerals are generally sufficient in the diet when the minerals listed above are present: chloride, chromium, copper, fluoride, iodine, manganese, molybdenum, sodium, and sulfur. For information on functions and food sources, consult a nutrition book.

Nutritional values

The recipes in this book have been analyzed for significant nutrients to help you evaluate your diet and balance your meals throughout the day. Using these calculations, along with the other information in this book, you can create meals that have the optimal balance of nutrients. Having the following nutritional values at your fingertips will help you plan healthful meals.

Keep in mind that the calculations reflect nutrients per serving unless otherwise noted. Not included in the calculations are optional ingredients or those added to taste, or that are suggested as an alternative or used as a substitution in the recipe. For recipes that yield a range of servings, the calculations are for the middle of that range. Many recipes call for a specific amount of salt and also suggest seasoning food to taste; however, if you are on a low-sodium diet, it is prudent to reduce or omit salt. If you have particular concerns about any nutrient needs, consult your doctor. The numbers for all nutritional values have been rounded using the guidelines required for reporting nutrient levels in the "Nutrition Facts" panel on U.S. food labels.

The best way to acquire the nutrients your body needs is through food. However, a balanced multivitamin-mineral supplement is a safe addition to your diet.

WHAT COUNTS AS A SERVING?	HOW MANY SERVINGS DO YOU NEED EACH DAY?		
	For a 1,600-calorie-per-day diet *(children 2–6, sedentary women, some older adults)*	For a 2,200-calorie-per-day diet *(children over 6, teen girls, active women, sedentary men)*	For a 2,800-calorie-per-day diet *(teen boys, active men)*
Fruit Group 1 medium whole fruit such as apple, orange, banana, or pear ½ cup (2–3 oz/60–90 g) chopped, cooked, or canned fruit ¼ cup (3 oz/90 g) dried fruit ¾ cup (6 fl oz/180 ml) fruit juice	2	3	4
Vegetable Group 1 cup (1 oz/30 g) raw, leafy vegetables ½ cup (2–3 oz/60–90 g) other vegetables, cooked or raw ¾ cup (6 fl oz/180 ml) vegetable juice	3	4	5
Bread, Cereal, Rice, and Pasta Group 1 slice of bread 1 cup (6 oz/180 g) ready-to-eat cereal ½ cup (2.5 oz/80 g) cooked cereal, rice, pasta	6	9	11

Adapted from USDA Dietary Guidelines (2005).

Purple & blue		CALORIES	PROTEIN/ GM	CARBS/ GM	TOT. FAT/ GM	SAT. FAT/ GM	CHOL/ MG	FIBER/ GM	SODIUM/ MG
p.27	Eggplant crisps with yogurt dipping sauce	150	5	14	9	2	4	5	208
p.27	Roasted purple carrots & fennel	123	2	16	6	1	0	5	387
p.28	Grilled pizzas with blue potatoes & onions	359	13	41	16	6	26	2	389
p.31	Purple asparagus with orange vinaigrette	39	2	7	1	0	0	1	2
p.31	Scallops with bell pepper dressing	163	10	5	11	2	19	1	95
p.32	Grilled eggplant & feta cheese rolls	153	8	9	11	5	13	4	470
p.32	Purple carrots glazed with red wine	89	1	11	2	1	5	3	81
p.37	Fig & purple endive salad	168	1	17	12	1	0	3	231
p.37	Halibut & purple grapes	227	36	6	6	2	59	0	529
p.38	Roasted tuna with olives, grapes & pine nuts	369	35	10	21	3	64	1	924
p.38	Roasted turkey breast with figs & lavender	308	38	17	10	3	95	3	487
p.41	Chicken & eggplant salad	464	39	16	27	4	94	7	738
p.41	Chicken & fig skewers	354	32	23	15	4	116	5	105
p.42	Roasted pork & prunes	364	28	29	15	5	82	3	590
p.47	Baked pilaf with currants, lavender & almonds	321	8	52	10	2	8	5	1174
p.47	Herbed blue potatoes	235	5	39	7	1	0	4	600
p.48	Salmon with wild blueberry & rhubarb sauce	238	24	18	8	1	53	2	59
p.51	Stir-fried pork with black plums	198	17	22	5	1	51	3	63
p.51	Duck with purple cabbage, blackberries & port	319	25	16	16	3	128	3	92

Purple & blue

		CALORIES	PROTEIN/ GM	CARBS/ GM	TOT. FAT/ GM	SAT. FAT/ GM	CHOL/ MG	FIBER/ GM	SODIUM/ MG
p.52	Sichuan beef with eggplant	372	23	33	16	4	28	4	333
p.57	Wild rice with purple bell pepper & pecans	209	4	22	13	2	0	3	4
p.57	Pan-fried blue potatoes with sage	85	1	10	5	1	0	1	2
p.58	Grilled plums with kirsch cream	214	2	17	16	10	58	1	15
p.58	Grilled berry parcels	159	2	39	1	0	0	7	2
p.61	Purple fruits with lavender syrup	194	1	43	3	2	8	1	1
p.61	Roasted black plums with star anise	62	0	12	2	1	5	1	0
p.62	Blackberry crêpes	452	10	75	12	7	83	4	258
p.62	Pomegranate-glazed figs	168	2	24	9	5	23	3	13

Green

		CALORIES	PROTEIN/ GM	CARBS/ GM	TOT. FAT/ GM	SAT. FAT/ GM	CHOL/ MG	FIBER/ GM	SODIUM/ MG
p.69	Belgian endive with blue cheese & walnuts	321	10	7	30	8	21	3	688
p.69	Green onions with anchovy sauce	112	4	5	9	1	10	2	485
p.70	Grilled fish tacos with green cabbage salad	538	24	39	34	5	56	11	995
p.73	Roasted broccolini with lemon	75	2	5	5	1	0	1	308
p.73	Roasted zucchini with anchoïade	256	6	4	24	4	15	1	951
p.74	Spinach soufflé	272	13	11	20	11	252	1	761
p.79	Stir-fried chicken with broccoli & mushrooms	275	18	29	10	2	31	4	455
p.79	Dry-fried long beans	85	2	8	6	0	0	3	9

Green		CALORIES	PROTEIN/ GM	CARBS/ GM	TOT. FAT/ GM	SAT. FAT/ GM	CHOL/ MG	FIBER/ GM	SODIUM/ MG
p.80	Chicken breasts stuffed with goat cheese & arugula	391	44	14	16	5	111	3	262
p.83	Trout & green pear salad	353	32	14	18	3	86	3	82
p.83	Grilled halibut with limes	373	27	4	27	5	84	1	171
p.84	Chicken, avocado & spinach salad	525	41	20	33	5	96	9	322
p.89	Roasted asparagus with eggs & parmesan	133	9	5	9	2	212	2	237
p.89	Cod on a bed of cucumbers	117	23	3	1	0	54	1	310
p.90	Baked pasta with dandelion greens & sausage	582	31	55	28	8	87	5	1263
p.93	Lamb chops with arugula pesto	421	24	3	35	6	85	1	350
p.93	Broccoli gratin	301	11	20	21	5	17	3	537
p.94	Fettuccine with fava beans, artichokes & asparagus	528	24	82	15	3	6	19	228
p.94	Lemon sole with peas	270	35	12	8	4	97	3	143
p.97	Duck & Brussels sprouts	358	22	11	24	3	60	5	88
p.101	Stir-fried calamari & pea shoots	375	24	39	17	3	198	5	244
p.101	Chicken with tomatillo sauce	180	24	5	6	1	63	1	76
p.102	Okra with yellow plum tomatoes	66	2	8	4	1	0	3	15
p.102	Swiss chard with lemon & anchovy	134	3	7	11	2	2	2	304
p.105	Green figs with almond custard	224	5	39	6	3	110	3	35
p.106	Green apples baked with dried cranberries	264	0	56	6	4	15	3	13
p.106	Green pear & grape clafoutis	254	5	36	10	6	101	1	49

White & tan	CALORIES	PROTEIN/ GM	CARBS/ GM	TOT. FAT/ GM	SAT. FAT/ GM	CHOL/ MG	FIBER/ GM	SODIUM/ MG
p.113 Mushroom bruschetta	316	12	46	9	2	6	6	*777*
p.113 Mustard-honey leeks	165	1	9	14	2	0	1	74
p.114 Baked onion & white eggplant purée	72	2	15	2	0	0	6	586
p.114 Mashed Jerusalem artichokes with truffle oil	142	3	21	6	2	10	2	589
p.117 White asparagus mimosa with browned butter	82	3	3	7	4	68	1	18
p.117 Potato galettes with smoked salmon	156	5	16	8	1	5	1	429
p.118 Turkey sandwiches with sweet onions	415	34	32	17	3	56	2	858
p.118 Grilled white corn salad	139	3	22	6	1	0	3	211
p.123 Pork pot roast with parsnips, carrots & apples	425	38	20	22	8	123	4	749
p.124 Sicilian shrimp with cauliflower & almonds	277	20	26	12	2	129	5	328
p.124 Potatoes with chorizo & parsley	189	6	29	4	2	9	3	143
p.127 Turkey fricassee with kohlrabi, pears, & mushrooms	293	25	28	10	1	34	4	599
p.127 Pork chops smothered in onions & apples	296	25	15	14	3	67	2	359
p.128 Monkfish with roasted white corn salsa	300	25	17	16	3	40	5	48
p.133 White eggplant & green onion salad	120	2	9	9	1	0	4	6
p.133 Grilled fennel with Indian spices	113	4	12	6	1	2	4	229
p.134 Cuban-style pork & plantains	452	32	33	22	7	86	2	362
p.137 Mu shu pork	593	29	68	22	5	54	6	990
p.138 Spicy cauliflower gratin	161	7	19	7	4	19	4	751

White & tan		CALORIES	PROTEIN/ GM	CARBS/ GM	TOT. FAT/ GM	SAT. FAT/ GM	CHOL/ MG	FIBER/ GM	SODIUM/ MG
p.138	Parsley portobellos	134	4	8	11	2	0	2	311
p.143	Roasted fennel with fennel seed	143	2	14	6	7	1	0	92
p.143	Celery root & potato gratin	210	5	20	13	8	42	3	301
p.144	Turnips with peas & mushrooms	86	5	12	3	0	0	5	174
p.144	Chicken with caramelized shallots & wine	261	25	16	8	4	78	1	81
p.147	White nectarines with raw sugar & rum	142	1	22	3	2	8	2	0
p.147	Baked bananas & tapioca pudding	233	5	38	7	4	53	2	59

Yellow & orange		CALORIES	PROTEIN/ GM	CARBS/ GM	TOT. FAT/ GM	SAT. FAT/ GM	CHOL/ MG	FIBER/ GM	SODIUM/ MG
p.153	Yellow tomatoes with mint & pecorino	92	5	9	5	2	6	2	159
p.153	Grilled pumpkin with pumpkin seed dressing	112	2	7	9	1	0	1	2
p.154	Corn & crab quesadillas	360	17	30	19	8	62	2	916
p.154	Scallops with golden beets	165	10	18	6	1	14	3	632
p.157	Spanish tortilla with golden potatoes	190	6	17	11	2	90	1	348
p.158	Grilled salmon, yellow potato & corn salad	558	36	32	32	5	90	4	96
p.163	Grilled duck breast with papaya	423	43	14	21	5	231	3	308
p.164	Grilled snapper & mandarin salad	246	36	16	5	1	60	4	308
p.164	Mahimahi & mango salsa	217	32	11	5	1	124	1	236
p.167	Halibut with roasted nectarine chutney	327	32	28	10	3	53	4	951

Yellow & orange		CALORIES	PROTEIN/ GM	CARBS/ GM	TOT. FAT/ GM	SAT. FAT/ GM	CHOL/ MG	FIBER/ GM	SODIUM/ MG
p.167	Roasted sea bass with carrot purée	256	34	8	9	4	92	2	469
p.168	Rack of lamb with orange bell pepper relish	197	22	6	10	3	81	1	768
p.168	Baked sweet potato & rutabaga mash	132	2	18	6	4	15	4	334
p.173	Spaghetti squash agio e olio	107	3	13	5	1	4	3	857
p.173	Turban squash with honey butter	206	3	41	6	4	15	5	302
p.174	Baked stew of curried root vegetables	270	5	21	20	16	15	6	529
p.177	Chicken with yellow peppers & passion fruit	345	29	33	11	2	67	3	64
p.177	Stuffed squash blossoms	368	15	21	24	8	32	1	287
p.178	Shrimp with papaya & coconut	184	15	18	6	2	126	2	149
p.178	Apricot-stuffed chicken breasts	484	40	44	10	5	116	4	192
p.183	Rutabaga & golden beets with pomegranate seeds	96	3	14	4	1	0	3	80
p.183	Indian-spiced squash with cashews	57	1	4	5	2	5	1	189
p.184	Ham & sweet potato hash	178	10	14	9	2	219	2	258
p.184	Butternut squash & pears with rosemary	98	1	17	4	0	0	3	4
p.187	Grilled apricots with sabayon	225	4	36	8	2	205	2	10
p.188	Pumpkin flan	343	10	42	16	8	245	1	218
p.191	Winter peach shortcake	496	6	59	26	16	76	3	482

Red	CALORIES	PROTEIN/ GM	CARBS/ GM	TOT. FAT/ GM	SAT. FAT/ GM	CHOL/ MG	FIBER/ GM	SODIUM/ MG
p.197 Grilled radicchio	131	4	7	10	3	6	1	172
p.197 Liver & onion bruschetta	360	21	39	12	3	201	4	542
p.198 Grilled calamari with about ⅓ cup Romesco sauce per serving	284	27	19	12	1	330	3	125
p.201 Roasted tomato tart	203	4	21	12	5	37	2	489
p.202 Warm tomato & olive bruschetta	139	5	19	5	1	0	5	346
p.202 Red wine spaghetti with red bell pepper & onion	581	17	78	10	2	6	14	117
p.207 Shrimp with watermelon, feta, & mint	272	28	11	13	5	198	1	633
p.207 Grilled cherry tomatoes	31	1	3	2	0	0	1	101
p.208 Sautéed trout with red grape sauce	419	36	14	14	6	122	0	54
p.211 Mahimahi with red potato, red bell pepper & rosemary	311	23	18	15	2	83	3	688
p.211 Baked mackerel with red currants	436	35	4	30	9	120	1	704
p.212 Game hens with pears	432	29	26	24	7	168	3	1247
p.212 Roasted chicken & red onion	508	45	8	32	9	150	1	717
p.215 Duck with blood orange sauce	482	44	33	19	5	231	2	448
p.215 Turkey tenderloin with cranberry compote	212	27	16	5	1	56	3	78
p.219 Pork tenderloin with sour cherry sauce	239	19	17	10	3	55	1	49
p.219 Red-hot hash browns	111	2	19	4	0	0	2	5
p.220 Lamb kebabs with blood orange salad	377	23	26	21	5	74	10	214
p.223 Veal with red plum sauce	301	33	11	13	4	131	1	555

Red		CALORIES	PROTEIN/ GM	CARBS/ GM	TOT. FAT/ GM	SAT. FAT/ GM	CHOL/ MG	FIBER/ GM	SODIUM/ MG
p.223	Chicken with cherry salsa	230	29	12	7	1	78	1	217
p.224	Baked pasta with radicchio & blue cheese	520	19	66	21	10	42	3	1001
p.229	Rib-eye steaks with baked plums	254	25	9	13	5	83	1	341
p.229	Roasted beets with Indian spices	150	3	19	8	1	0	6	732
p.230	Berry gratin	135	4	23	3	1	106	5	36
p.230	Deep-dish cherry pie	319	4	64	6	4	16	2	170
p.233	Caramelized red pears with cinnamon	309	1	68	1	1	3	7	6
p.233	Broiled grapes in yogurt & sour cream	237	3	45	6	4	19	1	45
p.234	Strawberries in red wine	246	3	25	13	8	72	2	51
p.234	Cherries & pound cake	325	3	61	6	3	63	2	123

Brown		CALORIES	PROTEIN/ GM	CARBS/ GM	TOT. FAT/ GM	SAT. FAT/ GM	CHOL/ MG	FIBER/ GM	SODIUM/ MG
p.241	Broiled polenta with mushroom ragout	287	10	23	18	8	29	5	1258
p.242	Chicken thighs with lima bean purée	632	40	25	40	13	168	6	1322
p.245	Broiled tuna with cannellini bean salad	570	48	33	26	4	65	9	1046
p.246	Chicken, mushroom & barley casserole	325	21	25	16	3	57	5	362
p.251	Duck sausage, tomato & cranberry bean casserole	367	21	30	18	7	55	11	1457
p.252	Turkey with red mole	361	33	40	9	1	56	5	106
p.255	Cashew chicken stir-fry	334	24	20	18	4	51	3	324

Brown		CALORIES	PROTEIN/ GM	CARBS/ GM	TOT. FAT/ GM	SAT. FAT/ GM	CHOL/ MG	FIBER/ GM	SODIUM/ MG
p.259	Bulgur salad with zucchini, asparagus & green onions	240	8	36	9	1	0	9	515
p.260	Pork, quinoa & chile casserole	365	28	18	20	5	71	2	320
p.263	Lima beans baked with ham	330	35	35	5	2	51	12	2024
p.263	Tamarind shrimp with peanuts	412	24	45	15	2	129	4	834
p.264	Ginger couscous with dried fruit	244	5	38	10	1	0	5	586
p.264	Split peas with yogurt & mint	218	13	33	4	1	3	16	913
p.269	Black bean & white corn salad	132	6	22	3	0	0	6	23
p.269	Lentils with shallots & serrano ham	181	13	24	5	1	6	9	202
p.270	Mango chicken with toasted quinoa	389	39	37	10	2	94	4	97
p.270	Kasha with walnuts & pasta	292	7	37	15	1	0	5	178
p.273	Maple panna cotta with candied walnuts	392	7	22	32	12	61	1	53
p.274	Pear, cranberry & walnut crisp	401	4	51	22	10	40	5	100
p.274	Oatmeal & dried peach muffins	190	3	28	8	1	25	1	144

Glossary

almonds: See Nuts.

anaheim chiles: See Chiles.

ancho chiles: See Chiles.

anchovies: These tiny Mediterranean fish are high in heart-healthy omega-3 fatty acids. They are generally boned, cured, packed in oil and sold in small cans or jars.

apples: The major portion of the apple's nutrition is in its skin, which contains the flavonoid quercetin, an antioxidant that fights viruses and allergies and is thought to be anticarcinogenic. Apple flesh is an important source of pectin, a fiber that lowers cholesterol.

apricots: The apricot's color is due to the pigments beta-carotene and lycopene, which promote eye health and heart health, lower the risk of some cancers, and strengthen the immune system. Apricots are also high in vitamin C, potassium, and fiber.

artichokes: The artichoke's fleshy heart provides a complex of heart-healthy phytochemicals, including cynarin; it also contains chlorophyll and beta-carotene and provides a wide range of vitamins and minerals. Baby artichokes are completely edible and the chokes can be sliced and eaten raw.

arugula (rocket): A peppery green, arugula is eaten both cooked and raw. It is a good source of iron and vitamins A and C and contains lutein, which protects eye health.

Asian chile sauce or paste: Used as a seasoning or condiment to add heat in Chinese and Southeast Asian dishes, this seasoning is made from fresh or dried red chiles. You can find it at Asian groceries and specialty-food stores.

Asian dark sesame oil: This dark sesame oil is made from toasted or roasted sesame seeds. Heat harms its flavor, so add it after cooking and use it to give sauces and dressings a toasted flavor. It is sold in the ethnic sections of well-stocked supermarkets and in Asian and specialty-food stores.

asparagus: This vegetable is one of the best sources of folate, a B vitamin that helps fight heart disease and keeps the female reproductive system healthy. It is also rich in phytochemicals, depending on its color (it comes in green, white, and purple).

avocados: Technically a fruit, the avocado is high in fat, but most of it is monounsaturated, which helps to lower cholesterol. It also contains beta-sitosterol, a plant cholesterol that lowers cholesterol as well, and may prevent the growth of cancer cells. Avocados are high in vitamins and minerals, especially vitamins A, C, B_6, folate, and potassium.

bananas: Bananas are high in potassium, which balances sodium and helps regulate blood pressure, and may reduce arterial plaque formation. Potassium also helps to prevent strokes by lowering platelet activity and reducing blood clots. Bananas are also high in vitamins C and B_6, and contain a kind of fiber that is believed to protect against colon cancer.

barley: This grain contributes fiber, vitamins, minerals, and phytochemicals to the diet. Hulled barley retains its bran and germ, and so provides more nutrients as well as antioxidants. Pearl barley, which has been refined, steamed, and polished, lacks the nutrients of hulled and is not considered a whole grain.

basil: Traditionally used in kitchens throughout the Mediterranean and in Southeast Asia, basil is one of the world's best-loved herbs and is a source of green phytonutrients. Although related to mint, basil tastes faintly of anise and cloves. Italian cooks use it in pesto and often pair it with tomatoes. In Thailand and Vietnam, basil is often combined with fresh mint for seasoning stir-fries, curries, and salads.

beans, black: Also called turtle, Mexican, or Spanish black beans, these beans have a robust taste. Used widely in Latin American cooking for soups and dips. Like all dried beans, black beans contain protein, iron, calcium, and phosphorus; they are especially high in fiber.

beans, cannellini: These tan-colored kidney beans, used in Italian cooking, have a buttery texture and a delicate taste. Great Northern beans may be substituted.

beans, cranberry (borlotti): Usually eaten dried, cranberry beans are cream colored with many red speckles. High in fiber and protein, they also contain folic acid, iron, and potassium.

beans, fava: A type of shell bean also known as bread beans, fresh favas are only in season in spring. The beans contain folate, vitamin B_1, zinc, and protein. They are also a source of L-dopa, known to fight Parkinson's disease.

beans, fermented black: These beans, actually dried black soybeans fermented in salt and other spices, add a burst of salt and sourness to a dish. They can be found at Asian markets and specialty-food stores.

beans, lima: Also called butter beans, lima beans are high in fiber and a good source of protein. They contain beneficial minerals such as molybdenum, which helps your body detoxify sulfites; magnesium; and folic acid.

beets: Red beets get their color from the phytochemical betacyanin, which is believed to reduce tumor growth. They also contain betaine, which helps protect the heart, and salicylic acid, which has anti-inflammatory properties, and are especially high in folate. The phytochemicals in golden beets help promote eye health and boost immunity.

Belgian endive (chicory/witloof): A member of the chicory family, Belgian endive is blanched (grown in darkness) to prevent it from turning green. It does contain phytochemicals based on the color of the tips, purple or green.

bell peppers (capsicums): All bell peppers are high in cancer-fighting phytochemicals; the various compounds that give them their different colors also promote eye health (green, yellow, orange, and red); the anti-oxidants in purple bell peppers aid memory function and promote healthy aging. Red peppers are high in vitamin C.

blackberries: Their dark purple color, caused by anthocyanins, helps to lower the risk of some cancers and promote urinary tract health. Second only to blueberries in their antioxidant content, they are also high in vitamin C, potassium, folate, and fiber. Varieties include marionberries, loganberries, boysenberries, and olallieberries.

blood oranges: See Oranges.

blueberries: These native American berries are so high in antioxidant and anti-inflammatory compounds that they are considered "brain food". they contain a range of anthocyanins, which are thought to help fight cancer and have antiaging capabilities. Blueberries are available fresh, dried, and frozen.

bread crumbs: Whether ground from stale bread a few days past its peak (fresh) or bread that has dried completely (dried), bread crumbs add texture and body to many recipes. Seek out unseasoned crumbs, which don't contain added salt, dried cheese, or other flavorings.

broccoli: Extremely high in vitamin C and even higher in vitamin K, broccoli also contains vitamin A and cancer-fighting phytochemicals. Broccoli sprouts also contain high levels of these compounds.

Brussels sprouts: These miniature green cabbages contain the same cancer-fighting compounds as their larger cousins, and are even higher in vitamin C and K than broccoli; just 4 Brussels sprouts contain 243 percent of the Daily Value of vitamin K, which promotes proper blood clotting.

buckwheat flour: A gluten-free alternative to wheat flour, buckwheat flour is a rich source of magnesium, phosphorus, and B vitamins. It is also high in phytochemicals.

bulgur wheat: Like other whole grains, bulgur wheat is rich in selenium, an antioxidant that is believed to fight cancer. Bulgur wheat kernels have been steamed, dried, and crushed, and are available in various grinds.

cabbage: The patriarch of the cruciferous vegetable family, cabbage can be found in red and green and is high in vitamins C and K, but its real value is its concentration of isothio-

cyanates, powerful cancer-fighting compounds. Red cabbage, which is actually purple, contains more vitamin C than green cabbage, along with the antioxidant anthocyanin.

Cajun spice mix: This potent blend of spices includes ground red chile and may also contain garlic, paprika, sage, and mustard.

calabaza squash: See Squash, Winter.

caper berries: The fruit of the same shrub that produces capers. Olive-shaped with long stems, caper berries are pickled or salted, and like capers, they must be rinsed before use.

cashews: See Nuts.

cauliflower: Another member of the cruciferous family, cauliflower, traditionally was blanched, or covered during growing, to keep the head white; now it has been bred to be naturally white. Even so, it still contains the cancer-fighting compounds of its cousins, along with phytochemicals that promote hearth health. Purple cauliflower offers a colorful change of pace from the common white cauliflower.

celery: Like other green vegetables, celery helps to fight certain cancers, promotes eye health, strengthens the immune system, and helps build strong bones and teeth. It is also high in fiber.

celery root: Also called celeriac, this vegetable is the root of a celery plant grown specifically for its root. Once the knobby brown root is peeled, its tender ivory flesh is delicious. It is lower in carbohydrates than other root vegetables and contains phosphorus and potassium.

cheese, feta: Young cheese traditionally made from sheep's milk and used in Greek cuisine. It is known for its crumbly texture; some versions are also creamy. Feta's saltiness is heightened by the brine in which the cheese is pickled. Feta is also produced from cow's or goat's milk. Reduced-fat feta is also available.

cheese, ricotta: This mild, soft cheese, sold in tubs, is made by heating the whey left over from making sheep's, cow's, or goat's milk cheeses. Most Italian ricotta is made from sheep's milk. It can be served in sweet or savory preparations and is available in low-fat versions.

cherries: Tart red and sweet dark red cherries derive their color from anthocyanin pigments and other antioxidants, which help protect the heart and brain, lower the risk of some cancers, and are powerful anti-inflammatories. Both sweet and tart cherries also contain a terpenoid that appears to prevent the growth of tumors.

chicken broth: Most commercial brands are high in sodium and may contain MSG, sugar, and other ingredients. When shopping, look for varieties that are organic or free-range as well as natural, low-sodium, and fat free.

chickpeas (garbanzo beans): These crumpled-looking dried beans are meaty and hearty-flavored when cooked. They are popular in soups and purées and are the basis for hummus, the Middle Eastern dip.

chile sauce, Thai sweet: A purée of chiles with a sweet flavor in addition to heat, this sauce is often used to season shrimp and noodle dishes in Southeast Asia. It is commonly used as a condiment.

chiles: All chiles contain the phytochemical capsaicin, which gives them their hot taste and also acts as a cancer fighter. Although usually eaten only in small amounts, they are nutrient rich, containing vitamins A, C, and E, along with folic acid and potassium. Brick red–colored anchos are the dried form of fresh poblano chiles. They have a sweet, rich, and fruity flavor. Anaheims are fresh, mild green chiles that turn a deep burgundy color when dried.

Chinese broccoli: Called *gai lan* or Chinese kale, this cruciferous vegetable has slender, crisp stems and dark, blue-green leaves. Sometimes it has small white flowers. It is a good candidate for steaming, or blanching and then stir-frying. Look for it at Asian groceries and specialty-food stores.

Chinese five-spice powder: This distinctive spice blend varies in its makeup, but usually contains cloves, aniseed or fennel seeds, star anise, cinnamon, and Sichuan peppercorns.

chives: These slender, bright green stems are used to give an onionlike flavor without the bite. The grasslike leaves can be snipped with a pair of kitchen scissors and scattered over scrambled eggs, stews, salads, soups, tomatoes, or any dish that would benefit from a boost of mild oniony flavor. Chives do not take well to long cooking—they lose flavor and crispness and turn a dull grayish green.

chocolate: Because chocolate is a plant food, it also contains phytochemicals, in the form of a group of antioxidants called catechins, also found in red wine. Dark chocolate is higher in these flavonoids (and lower in fat and sugar) than milk chocolate.

cilantro: Also called fresh coriander and Chinese parsley, cilantro is a distinctively flavored herb with legions of loyal followers. Used extensively in the cuisines of Mexico, India, Egypt, Thailand, Vietnam, and China, cilantro asserts itself with a flavor that can't be missed. Cilantro Is thought to help rid the body of toxins such as lead and mercury as well as combat anxiety.

cinnamon: The dried bark of a tropical tree, the essential oils of this fragrant spice may serve as an anti-inflammatory, prevent the growth of bacteria, and help diabetics regulate their blood sugar by boosting their response to insulin.

coconut: The world's largest nut, coconuts contain a fleshy, white, edible interior and sweet, watery liquid that contains fiber, antioxidants, vitamins, and minerals. Coconut meat is sold flaked and shredded, but it is often sweetened. Look for unsweetened coconut in specialty-food or health-food stores.

coffee: Like all plant foods, coffee contains beneficial phytochemicals. It is also high in the stimulant caffeine, to which some people are sensitive to which is being studied for its effects in countering Parkinson's disease and diabetes.

corn: Corn is rich in vitamins, minerals, protein, and fiber. Yellow corn is given its color by carotenoids that not only fight heart disease and cancer, but also protect against macular degeneration.

couscous: A pasta made from high-protein durum wheat, couscous is also available in whole-wheat (wholemeal) form, which cooks just as quickly and is virtually indistinguishable from regular couscous.

cranberries: High in both fiber and vitamin C, these red berries are excellent for preventing urinary tract infections due to their polyphenols. The anthocyanins that make cranberries red have antioxidant properties that protect the heart and may guard against cancer. Fresh, frozen, and dried cranberries, even juice, are all equally beneficial to health.

cucumbers: A member of the gourd family, the most available cucumber is sold with a waxed coating, which must be peeled, thus removing the beneficial phytochemicals of its skin. The unwaxed, thinner skin of English (hothouse) cucumbers can be eaten, as can that of Armenian cucumbers, similar to English cucumbers but smaller.

currants, dried: Dried currants are actually dried Zante grapes. Although smaller than raisins, they have most of the same nutrients.

currants, fresh red: Ripe red currants have a slightly tart taste and are in season at the height of summer (July through early August). They are high in pectin, a natural gelling agent that helps lower cholesterol.

dandelion greens: The sharply saw-toothed leaves of the dandelion have a pleasantly bitter flavor. Like other leafy greens, they contain calcium and iron as well as potassium and vitamins A and C. Be wary of picking the wild greens, which may have been treated with lawn chemicals.

dill: The fine, feathery leaves of this herb have a distinct aromatic flavor. Dill is used in savory pastries, baked vegetables, and, of course, in the making and jarring of pickles (pickled cucumber).

eggplants (aubergines): The purple skin of the familiar globe eggplant is rich in heart- and brain-healthy anthocyanins, while its flesh contains saponins, antioxidants that help lower cholesterol levels. Other varieties may be slightly smaller and have lavender, white, rose, or variegated skin.

farro: This ancient, unhybridized wheat from Italy is ground and used to make dark, nutty-tasting pasta. The whole grain is also used in soups and salads. You can find it in specialty-food stores and Italian markets.

fennel: Mild and sweet with an aniselike flavor, this pale green bulb contains the phytonutrient anethole, found to reduce inflammation and prevent cancer. Fennel is also a good source of antioxidants, fiber, and vitamin C.

fennel seeds: The seed of the fennel has a licorice-like flavor and may be used ground or whole in savory dishes such as stews and roasts. It is also used in some breads and desserts and to flavor liqueurs.

figs: Whether fresh (available in summer and early fall) or dried, figs provide phosphorus, calcium, and iron.

fish sauce: Made from a mixture of salted and fermented fish, often anchovies, this salty-tart Southeast Asian sauce adds a depth of flavor to dishes that regular salt can't match.

garam masala: In India, each region or cook has a different recipe for this aromatic blend of roasted, ground spices. It commonly includes cumin, fennel, cardamom, cloves, cinnamon, nutmeg, ginger, coriander, and turmeric, the source of its warm yellow color.

garlic: Unusually rich in antioxidants and anti-inflammatories, garlic forms organosulfur compounds when chopped, crushed, or sliced. These substances lower blood pressure, slow clotting, and promote heart health.

ginger: Found most often in Chinese cuisine and prized for its culinary and medicinal uses, ginger helps the body with digestion and lowers cholesterol. It contains both antioxidant and antimicrobial compounds.

grapes: The dark purple Concord grape, which is usually made into grape juice, is extremely high in antioxidants, making grape juice an important heart-healthy food. Red table grapes also promote immunity and heart health, and green grapes can help lower cancer risk and promote eye health.

green beans: High in vitamins A and C, green beans also protect eye health because of their lutein content. Long beans or yard beans are commonly used In Chinese stir-fries. Their chewier texture and intense taste is a good match for spicy seasonings.

hazelnuts: Also known as filberts, hazelnuts have sweet, rich, cream-colored flesh. They are a good source of fiber, vitamin E, and many minerals including phosphorus, potassium and magnesium.

Jerusalem artichokes (sunchokes): These tubers, not true artichokes but a kind of sunflower, have a nutty taste slightly reminiscent of artichokes. They are particularly high in iron and may be eaten either raw or cooked.

jicama: Technically a legume, crisp jicama is eaten both raw and cooked. It provides vitamin C and potassium.

kasha: The tan colored, pyramid shaped roasted seeds of buckwheat, kasha has a pleasantly sour, nutlike taste and robust texture. It is high in protein.

kirsch: Named for the German word for "cherry," this dry, clear brandy is made from distilled fermented cherry juice and pits.

kohlrabi: A member of the turnip family and also known as a cabbage turnip, this crisp, mildly sweet vegetable looks like a regular turnip and tastes like a mildly sweet form of broccoli or cabbage. It is a good source of potassium and vitamin C.

lavender: You'd have to consume quite a bit of lavender to reap its phytochemical benefits, but it does contain perillyl alcohol, thought to have anti-cancer properties. Lavender's fragrance is also well known for its calming properties.

leeks: By virtue of their membership in the onion family, leeks contain organosulfur compounds, which are thought to fight cancer and heart disease. They also help improve the body's good–bad cholesterol ratio.

lemongrass: A tough, grayish green grass with a bulblike base and mild lemon flavor, lemongrass is an herb of Southeast Asia. It contains a phytochemical, limonene, which is being studied for its anti-tumor properties.

lemons: High in vitamin C, lemons are a flavor enhancer; add lemon juice to raw and cooked fruits and use it to replace salt at the table for vegetables and fish.

lentils: High in protein, like all beans, lentils come in a wide variety of colors. They also provide iron, phosphorus, calcium, and vitamins A and B-complex.

lettuces: Lettuce can be divided into four major groups: butterhead, crisphead, leaf, and romaine (cos). Most lettuces are high in vitamins A and C; they also provide calcium and iron. The darker the green, the higher the level of its beneficial phytochemicals.

limes: High in vitamin C, like all citrus, lime juice also contains lutein, which benefits eye health. The Persian lime is widely available, while the yellowish green Key lime is usually found fresh only in Florida and Latin markets. The juice is available in bottles.

long beans: See Green Beans.

mâche: Also called lamb's lettuce, since it appears in early spring, this delicate green is mild and grows in small, loose bunches. Like other dark greens, it contains vitamin C, beta-carotene, and folic acid, but also includes vitamin B_9, which combats stress and fatigue.

mango: Rich in beta-carotene, vitamin C, and many other protective phytochemicals, mangoes are also a low-fat source of vitamin E. Select ripe mangoes that are aromatic at their stem end and give slightly when gentle pressure is applied.

mint: A refreshing herb available in many varieties, with spearmint the most common. Used fresh to flavor a broad range of savory preparations, including spring lamb, poultry, and vegetables, or to garnish desserts.

mushrooms: Neither vegetables nor fruits but fungi, mushrooms come in a variety of forms and are available wild and cultivated. They are rich in riboflavin, niacin, and pantothenic acid, all B-complex vitamins, and also contain the valuable minerals copper and selenium.

nectarines: A close relative of the peach, the nectarine has an edible skin that contains many of its phytochemicals. Yellow nectarines contain beta-carotene, while the pink-skinned, white-fleshed variety has its own group of beneficial compounds.

nuts: High in fiber, most nuts also contain folate, riboflavin, and magnesium. They are high in beneficial omega-3 fatty acids and vitamin E, an antioxidant that protects brain cells, promotes heart health, and lowers LDL (bad) cholesterol.

oats: Oat groats are whole grains that may be cut into pieces to make Scottish, steel-cut, or Irish oats, or steamed and rolled into old-fashioned, or rolled, oats. When the groats are cut into pieces and rolled thinner, they become quick-cooking oats. All of these forms retain their selenium and cholesterol-fighting nutrients, unlike instant oats. They are also high in vitamins B_1, B_6, and E.

okra: A slender, grayish green, ridged pod that contains numerous small, edible seeds, okra has a mild flavor similar to green beans. When cooked, it has a viscous quality that helps thicken soups such as gumbo. It is high in fiber and a good source of vitamin C, folate, and magnesium.

olives: One of the world's most renowned crops, olives have helped sustain people in the Mediterranean for thousands of years. Too bitter to eat fresh, olives are either pressed to make oil, which is prized for its high levels of vitamin E and heart-healthy monounsaturated fat, or cured.

onions: All onions contain organosulfur compounds that are thought to fight cancer and to promote heart health. Yellow and red onions also contain quercetin, which boosts these actions, while red onions have the added benefit of the antioxidant anthocyanin.

oranges: Famed for their extremely high vitamin C content, oranges are also high in folate and potassium. Blood oranges have berry-flavored red flesh that is high in anthocyanin, an important antioxidant that gives them their dramatic color.

papayas: With flesh ranging from yellow to orange to red, depending on their type, papayas are high in antioxidant carotenoids, which guard against certain cancers.

paprika: Made from ground dried red pimento peppers, the best paprikas come from Hungary and Spain. Most paprikas are mild and sweet, although you can find hot paprika as well. Seek out smoked Spanish pimentòn for added depth of flavor.

parsley: With its refreshing, faintly peppery flavor, this vibrant herb is not only widely used, but is also very good for you. It contains cancer-fighting oils, including myristicin, as well as vitamin C, beta-carotene, and folic acid.

parsnips: Related to carrots, parsnips are ivory-colored with a sweet flavor that is enhanced when roasted. They contain vitamin C, folic acid, magnesium, and potassium.

passion fruit: Named by a missionary for the Passion of Christ rather than for any earthly romantic feelings, this aromatic fruit has a tart, tropical flavor. Passion fruits are ripe when their inedible skins are wrinkled. Choose one that feels heavy for its size. The pulp and seeds are the parts you eat.

pea shoots: Fresh pea shoots are the young greens and tendrils from the tips of edible pea plant branches. They may be found at farmers' markets in the spring and carry the same nutritional value as regular peas.

peaches: While its fuzzy skin is usually not eaten, the yellow or white flesh of the peach is high in vitamins A and C. Peaches are available either freestone or clingstone and can be found fresh, dried, frozen, and canned.

peanuts: Although they are not truly nuts, but legumes, peanuts are high in fat. They are a good source of protein, but they should be eaten in small amounts. Like most nuts, the fat they contain is largely monounsaturated.

pears: The beneficial pigments of pears are concentrated in their skin; as the skin is quite thin (except in the tan-skinned varieties), they can be eaten unpeeled, whether raw or cooked. The flesh contains vitamin A, as well as some phosphorus.

peas, English: Also called green or garden peas, they should be eaten soon after picking; they are also available frozen. They provide niacin and iron, along with vitamins A and C.

peas, split: When dried, the yellow or green field pea may be split at its natural seam for faster cooking in soups or purées. They are especially high in fiber and contain vitamin A.

peas, sugar snap: Sugar snaps are a cross between the English pea and the snow pea

(mangetout). They resemble the former but are entirely edible either cooked or raw. They provide vitamins A and C, along with folate, iron, phosphorus, and thiamin.

Pernod: This anise-flavored liqueur is popular in France. Mixed with water, it is served as an aperitif. It is also used in cooking as a flavoring.

pine nuts: Delicate, buttery pine nuts contain both iron and thiamin. They are a favorite garnish for salads and cooked foods.

pineapples: The pineapple's sweet, juicy flesh provides manganese, vitamins A and C, and bromelain, an anti-inflammatory enzyme that is also a digestive aid. The tough waxy rind may be dark green, orange-yellow, or reddish when the pineapple is ripe.

plantains: A plantain tastes like a less sweet, blander version of its close relative the banana. Its high starch content allows it to be cooked in many ways, and its often neutral flavor lets it pair well with a wide variety of ingredients.

plums: The edible skin of the plum, which comes in a variety of colors, contains most of its phyto-chemicals, although the yellow, purple, or red flesh also contains beneficial compounds. They are a good source of vitamin C. When they are not in season, enjoy them as prunes, their dried form.

polenta (corn): Although polenta may be made from other dried grains or white corn, usually it is coarsely or finely ground yellow cornmeal. Only stone-ground cornmeal is whole grain; store it in an airtight container in the refrigerator.

pomegranates: The fleshy seeds of this fruit are high in vitamin C, potassium, and heart-healthy anthocyanins. The fruit is in season during the autumn months, while pomegranate juice is available year-round in natural foods stores and some other markets.

potatoes: The deeper the color of its pigment, the more healthful phytochemicals a potato possesses, but all potatoes are extremely rich in vitamins and minerals if eaten with the skin; they are also high in fiber. Make sure to buy organic potatoes if you plan to eat the skins.

prunes: These dried prune plums, now also called dried plums, are rich in vitamin A, potassium, and

fiber. They are higher in antioxidants than any other fruit or vegetable, making them the top antiaging food.

pumpkin seeds: High in fiber, protein, and various minerals, pumpkin seeds also contain beta-sisterol, which lowers cholesterol and slows the growth of abnormal cells. Look for them in natural foods stores or Latin markets (they are also called pepitas).

pumpkins: The flesh of the pumpkin is nutrient rich with vitamin A and carotenoids, specifically the cancer-fighters alpha- and beta-carotene and lutein.

quinoa: An ancient Incan grain, quinoa is higher in protein than all other grains, and its protein is complete. It is also rich in nutrients and unsaturated fat.

radicchio: A red-leafed member of the chicory family, radicchio comes in the loose-headed Verona variety and the tighter, more oblong Treviso variety. Both kinds have an assertive bitter flavor, and both provide beneficial antioxidants such as anthocyanins and lycopene. Radicchio may be eaten raw, grilled, baked, or sautéed.

raisins: Antioxidant rich, raisins are also high in vitamins, minerals, and fiber. Both dark raisins and golden raisins (sultanas) start as green grapes, but golden raisins are treated with sulfur dioxide to prevent oxidation.

raspberries: Red raspberries have more fiber than most other fruits; they are also high in vitamin C and folate and extremely high in cancer-fighting antioxidants. Golden raspberries are rarer, but they contain heart- and eye-healthy bioflavonoids. Although fresh raspberries are often fragile, frozen unsweetened raspberries retain their flavor and are available year-round.

rhubarb: These tart red stalks are one of the first signs of spring in the market. High in vitamin A and beneficial phytochemicals, rhubarb helps protect the heart, boost the immunity, and lower the risk of some cancers.

rice, brown: This whole grain retains its bran covering, making it high in fiber. Brown rice is available in long-, medium-, and short-grain varieties. Like other whole grains, it is high in fiber and selenium; because the bran can become rancid at room temperature, brown rice should be kept refrigerated.

rutabagas: Another member of the cabbage family, this yellow-skinned root vegetable has a mild-tasting yellow flesh. It contains vitamins A and C, as well as fiber and potassium.

shallots: A member of the onion family, the shallot contains the same heart-healthy organosulfides as its relatives. It is milder in taste in small amounts than the onion.

spaghetti squash: See Squash, Winter.

spinach: High in a multitude of nutrients, from vitamins A, C, and K to folate and potassium, spinach is also one of the best sources of lutein, the carotenoid that prevents macular degeneration.

squash, winter: The flesh of winter squash is rich with vitamins and cancer-fighting carotenoids. Bright yellow, oval-shaped spaghetti squash has flesh that forms long, thin strands when cooked. Turban squash has an exotic appearance, and a multihued skin in oranges, yellows, and greens.

star anise: Unrelated to and slightly more bitter in flavor than aniseed, this seed-bearing pod is from a Chinese evergreen tree. This uniquely shaped spice flavors teas and savory dishes throughout Asia.

strawberries: Rich in antioxidant content, partly due to their anthocyanin pigments, strawberries are also extremely high in vitamin C. Because of these compounds, as well as their phenolic acids, these berries are thought to be important cancer-fighters.

sugar, raw: Similar in color and flavor to brown sugar, "raw" sugar in the United States is actually partially refined; however, it may still retain some of the nutrients from the sugarcane plant, which are lost in more refined sugars. Jaggery sugar, also called palm sugar, is an unrefined, dark, coarse-grained sugar used in Southeast Asia and India.

sunflower seeds: These mild, nutty-tasting seeds are high in polyunsaturated fats and vitamin E. They also contain magnesium, which is essential for healthy bones and providing energy, and selenium, an important cancer-fighting mineral.

sweet potatoes: This common root vegetable, often erroneously referred to as a yam, is available in pale yellow and dark orange. Both are high in fiber, vitamins A and C, and a host of other vitamins and minerals, as well as more beta-carotene than any other vegetable.

Swiss chard: Another important member of the cruciferous vegetable family, chard has dark green leaves and either white, yellow, or red stalks and ribs. Along with cancer-fighting phytochemicals, it contains iron and vitamins A and C.

tahini: A paste made from ground sesame seeds, tahini has a rich, creamy, concentrated flavor. It is most popular as an essential ingredient in such Mediterranean spreads as hummus and baba ghanoush and provides many of the same benefits as sesame oil.

tapioca: A starchy substance derived from the root of the cassava plant, tapioca comes in three basic forms: pearl (small dried balls of tapioca starch), granulated (coarsely broken-up pearl tapioca), and quick cooking, also called instant (very finely granulated pearl tapioca).

tomatillos: Sometimes called Mexican green tomatoes, tomatillos are firmer and less juicy than tomatoes and grow to ripeness inside a pale-green papery sheath. Used both raw and cooked, they are an essential sweet-sour ingredient in many Mexican green sauces. Look for fresh or canned tomatillos in well-stocked supermarkets or Latin markets.

tomatoes: Not only are tomatoes high in vitamin C, they are also high in fiber and many other vitamins and minerals. They are also high in lycopene, which lowers cancer risk. The body absorbs this antioxidant better when tomatoes are cooked, making tomato sauce and tomato paste especially healthful.

turban squash: See Squash, Winter.

turnips: With crisp white flesh and a purple cap, this root vegetable has a mild, sweet flavor when young and is woodier with age.

vinegar: Made from a variety of red or white wines or, like cider vinegar and rice vinegar, from fruits and grains. All are a healthy, low-fat way to season a range of foods.

walnuts: Rich, assertive walnuts contain ellagic acid, an important disease and cancer fighter. They are also high in heart-healthy, cholesterol-lowering omega-3 fatty acids and vitamin E. In addition, walnuts protect brain function and contain melatonin, a hormone that aids sleep.

water chestnuts: Water chestnuts are walnut-sized, dark brown tubers grown in ponds, streams, and rivers. The white flesh inside this vegetable is sweet and slightly starchy with a crunchy texture. Canned water chestnuts should be rinsed before using.

watercress: This spicy green is, surprisingly, a cruciferous vegetable. It contains good amounts of vitamins A and C. The peppery taste of watercress is due to a certain isothiocyanate that has shown the potential to help combat lung cancer.

watermelon: Despite its high water content, this melon provides vitamins A and C, along with the anthocyanins that give it its color.

wine: The colors of red and rosé wines are due to the skins of the purple grapes used to make them; red wine has more beneficial flavonoids than grape juice. These phytochemicals have been shown to help increase HDL (good) cholesterol.

winter savory: This shrublike Mediterranean evergreen herb has a strong, spicy flavor that some cooks liken to thyme. It complements dried beans and lentils, meats, poultry, and tomatoes.

yogurt: The bacterial cultures in yogurt are prized as a digestive aid. Like the milk it is made from, yogurt can be full fat, low fat, or nonfat.

zucchini (courgettes): Most of the zucchini's nutrients are found in its skin, which contains phytochemicals that strengthen the eyes, bones, and teeth; help to boost immunity; and lower the risk of some cancers.

Index

A

Almonds
  Baked Pilaf with Currants, Lavender, and
    Almonds, 47
  Romesco Sauce, 198
  Sicilian Shrimp with Cauliflower and
    Almonds, 124
  toasting, 84
  Amaranth, Popped, 266
Anchovies, 290
  Green Onions with Anchovy Sauce, 69
  Red Bell Peppers Baked with Anchovies, 217
  Roasted Zucchini with Anchoïade, 73
  Swiss Chard with Lemon and Anchovy, 102
Antioxidants, 12
Apples, 290
  Crisp Green Apple and Celery Salad, 76
  Green Apples Baked with Dried Cranberries, 106
  Pork Chops Smothered in Onions and
    Apples, 127
  Pork Pot Roast with Parsnips, Carrots, and
    Apples, 123
Apricots, 290
  Apricot-Stuffed Chicken Breasts, 178
  Grilled Apricots with Sabayon, 187
  Wild Rice with Apricots, 170
Artichokes, 290
  Fettuccine with Fava Beans, Artichokes,
    and Asparagus, 94
  Grilled Artichoke Salad, 76
Arugula, 290
  Chicken Breasts Stuffed with Goat Cheese
    and Arugula, 80
  Lamb Chops with Arugula Pesto, 93
Asparagus, 290
  Bulgur Salad with Zucchini, Asparagus,
    and Green Onions, 259
  Fettuccine with Fava Beans, Artichokes,
    and Asparagus, 94
  Purple Asparagus with Orange Vinaigrette, 31
  Roasted Asparagus with Eggs and
    Parmesan, 89
  White Asparagus Mimosa with Browned
    Butter, 117
Avocados, 290

B

Bananas, 290
  Baked Bananas and Tapioca Pudding, 147
Barley, 290
  Chicken, Mushroom, and Barley
    Casserole, 246
Basil, 290
Beans, 290, 292–93. See also Chickpeas
  Black Bean and White Corn Salad, 269
  Broiled Tuna with Cannellini Bean Salad, 245
  Chicken Thighs with Lima Bean Purée, 242
  Dry-Fried Long Beans, 79
  Duck Sausage, Tomato, and Cranberry Bean
    Casserole, 251
  Fettuccine with Fava Beans, Artichokes,
    and Asparagus, 94
  Grilled Favas, 77
  Lima Beans Baked with Ham, 263
  Red Kidney Bean Quesadillas, 249
  Shrimp, Beans, and Tomatoes, 248
  White Beans with Tomato and Bacon, 266
Beef
  Rib-Eye Steaks with Baked Plums, 229
  Sichuan Beef with Eggplant, 52
Beets, 290
  Roasted Beet Salad with Eggs, 217
  Roasted Beets with Indian Spices, 229
  Rutabaga and Golden Beets with
    Pomegranate Seeds, 183
  Scallops with Golden Beets, 154
  Sweet and Sour Beets, 204
Belgian endive, 290
  Belgian Endive with Blue Cheese and
    Walnuts, 69
  Fig and Purple Endive Salad, 37
Bell peppers, 290
  Chicken with Yellow Peppers and Passion
    Fruit, 177
  Grilled Red Bell Peppers, 205
  Hungarian Red Peppers, 227
  Mahimahi with Red Potato, Red Bell Pepper,
    and Rosemary, 211
  Orange Gazpacho, 160
  Rack of Lamb with Orange Bell Pepper
    Relish, 168
  Red Bell Peppers Baked with Anchovies, 217
  Red Wine Spaghetti with Red Bell Pepper
    and Onion, 202
  Romesco Sauce, 198
  Scallops with Bell Pepper Dressing, 31
  Wild Rice with Purple Bell Pepper and
    Pecans, 57
Blackberries, 291
  Blackberry Crêpes, 62
  Duck with Purple Cabbage, Blackberries,
    and Port, 51
  Grilled Berry Parcels, 58
  Savory and Spicy Blackberry Sauce, 54
Blueberries, 291
  Blueberries with Lemon, 55
  Grilled Berry Parcels, 58
  Salmon with Wild Blueberry and Rhubarb
    Sauce, 48
  Sweet Blueberry Flat Bread, 45
Blue recipes. See Purple and blue recipes
Bok Choy, Hot and Sour, 141
Bread. See also Bruschetta
  crumbs, 251, 291
  Sweet Blueberry Flat Bread, 45
  Turkey Sandwiches with Sweet Onions, 118
Broccoli, 291
  Broccoli Braised with Garlic and Chile, 87
  Broccoli Gratin, 93
  Stir-Fried Chicken with Broccoli and
    Mushrooms, 79
  Broccolini, Roasted, with Lemon, 73
Brown recipes, 13, 238, 288–89
  Baked Potatoes with Flaxseed and
    Cheddar, 256
  Black Bean and White Corn Salad, 269
  Broiled Polenta with Mushroom Ragout, 241
  Broiled Tuna with Cannellini Bean Salad, 245
  Bulgur Salad with Zucchini, Asparagus,
    and Green Onions, 259
  Cashew Chicken Stir-Fry, 255
  Chicken, Mushroom, and Barley Casserole, 246
  Chicken Thighs with Lima Bean Purée, 242
  Chickpeas with Baby Spinach, 249
  Crunchy Breakfast Topping, 267
  Duck Sausage, Tomato, and Cranberry
    Bean Casserole, 251
  Ginger Couscous with Dried Fruit, 264
  Grilled Rice Patties with Asian Flavors, 248
  Kasha with Walnuts and Pasta, 270
  Lentils with Shallots and Serrano Ham, 269
  Lima Beans Baked with Ham, 263

Mango Chicken with Toasted Quinoa, 270
Maple Panna Cotta with Candied Walnuts, 273
Oatmeal and Dried Peach Muffins, 274
Peanut Sambal, 267
Pear, Cranberry, and Walnut Crisp, 274
Popped Amaranth, 266
Pork, Quinoa, and Chile Casserole, 260
Pumpkin Seed Crust for Fish, 257
Red Kidney Bean Quesadillas, 249
Roasted Chestnuts with Savoy Cabbage, 257
Roasted Pine Nuts and Raisin Sauce, 256
Shrimp, Beans, and Tomatoes, 248
Split Peas with Yogurt and Mint, 264
Tamarind Shrimp with Peanuts, 263
Turkey with Red Mole, 252
White Beans with Tomato and Bacon, 266

Bruschetta
Liver and Onion Bruschetta, 197
Mushroom Bruschetta, 113
Warm Tomato and Olive Bruschetta, 202

Brussels sprouts, 291
Brussels Sprouts with Capers and Lemon, 99
Duck and Brussels Sprouts, 97

Buckwheat flour, 291

Bulgur wheat, 291
Bulgur Salad with Zucchini, Asparagus, and
Green Onions, 259

C

Cabbage, 291
Duck with Purple Cabbage, Blackberries,
and Port, 51
Grilled Fish Tacos with Green Cabbage
Salad, 70
Grilled Purple Cabbage, 35
Purple Cabbage with Raisins, 55
Roasted Chestnuts with Savoy Cabbage, 257

Cajun spice mix, 291
Cake, Pound, and Cherries, 234
Calamari. See Squid
Caper berries, 291
Caponata, Eggplant, 52
Carbohydrates, 10, 13, 276

Carrots
Baked Stew of Curried Root Vegetables, 174
Moroccan Carrot Salad, 160
Pork Pot Roast with Parsnips, Carrots,
and Apples, 123

Purple Carrots Glazed with Red Wine, 32
Roasted Purple Carrots and Fennel, 27
Roasted Sea Bass with Carrot Purée, 167

Cashews
Cashew Chicken Stir-Fry, 255
Indian-Spiced Squash with Cashews, 183

Cauliflower, 291
Baked Stew of Curried Root Vegetables, 174
Sicilian Shrimp with Cauliflower and
Almonds, 124
Spicy Cauliflower Gratin, 138

Celery, 291
Crisp Green Apple and Celery Salad, 76

Celery root, 291
Celery Root and Potato Gratin, 143

Cheese, 291
Baked Pasta with Radicchio and Blue
Cheese, 224
Baked Potatoes with Flaxseed and
Cheddar, 256
Belgian Endive with Blue Cheese and
Walnuts, 69
Chicken Breasts Stuffed with Goat Cheese
and Arugula, 80
Corn and Crab Quesadillas, 154
Figs with Ricotta, 35
Grilled Eggplant and Feta Cheese Rolls, 32
Poblano Chiles Stuffed with Goat Cheese, 86
Red Kidney Bean Quesadillas, 249
Shrimp with Watermelon, Feta, and Mint, 207
Yellow Tomatoes with Mint and Pecorino, 153

Cherries, 291
Cherries and Pound Cake, 234
Chicken with Cherry Salsa, 223
Deep-Dish Cherry Pie, 230
Pork Tenderloin with Sour Cherry Sauce, 219

Chestnuts, Roasted, with Savoy Cabbage, 257

Chicken
Apricot-Stuffed Chicken Breasts, 178
broth, 291
Cashew Chicken Stir-Fry, 255
Chicken and Eggplant Salad, 41
Chicken and Fig Skewers, 41
Chicken, Avocado, and Spinach Salad, 84
Chicken Breasts Stuffed with Goat Cheese
and Arugula, 80
Chicken, Mushroom, and Barley Casserole, 246
Chicken Thighs with Lima Bean Purée, 242

Chicken with Caramelized Shallots and
Wine, 144
Chicken with Cherry Salsa, 223
Chicken with Tomatillo Sauce, 101
Chicken with Yellow Peppers and Passion
Fruit, 177
Mango Chicken with Toasted Quinoa, 270
Roasted Chicken and Red Onion, 212
Stir-Fried Chicken with Broccoli and
Mushrooms, 79

Chickpeas, 291
Bulgur Salad with Zucchini, Asparagus, and
Green Onions, 259
Chickpeas with Baby Spinach, 249

Chiles, 291
Grilled Chile Sauce, 204
Poblano Chiles Stuffed with Goat Cheese, 86
Pork, Quinoa, and Chile Casserole, 260
sauces, 290, 291

Chinese broccoli, 291
Chinese Broccoli with Oyster Sauce, 98

Chives, 291–92
Chocolate, 292
Chutney, Raisin and Prune, with Lemon, 45
Cilantro, 292
Cinnamon, 292
Clafoutis, Green Pear and Grape, 106
Coconut, 292
Coffee, 292

Corn, 292
Black Bean and White Corn Salad, 269
Corn and Crab Quesadillas, 154
Grilled Salmon, Yellow Potato, and Corn
Salad, 158
Grilled White Corn Salad, 118
Grilled White Corn with Herb Butter, 120
Monkfish with Roasted White Corn Salsa, 128
Sautéed Summer Squash with Corn, 181

Couscous, 292
Ginger Couscous with Dried Fruit, 264

Crab and Corn Quesadillas, 154

Cranberries, 292
Cranberry and Blood Orange Sauce, 216
Green Apples Baked with Dried Cranberries, 106
Pear, Cranberry, and Walnut Crisp, 274
Turkey Tenderloin with Cranberry Compote, 215

Crêpes, Blackberry, 62
Crisp, Pear, Cranberry, and Walnut, 274

Crumble, Tan Pear, with Lavender, 131
Cucumbers, 292
    Cod on a Bed of Cucumbers, 89
Currants, 292

D

Dandelion greens, 292
    Baked Pasta with Dandelion Greens and
        Sausage, 90
Dill, 292
Duck
    Duck and Brussels Sprouts, 97
    Duck Sausage, Tomato, and Cranberry Bean
        Casserole, 251
    Duck with Blood Orange Sauce, 215
    Duck with Purple Cabbage, Blackberries,
        and Port, 51
    Grilled Duck Breast with Papaya, 163

E

Eggplants, 292
    Baked Onion and White Eggplant Purée, 114
    Chicken and Eggplant Salad, 41
    Eggplant Caponata, 52
    Eggplant Crisps with Yogurt Dipping Sauce, 27
    Grilled Eggplant and Feta Cheese Rolls, 32
    Roasted Eggplant, Asian Style, 44
    Sichuan Beef with Eggplant, 52
    White Eggplant and Green Onion Salad, 133
Eggs
    Roasted Asparagus with Eggs and Parmesan, 89
    Roasted Beet Salad with Eggs, 217
    Spanish Tortilla with Golden Potatoes, 157
    Spinach Soufflé, 74

F

Farro, 292
Fats, 10, 21, 277
Fennel, 292
    Grilled Fennel with Indian Spices, 133
    Roasted Fennel with Fennel Seed, 143
    Roasted Purple Carrots and Fennel, 27
    seeds, 292
    trimming, 27
Fiber, 13
Figs, 292
    Chicken and Fig Skewers, 41
    Fig and Purple Endive Salad, 37

Figs with Ricotta, 35
    Green Figs with Almond Custard, 105
    Pomegranate-Glazed Figs, 62
    Roasted Turkey Breast with Figs and
        Lavender, 38
Fish. *See also* Anchovies; Halibut; Mahimahi;
    Salmon; Trout; Tuna
    Baked Mackerel with Red Currants, 211
    Cod on a Bed of Cucumbers, 89
    Grilled Fish Tacos with Green Cabbage
        Salad, 70
    Grilled Snapper and Mandarin Salad, 164
    Lemon Sole with Peas, 94
    Monkfish with Roasted White Corn Salsa, 128
    Pumpkin Seed Crust for Fish, 257
    Roasted Sea Bass with Carrot Purée, 167
Fish sauce, 292
Five-spice powder, 291
Flan, Pumpkin, 188
Fruits, 8–9, 11, 12, 20. *See also individual fruits*

G

Galettes, Potato, with Smoked Salmon, 117
Game Hens with Pears, 212
Garam masala, 292
Garlic, 292
    Garlic Chips, 140
    Roasted Garlic Spread with Thyme, 131
Gazpacho, Orange, 160
Ghee, 183
Ginger, 292
Grains, 9, 11, 13. *See also individual grains*
Grapefruit
    Grapefruit Baked with Brown Sugar, 170
    Warm Ruby Grapefruit Salad, 226
Grapes, 292
    Broiled Grapes in Yogurt and Sour
        Cream, 233
    Green Pear and Grape Clafoutis, 106
    Halibut and Purple Grapes, 37
    Prosciutto Grapes, 226
    Purple Fruits with Lavender Syrup, 61
    Roasted Tuna with Olives, Grapes, and
        Pine Nuts, 38
    Sautéed Trout with Red Grape Sauce, 208
Green onions
    Green Onions with Anchovy Sauce, 69
    White Eggplant and Green Onion Salad, 133

Green recipes, 66, 282–83
    Baked Pasta with Dandelion Greens and
        Sausage, 90
    Belgian Endive with Blue Cheese and
        Walnuts, 69
    Broccoli Braised with Garlic and Chile, 87
    Broccoli Gratin, 93
    Brussels Sprouts with Capers and Lemon, 99
    Chicken, Avocado, and Spinach Salad, 84
    Chicken Breasts Stuffed with Goat Cheese
        and Arugula, 80
    Chicken with Tomatillo Sauce, 101
    Chinese Broccoli with Oyster Sauce, 98
    Cod on a Bed of Cucumbers, 89
    Crisp Green Apple and Celery Salad, 76
    Dry-Fried Long Beans, 79
    Duck and Brussels Sprouts, 97
    Fettuccine with Fava Beans, Artichokes, and
        Asparagus, 94
    French Peas and Lettuce, 98
    Garlic Spinach, 99
    Gratinéed Swiss Chard, 87
    Green Apples Baked with Dried Cranberries, 106
    Green Figs with Almond Custard, 105
    Green Onions with Anchovy Sauce, 69
    Green Pear and Grape Clafoutis, 106
    Grilled Artichoke Salad, 76
    Grilled Favas, 77
    Grilled Fish Tacos with Green
        Cabbage Salad, 70
    Grilled Halibut with Limes, 83
    Honeydew Prosciutto Wraps, 77
    Lamb Chops with Arugula Pesto, 93
    Lemon Sole with Peas, 94
    Okra with Yellow Plum Tomatoes, 102
    Poblano Chiles Stuffed with Goat Cheese, 86
    Roasted Asparagus with Eggs and Parmesan, 89
    Roasted Broccolini with Lemon, 73
    Roasted Zucchini with Anchoïade, 73
    Sautéed Spinach with Peanuts and Soy
        Sauce, 86
    Spinach Soufflé, 74
    Stir-Fried Calamari and Pea Shoots, 101
    Stir-Fried Chicken with Broccoli and
        Mushrooms, 79
    Swiss Chard with Lemon and Anchovy, 102
    Trout and Green Pear Salad, 83
Grilling tips, 14–15

H

Halibut
  Grilled Fish Tacos with Green Cabbage
    Salad, 70
  Grilled Halibut with Limes, 83
  Halibut and Purple Grapes, 37
  Halibut with Roasted Nectarine
    Chutney, 167
Ham. *See also* Prosciutto
  Ham and Sweet Potato Hash, 184
  Lentils with Shallots and Serrano Ham, 269
  Lima Beans Baked with Ham, 263
Hash, Ham and Sweet Potato, 184
Hash Browns, Red-Hot, 219
Hazelnuts, 293
Herbs, 21. *See also individual herbs*
Hominy, 293
Honeydew Prosciutto Wraps, 77

J

Jerusalem artichokes, 293
  Mashed Jerusalem Artichokes with Truffle
    Oil, 114
Jicama, 293

K

Kasha, 293
  Kasha with Walnuts and Pasta, 270
Kirsch, 293
Kohlrabi, 293
  Turkey Fricassee with Kohlrabi, Pears, and
    Mushrooms, 127

L

Lamb
  Lamb Chops with Arugula Pesto, 93
  Lamb Kebabs with Blood Orange Salad, 220
  Rack of Lamb with Orange Bell Pepper
    Relish, 168
Lavender, 293
Leeks, 293
  Mustard-Honey Leeks, 113
Legumes, 9, 11, 13. *See also individual legumes*
Lemongrass, 293
Lemons, 293
Lentils, 293
  Lentils with Shallots and Serrano Ham, 269

Lettuce, 293
Limes, 293
Liver and Onion Bruschetta, 197

M

Mâche, 293
Mahimahi
  Mahimahi and Mango Salsa, 164
  Mahimahi with Red Potato, Red Bell Pepper,
    and Rosemary, 211
Mangoes, 293
  Mahimahi and Mango Salsa, 164
  Mango Chicken with Toasted Quinoa, 270
Meal planning, 20–21
Meat, 20–21. *See also individual meats*
Minerals, 10–11, 279
Mint, 293
Muffins, Oatmeal and Dried Peach, 274
Mushrooms, 293
  Broiled Polenta with Mushroom Ragout, 241
  Chicken, Mushroom, and Barley Casserole, 246
  Mushroom Bruschetta, 113
  Pan-Seared Mushrooms, 140
  Parsley Portobellos, 138
  Pesto Portobellos, 121
  Roasted Mushrooms with Sage Butter, 130
  Stir-Fried Chicken with Broccoli and
    Mushrooms, 79
  Turkey Fricassee with Kohlrabi, Pears, and
    Mushrooms, 127
  Turnips with Peas and Mushrooms, 144

N

Nectarines, 293
  Halibut with Roasted Nectarine Chutney, 167
  White Nectarines with Raw Sugar and Rum, 147
Nutrition, 8–13, 276–89
Nuts, 9, 13, 293. *See also individual nuts*

O

Oats, 293
  Oatmeal and Dried Peach Muffins, 274
Oils, 21
Okra, 293
  Okra with Yellow Plum Tomatoes, 102
Olives, 293
Onions, 293. *See also* Green onions
  Baked Onion and White Eggplant Purée, 114

Liver and Onion Bruschetta, 197
  Red Onions with Fennel, 205
  Roasted Onions with Balsamic and Pepper, 130
Orange recipes. *See* Yellow and orange recipes
Oranges, 293
  Cranberry and Blood Orange Sauce, 216
  Duck with Blood Orange Sauce, 215
  Lamb Kebabs with Blood Orange Salad, 220
  Purple Asparagus with Orange Vinaigrette, 31

P

Panna Cotta, Maple, with Candied Walnuts, 273
Papayas, 293 94
  Grilled Duck Breast with Papaya, 163
  Shrimp with Papaya and Coconut, 178
Paprika, 293
Parsley, 294
Parsnips, 294
  Baked Stew of Curried Root Vegetables, 174
  Grilled Parsnip Chips with Lemon and
    Honey, 121
  Pork Pot Roast with Parsnips, Carrots, and
    Apples, 123
Passion fruit, 294
  Chicken with Yellow Peppers and Passion
    Fruit, 177
Pasta. *See also* Couscous
  Baked Pasta with Dandelion Greens and
    Sausage, 90
  Baked Pasta with Radicchio and Blue
    Cheese, 224
  Fettuccine with Fava Beans, Artichokes,
    and Asparagus, 94
  Kasha with Walnuts and Pasta, 270
  Red Wine Spaghetti with Red Bell Pepper
    and Onion, 202
Peaches, 294
  Ginger Couscous with Dried Fruit, 264
  Oatmeal and Dried Peach Muffins, 274
  Winter Peach Shortcake, 191
Peanuts, 294
  Peanut Sambal, 267
  Sautéed Spinach with Peanuts and Soy
    Sauce, 86
  Tamarind Shrimp with Peanuts, 263
Pears, 294
  Butternut Squash and Pears with Rosemary, 184
  Caramelized Red Pears with Cinnamon, 233

Game Hens with Pears, 212
Ginger Couscous with Dried Fruit, 264
Green Pear and Grape Clafoutis, 106
Pear, Cranberry, and Walnut Crisp, 274
Peppered Yellow Pears with Honey, 180
Tan Pear Crumble with Lavender, 131
Trout and Green Pear Salad, 83
Turkey Fricassee with Kohlrabi, Pears, and
    Mushrooms, 127
Peas, 294
    French Peas and Lettuce, 98
    Lemon Sole with Peas, 94
    Split Peas with Yogurt and Mint, 264
    Turnips with Peas and Mushrooms, 144
Pea shoots, 294
    Stir-Fried Calamari and Pea Shoots, 101
Pecans, Wild Rice with Purple Bell Pepper and, 57
Pernod, 294
Persimmons, Savory Sautéed, 181
Pesto
    Arugula Pesto, 93
    Pesto Portobellos, 121
Phytochemicals, 11, 12, 13
Pie, Deep-Dish Cherry, 230
Pilaf, Baked, with Currants, Lavender, and
    Almonds, 47
Pineapple, 294
    Grilled Pineapple, 161
    Pineapple with Preserved Ginger, 180
Pine nuts, 294
    Roasted Pine Nuts and Raisin Sauce, 256
    toasting, 37
Pizzas, Grilled, with Blue Potatoes
    and Onions, 28
Plantains, 294
    Cuban-Style Pork and Plantains, 134
    Plantain with Jalapeño, 141
Plums, 294
    Grilled Plums with Kirsch Cream, 58
    Purple Fruits with Lavender Syrup, 61
    Rib-Eye Steaks with Baked Plums, 229
    Roasted Black Plums with Star Anise, 61
    Stir-Fried Pork with Black Plums, 51
    Veal Chops with Red Plum Sauce, 223
Polenta, 294
    Broiled Polenta with Mushroom Ragout, 241
Pomegranates, 294
    Pomegranate-Glazed Figs, 62

Rutabaga and Golden Beets with
    Pomegranate Seeds, 183
Pomelo, Broiled, 161
Pork
    Cuban-Style Pork and Plantains, 134
    Mu Shu Pork, 137
    Pork Chops Smothered in Onions and
        Apples, 127
    Pork Pot Roast with Parsnips, Carrots, and
        Apples, 123
    Pork, Quinoa, and Chile Casserole, 260
    Pork Tenderloin with Sour Cherry Sauce, 219
    Roasted Pork and Prunes, 42
    Stir-Fried Pork with Black Plums, 51
Potatoes, 294
    Baked Potatoes with Flaxseed and Cheddar, 256
    Baked Stuffed Blue Potatoes, 44
    Celery Root and Potato Gratin, 143
    Grilled Blue Potatoes, 34
    Grilled Pizzas with Blue Potatoes and Onions, 28
    Grilled Salmon, Yellow Potato, and Corn
        Salad, 158
    Herbed Blue Potatoes, 47
    Mahimahi with Red Potato, Red Bell Pepper,
        and Rosemary, 211
    Pan-Fried Blue Potatoes with Sage, 57
    Potatoes with Chorizo and Parsley, 124
    Potato Galettes with Smoked Salmon, 117
    Red-Hot Hash Browns, 219
    Spanish Tortilla with Golden Potatoes, 157
Prosciutto
    Honeydew Prosciutto Wraps, 77
    Prosciutto Grapes, 226
Protein, 277
Prunes, 294
    Bacon-Wrapped Prunes, 34
    Raisin and Prune Chutney with Lemon, 45
    Roasted Pork and Prunes, 42
Pudding, Baked Bananas and Tapioca, 147
Pumpkins, 294
    Grilled Pumpkin with Pumpkin Seed
        Dressing, 153
    Pumpkin Flan, 188
    Roasted Pumpkin Purée, 171
Pumpkin seeds, 294
    Grilled Pumpkin with Pumpkin Seed
        Dressing, 153
    Pumpkin Seed Crust for Fish, 257

Purple and blue recipes, 24, 281–82
    Bacon-Wrapped Prunes, 34
    Baked Pilaf with Currants, Lavender, and
        Almonds, 47
    Baked Stuffed Blue Potatoes, 44
    Blackberry Crêpes, 62
    Blueberries with Lemon, 55
    Chicken and Eggplant Salad, 41
    Chicken and Fig Skewers, 41
    Duck with Purple Cabbage, Blackberries,
        and Port, 51
    Eggplant Caponata, 52
    Eggplant Crisps with Yogurt Dipping Sauce, 27
    Fig and Purple Endive Salad, 37
    Figs with Ricotta, 35
    Grilled Berry Parcels, 58
    Grilled Blue Potatoes, 34
    Grilled Eggplant and Feta Cheese Rolls, 32
    Grilled Pizzas with Blue Potatoes
        and Onions, 28
    Grilled Plums with Kirsch Cream, 58
    Grilled Purple Cabbage, 35
    Halibut and Purple Grapes, 37
    Herbed Blue Potatoes, 47
    Pan-Fried Blue Potatoes with Sage, 57
    Pomegranate-Glazed Figs, 62
    Purple Asparagus with Orange Vinaigrette, 31
    Purple Cabbage with Raisins, 55
    Purple Carrots Glazed with Red Wine, 32
    Purple Fruits with Lavender Syrup, 61
    Raisin and Prune Chutney with Lemon, 45
    Roasted Black Plums with Star Anise, 61
    Roasted Eggplant, Asian Style, 44
    Roasted Pork and Prunes, 42
    Roasted Purple Carrots and Fennel, 27
    Roasted Tuna with Olives, Grapes, and
        Pine Nuts, 38
    Roasted Turkey Breast with Figs and
        Lavender, 38
    Salmon with Wild Blueberry and Rhubarb
        Sauce, 48
    Savory and Spicy Blackberry Sauce, 54
    Scallops with Bell Pepper Dressing, 31
    Sichuan Beef with Eggplant, 52
    Stir-Fried Pork with Black Plums, 51
    Sweet Blueberry Flat Bread, 45
    Wild Rice with Purple Bell Pepper and
        Pecans, 57

Q

Quesadillas
    Corn and Crab Quesadillas, 154
    Red Kidney Bean Quesadillas, 249
Quinoa, 294
    Mango Chicken with Toasted Quinoa, 270
    Pork, Quinoa, and Chile Casserole, 260
    rinsing, 260

R

Radicchio, 294
    Baked Pasta with Radicchio and Blue
       Cheese, 224
    Grilled Radicchio, 197
Raisins, 294
    Purple Cabbage with Raisins, 55
    Raisin and Prune Chutney with Lemon, 45
    Roasted Pine Nuts and Raisin Sauce, 256
Raspberries, 294
    Baked Golden Raspberries, 171
    Berry Gratin, 230
Red recipes, 194, 287–88
    Baked Mackerel with Red Currants, 211
    Baked Pasta with Radicchio and Blue
       Cheese, 224
    Berry Gratin, 230
    Broiled Grapes in Yogurt and Sour Cream, 233
    Caramelized Red Pears with Cinnamon, 233
    Cherries and Pound Cake, 234
    Chicken with Cherry Salsa, 223
    Cranberry and Blood Orange Sauce, 216
    Deep-Dish Cherry Pie, 230
    Duck with Blood Orange Sauce, 215
    Game Hens with Pears, 212
    Grilled Calamari, 198
    Grilled Cherry Tomatoes, 207
    Grilled Chile Sauce, 204
    Grilled Radicchio, 197
    Grilled Red Bell Peppers, 205
    Herbed Cherry Tomatoes, 227
    Hungarian Red Peppers, 227
    Lamb Kebabs with Blood Orange Salad, 220
    Liver and Onion Bruschetta, 197
    Mahimahi with Red Potato, Red Bell Pepper,
       and Rosemary, 211
    Pork Tenderloin with Sour Cherry Sauce, 219
    Prosciutto Grapes, 226

Red Bell Peppers Baked with Anchovies, 217
Red-Hot Hash Browns, 219
Red Onions with Fennel, 205
Red Wine Spaghetti with Red Bell Pepper
    and Onion, 202
Rib-Eye Steaks with Baked Plums, 229
Roasted Beet Salad with Eggs, 217
Roasted Beets with Indian Spices, 229
Roasted Chicken and Red Onion, 212
Roasted Tomato Tart, 201
Romesco Sauce, 198
Sautéed Trout with Red Grape Sauce, 208
Shrimp with Watermelon, Feta, and Mint, 207
Strawberries in Red Wine, 234
Sweet and Sour Beets, 204
Tomatoes Stuffed with Sausage, 216
Turkey Tenderloin with Cranberry Compote, 215
Veal Chops with Red Plum Sauce, 223
Warm Ruby Grapefruit Salad, 226
Warm Tomato and Olive Bruschetta, 202
Rhubarb, 294
    Salmon with Wild Blueberry and Rhubarb
       Sauce, 48
Rice, 294–95
    Baked Pilaf with Currants, Lavender, and
       Almonds, 47
    Grilled Rice Patties with Asian Flavors, 248
Roasting tips, 16–17
Romesco Sauce, 198
Rutabagas, 295
    Baked Sweet Potato and Rutabaga Mash, 168
    Rutabaga and Golden Beets with
       Pomegranate Seeds, 183

S

Salads
    Black Bean and White Corn Salad, 269
    Broiled Tuna with Cannellini Bean Salad, 245
    Bulgur Salad with Zucchini, Asparagus,
       and Green Onions, 259
    Chicken and Eggplant Salad, 41
    Chicken, Avocado, and Spinach Salad, 84
    Crisp Green Apple and Celery Salad, 76
    Fig and Purple Endive Salad, 37
    Grilled Artichoke Salad, 76
    Grilled Fish Tacos with Green Cabbage Salad, 70
    Grilled Salmon, Yellow Potato, and Corn
       Salad, 158

Grilled Snapper and Mandarin Salad, 164
Grilled White Corn Salad, 118
Lamb Kebabs with Blood Orange
    Salad, 220
Moroccan Carrot Salad, 160
Roasted Beet Salad with Eggs, 217
Trout and Green Pear Salad, 83
Warm Ruby Grapefruit Salad, 226
White Eggplant and Green Onion Salad, 133
Salmon
    Grilled Salmon, Yellow Potato, and Corn
       Salad, 158
    Potato Galettes with Smoked Salmon, 117
    Salmon with Wild Blueberry and Rhubarb
       Sauce, 48
Sambal, Peanut, 267
Sandwiches, Turkey, with Sweet Onions, 118
Sauces
    Arugula Pesto, 93
    Asian chile, 290
    Blueberries with Lemon, 55
    Cranberry and Blood Orange Sauce, 216
    fish, 292
    Grilled Chile Sauce, 204
    Roasted Pine Nuts and Raisin Sauce, 256
    Romesco Sauce, 198
    Savory and Spicy Blackberry Sauce, 54
    Thai sweet chile, 291
    Wild Blueberry and Rhubarb Sauce, 48
Sausage
    Baked Pasta with Dandelion Greens and
       Sausage, 90
    Duck Sausage, Tomato, and Cranberry Bean
       Casserole, 251
    Potatoes with Chorizo and Parsley, 124
    Tomatoes Stuffed with Sausage, 216
Sautéing tips, 18–19
Scallops
    Scallops with Bell Pepper Dressing, 31
    Scallops with Golden Beets, 154
Seeds, 9, 13. *See also individual seeds*
    Crunchy Breakfast Topping, 267
    toasting, 84
Serving size, 280
Sesame oil, 290
Shallots, 295
    Grilled Shallots, 120
Shortcake, Winter Peach, 191

Shrimp
　　Shrimp, Beans, and Tomatoes, 248
　　Shrimp with Papaya and Coconut, 178
　　Shrimp with Watermelon, Feta, and Mint, 207
　　Sicilian Shrimp with Cauliflower and
　　　　Almonds, 124
　　Tamarind Shrimp with Peanuts, 263
Soufflé, Spinach, 74
Spices, 21
Spinach, 295
　　Chicken, Avocado, and Spinach Salad, 84
　　Chickpeas with Baby Spinach, 249
　　Garlic Spinach, 99
　　Sautéed Spinach with Peanuts and Soy
　　　　Sauce, 86
　　Spinach Soufflé, 74
Squash, 295. See also Zucchini
　　Butternut Squash and Pears with Rosemary, 184
　　Indian-Spiced Squash with Cashews, 183
　　peeling, 183
　　Sautéed Summer Squash with Corn, 181
　　Spaghetti Squash Aglio e Olio, 173
　　Stuffed Squash Blossoms, 177
　　Turban Squash with Honey Butter, 173
Squid
　　Grilled Calamari, 198
　　Stir-Fried Calamari and Pea Shoots, 101
Star anise, 61, 295
Stir-frying tips, 19
Strawberries, 295
　　Berry Gratin, 230
　　Strawberries in Red Wine, 234
Sugar
　　palm, 61
　　raw, 295
Sunflower seeds, 295
Sweet potatoes, 295
　　Baked Stew of Curried Root Vegetables, 174
　　Baked Sweet Potato and Rutabaga Mash, 168
　　Ham and Sweet Potato Hash, 184
Swiss chard, 295
　　Gratinéed Swiss Chard, 87
　　Swiss Chard with Lemon and Anchovy, 102

T

Tacos, Grilled Fish, with Green Cabbage Salad, 70
Tahini, 295
Tamarind Shrimp with Peanuts, 263

Tan recipes. See White and tan recipes
Tapioca, 295
　　Baked Bananas and Tapioca Pudding, 147
Tarts
　　Roasted Tomato Tart, 201
　　Tart Shell, 201
Tomatillos, 295
　　Chicken with Tomatillo Sauce, 101
　　Monkfish with Roasted White Corn Salsa, 128
　　Turkey with Red Mole, 252
Tomatoes, 295
　　Duck Sausage, Tomato, and Cranberry Bean
　　　　Casserole, 251
　　Grilled Cherry Tomatoes, 207
　　Herbed Cherry Tomatoes, 227
　　Okra with Yellow Plum Tomatoes, 102
　　Orange Gazpacho, 160
　　Roasted Tomato Tart, 201
　　Romesco Sauce, 198
　　Shrimp, Beans, and Tomatoes, 248
　　Tomatoes Stuffed with Sausage, 216
　　Warm Tomato and Olive Bruschetta, 202
　　White Beans with Tomato and Bacon, 266
　　Yellow Tomatoes with Mint and Pecorino, 153
Tortilla, Spanish, with Golden Potatoes, 157
Tortillas
　　Corn and Crab Quesadillas, 154
　　Grilled Fish Tacos with Green Cabbage Salad, 70
　　Mu Shu Pork, 137
　　Red Kidney Bean Quesadillas, 249
Trout
　　Sautéed Trout with Red Grape Sauce, 208
　　Trout and Green Pear Salad, 83
Tuna
　　Broiled Tuna with Cannellini Bean Salad, 245
　　Roasted Tuna with Olives, Grapes, and
　　　　Pine Nuts, 38
Turkey
　　Roasted Turkey Breast with Figs
　　　　and Lavender, 38
　　Turkey Fricassee with Kohlrabi, Pears, and
　　　　Mushrooms, 127
　　Turkey Sandwiches with Sweet Onions, 118
　　Turkey Tenderloin with Cranberry
　　　　Compote, 215
　　Turkey with Red Mole, 252
Turnips, 295
　　Turnips with Peas and Mushrooms, 144

V

Veal Chops with Red Plum Sauce, 223
Vegetables, 8–9, 11, 12, 20. See also individual
　　vegetables
Vinegar, 295
Vitamins, 10–11, 278

W

Walnuts, 295
　　Belgian Endive with Blue Cheese and
　　　　Walnuts, 69
　　Kasha with Walnuts and Pasta, 270
　　Maple Panna Cotta with Candied Walnuts, 273
　　Pear, Cranberry, and Walnut Crisp, 274
Water chestnuts, 295
Watercress, 295
Watermelon, 295
　　Shrimp with Watermelon, Feta, and Mint, 207
White and tan recipes, 110, 284–85
　　Baked Bananas and Tapioca Pudding, 147
　　Baked Onion and White Eggplant Purée, 114
　　Celery Root and Potato Gratin, 143
　　Chicken with Caramelized Shallots and
　　　　Wine, 144
　　Cuban-Style Pork and Plantains, 134
　　Garlic Chips, 140
　　Grilled Fennel with Indian Spices, 133
　　Grilled Parsnip Chips with Lemon and
　　　　Honey, 121
　　Grilled Shallots, 120
　　Grilled White Corn Salad, 118
　　Grilled White Corn with Herb Butter, 120
　　Hot and Sour Bok Choy, 141
　　Mashed Jerusalem Artichokes with
　　　　Truffle Oil, 114
　　Monkfish with Roasted White Corn Salsa, 128
　　Mushroom Bruschetta, 113
　　Mu Shu Pork, 137
　　Mustard-Honey Leeks, 113
　　Pan-Seared Mushrooms, 140
　　Parsley Portobellos, 138
　　Pesto Portobellos, 121
　　Plantain with Jalapeño, 141
　　Pork Chops Smothered in Onions and
　　　　Apples, 127
　　Pork Pot Roast with Parsnips, Carrots, and
　　　　Apples, 123

Potatoes with Chorizo and Parsley, 124
Potato Galettes with Smoked Salmon, 117
Roasted Fennel with Fennel Seed, 143
Roasted Garlic Spread with Thyme, 131
Roasted Mushrooms with Sage Butter, 130
Roasted Onions with Balsamic and Pepper, 130
Sicilian Shrimp with Cauliflower and
    Almonds, 124
Spicy Cauliflower Gratin, 138
Tan Pear Crumble with Lavender, 131
Turkey Fricassee with Kohlrabi, Pears, and
    Mushrooms, 127
Turkey Sandwiches with Sweet Onions, 118
Turnips with Peas and Mushrooms, 144
White Asparagus Mimosa with Browned
    Butter, 117
White Eggplant and Green Onion Salad, 133
White Nectarines with Raw Sugar and Rum, 147
Wild rice
    Baked Pilaf with Currants, Lavender, and
        Almonds, 47
    Wild Rice with Apricots, 170
    Wild Rice with Purple Bell Pepper and
        Pecans, 57
Wine, 295
Winter savory, 295

Y

Yellow and orange recipes, 150, 285–86
    Apricot-Stuffed Chicken Breasts, 178
    Baked Golden Raspberries, 171
    Baked Stew of Curried Root Vegetables, 174
    Baked Sweet Potato and Rutabaga Mash, 168
    Broiled Pomelo, 161
    Butternut Squash and Pears with
        Rosemary, 184
    Chicken with Yellow Peppers and
        Passion Fruit, 177
    Corn and Crab Quesadillas, 154
    Grapefruit Baked with Brown Sugar, 170
    Grilled Apricots with Sabayon, 187
    Grilled Duck Breast with Papaya, 163
    Grilled Pineapple, 161
    Grilled Pumpkin with Pumpkin Seed
        Dressing, 153
    Grilled Salmon, Yellow Potato, and Corn
        Salad, 158
    Grilled Snapper and Mandarin Salad, 164

Halibut with Roasted Nectarine
    Chutney, 167
Ham and Sweet Potato Hash, 184
Indian-Spiced Squash with Cashews, 183
Mahimahi and Mango Salsa, 164
Moroccan Carrot Salad, 160
Orange Gazpacho, 160
Peppered Yellow Pears with Honey, 180
Pineapple with Preserved Ginger, 180
Pumpkin Flan, 188
Rack of Lamb with Orange Bell Pepper
    Relish, 168
Roasted Pumpkin Purée, 171
Roasted Sea Bass with Carrot Purée, 167
Rutabaga and Golden Beets with
    Pomegranate Seeds, 183
Sautéed Summer Squash with Corn, 181
Savory Sautéed Persimmons, 181
Scallops with Golden Beets, 154
Shrimp with Papaya and Coconut, 178
Spaghetti Squash Aglio e Olio, 173
Spanish Tortilla with Golden Potatoes, 157
Stuffed Squash Blossoms, 177
Turban Squash with Honey Butter, 173
Wild Rice with Apricots, 170
Winter Peach Shortcake, 191
Yellow Tomatoes with Mint and
    Pecorino, 153
Yogurt, 295

Z

Zucchini, 295
    Bulgur Salad with Zucchini, Asparagus,
        and Green Onions, 259
    Roasted Zucchini with Anchoïade, 73

Bibliography

The resources below were used in the creation
of this book, and are recommended for further
reading on the subject of colorful plant foods:

BOOKS
Gollman, Barbara, and Kim Pierce. *The Phytopia
Cookbook.* Dallas, Tex.: Phytopia, Inc., 1998.

Green, Eliza. *Field Guide to Produce.* Philadephia:
Quirk Books, 2004.

Heber, David, M.D., Ph.D. *What Color Is Your Diet?*
New York: Harper Collins, 2001.

Hess, Mary Abbott, L.H.D., M.S., R.D., F.A.D.A;
Dana Jacobi; and Marie Simmons.
Williams-Sonoma Essentials of Healthful Cooking.
Menlo Park, Calif.: Oxmoor House, 2003.

Joseph, James A., Ph.D.; Daniel A. Nadeau, M.D.;
and Anne Underwood. *The Color Code.*
New York: Hyperion, 2002.

Pivonka, Elizabeth, R.D., Ph.D., and Barbara Berry,
M.S., R.D. *5 a Day: The Better Health Cookbook.*
New York: Rodale, 2002.

Tantillo, Tony, and Sam Gugino. *Eat Fresh,
Stay Healthy.* New York: Macmillan General
Reference, 1997.

WEBSITES
Centers for Disease Control and Prevention:
http://www.cdc.gov

National Cancer Institute:
http://www.cancer.gov

Produce for Better Health Foundation:
http://www.5aday.org

United States Department of Agriculture:
http://www.usda.gov

University of California, Berkeley,
School of Public Health Wellness Letter:
http://www.wellnessletter.com

Originally published as Williams-Sonoma
New Healthy Kitchen series:

Grilling © 2007 Weldon Owen Inc. and Williams-Sonoma Inc.
Roasting © 2007 Weldon Owen Inc. and Williams-Sonoma Inc.
Sautéing © 2007 Weldon Owen Inc. and Williams-Sonoma Inc.

WILLIAMS-SONOMA

Founder & Vice-Chairman Chuck Williams

WELDON OWEN INC.

Chief Executive Officer, Weldon Owen Group John Owen
Chief Executive Officer and President Terry Newell
Vice President, Sales and New Business Development Amy Kaneko
Vice President and Creative Director Gaye Allen
Vice President and Publisher Hannah Rahill
Executive Editor Sarah Putman Clegg
Senior Editor Kim Goodfriend
Associate Editor Lauren Hancock
Assistant Editor Julia Humes
Art Director Marisa Kwek
Senior Designer Kara Church
Designer Ashley Martinez
Production Director Chris Hemesath
Production Manager Michelle Duggan
Color Manager Teri Bell
Co-edition and Reprint Coordinator Todd Rechner

THE WILLIAMS-SONOMA *EATING BY COLOR*

Conceived and produced by Weldon Owen Inc.
814 Montgomery Street, San Francisco, CA 94133
Telephone: 415 291 0100   Fax: 415 291 8841

In collaboration with Williams-Sonoma, Inc.
3250 Van Ness Avenue, San Francisco, CA 94109

A WELDON OWEN PRODUCTION
Copyright © 2007 by Weldon Owen Inc. and Williams-Sonoma Inc.

Set in Vectora.

Color separations by Mission Productions Limited.
Printed and bound in China by Midas Printing.

First printed in 2007.

10 9 8 7 6 5 4 3 2 1

Library of Congress Cataloging-in-Publication data is available.

ISBN 13: 978-0-8487-3190-8
ISBN 10: 0-8487-3190-5

ACKNOWLEDGMENTS
Weldon Owen wishes to thank the following people for their generous support in producing this book:
Copy Editor Carrie Bradley; Consulting Editor Sharon Silva; Proofreaders Kate Washington and Lesli Neilson; Indexer Ken DellaPenta;
Photographer Dan Goldberg; Photographer's Assistant Shawn Convey; Food Stylist Jen Straus; Assistant Food Stylist Max La Rivière-Hedrick;
Heather Belt; Alexa Hyman; Carolyn Miller; Eduardo Navarro; Leigh Noe; Jackie Mills; and Ryan Phillips.

CREDITS
Recipes Georgeanne Brennan 27, 38, 42, 44, 45, 47, 61, 73, 74, 86, 87, 89, 90, 93 (bottom), 97, 106, 114, 123, 128, 130, 131, 138, 143, 147, 154, 167, 168,
170, 171, 173, 174, 188, 201, 211, 212, 216, 217, 224, 229, 230, 233 (bottom), 246, 251, 256, 257, 260, 263 (top), 264 (bottom), 274; Dana Jacobi 31, 32
(bottom), 48, 51, 52, 54, 55, 57, 62, 79, 80, 94, 98, 99, 101, 102, 105, 117, 124, 127, 137, 140, 141, 144, 157, 177, 178, 180, 181, 183, 184, 191, 202, 208, 215,
219, 226, 227, 234, 252, 255, 263 (bottom), 264 (top), 266, 267, 269, 270, 273; Annabel Langbein 28, 32 (top), 34, 35, 37, 41, 58, 69, 70, 76, 77, 83, 84, 93
(top), 113, 118, 120, 121, 133, 134, 153, 158, 160, 161, 163, 164, 187, 197, 198, 204, 205, 207, 220, 223, 233 (top), 241, 242, 245, 248, 249, 259.

Photography Ben Dearnley: pages 22 (top left), 148 (bottom left), 193 (top right)

Annabel Langbein would like to thank the BBQ Factory, New Zealand, for kindly lending
the Brinkmann barbecue used to test these recipes.

A NOTE ON WEIGHTS AND MEASURES
All recipes include customary U.S. and metric measurements. Metric conversions are based on
a standard developed for these books and have been rounded off. Actual weights may vary.

Potatoes with Chorizo and Parsley, 124
Potato Galettes with Smoked Salmon, 117
Roasted Fennel with Fennel Seed, 143
Roasted Garlic Spread with Thyme, 131
Roasted Mushrooms with Sage Butter, 130
Roasted Onions with Balsamic and Pepper, 130
Sicilian Shrimp with Cauliflower and
    Almonds, 124
Spicy Cauliflower Gratin, 138
Tan Pear Crumble with Lavender, 131
Turkey Fricassee with Kohlrabi, Pears, and
    Mushrooms, 127
Turkey Sandwiches with Sweet Onions, 118
Turnips with Peas and Mushrooms, 144
White Asparagus Mimosa with Browned
    Butter, 117
White Eggplant and Green Onion Salad, 133
White Nectarines with Raw Sugar and Rum, 147
Wild rice
    Baked Pilaf with Currants, Lavender, and
        Almonds, 47
    Wild Rice with Apricots, 170
    Wild Rice with Purple Bell Pepper and
        Pecans, 57
Wine, 295
Winter savory, 295

Y

Yellow and orange recipes, 150, 285–86
    Apricot-Stuffed Chicken Breasts, 178
    Baked Golden Raspberries, 171
    Baked Stew of Curried Root Vegetables, 174
    Baked Sweet Potato and Rutabaga Mash, 168
    Broiled Pomelo, 161
    Butternut Squash and Pears with
        Rosemary, 184
    Chicken with Yellow Peppers and
        Passion Fruit, 177
    Corn and Crab Quesadillas, 154
    Grapefruit Baked with Brown Sugar, 170
    Grilled Apricots with Sabayon, 187
    Grilled Duck Breast with Papaya, 163
    Grilled Pineapple, 161
    Grilled Pumpkin with Pumpkin Seed
        Dressing, 153
    Grilled Salmon, Yellow Potato, and Corn
        Salad, 158
    Grilled Snapper and Mandarin Salad, 164

Halibut with Roasted Nectarine
    Chutney, 167
Ham and Sweet Potato Hash, 184
Indian-Spiced Squash with Cashews, 183
Mahimahi and Mango Salsa, 164
Moroccan Carrot Salad, 160
Orange Gazpacho, 160
Peppered Yellow Pears with Honey, 180
Pineapple with Preserved Ginger, 180
Pumpkin Flan, 188
Rack of Lamb with Orange Bell Pepper
    Relish, 168
Roasted Pumpkin Purée, 171
Roasted Sea Bass with Carrot Purée, 167
Rutabaga and Golden Beets with
    Pomegranate Seeds, 183
Sautéed Summer Squash with Corn, 181
Savory Sautéed Persimmons, 181
Scallops with Golden Beets, 154
Shrimp with Papaya and Coconut, 178
Spaghetti Squash Aglio e Olio, 173
Spanish Tortilla with Golden Potatoes, 157
Stuffed Squash Blossoms, 177
Turban Squash with Honey Butter, 173
Wild Rice with Apricots, 170
Winter Peach Shortcake, 191
Yellow Tomatoes with Mint and
    Pecorino, 153
Yogurt, 295

Z

Zucchini, 295
    Bulgur Salad with Zucchini, Asparagus,
        and Green Onions, 259
    Roasted Zucchini with Anchoïade, 73

Bibliography

The resources below were used in the creation of this book, and are recommended for further reading on the subject of colorful plant foods:

BOOKS

Gollman, Barbara, and Kim Pierce. *The Phytopia Cookbook.* Dallas, Tex.: Phytopia, Inc., 1998.

Green, Eliza. *Field Guide to Produce.* Philadephia: Quirk Books, 2004.

Heber, David, M.D., Ph.D. *What Color Is Your Diet?* New York: Harper Collins, 2001.

Hess, Mary Abbott, L.H.D., M.S., R.D., F.A.D.A; Dana Jacobi; and Marie Simmons. *Williams-Sonoma Essentials of Healthful Cooking.* Menlo Park, Calif.: Oxmoor House, 2003.

Joseph, James A., Ph.D.; Daniel A. Nadeau, M.D.; and Anne Underwood. *The Color Code.* New York: Hyperion, 2002.

Pivonka, Elizabeth, R.D., Ph.D., and Barbara Berry, M.S., R.D. *5 a Day: The Better Health Cookbook.* New York: Rodale, 2002.

Tantillo, Tony, and Sam Gugino. *Eat Fresh, Stay Healthy.* New York: Macmillan General Reference, 1997.

WEBSITES

Centers for Disease Control and Prevention: http://www.cdc.gov

National Cancer Institute: http://www.cancer.gov

Produce for Better Health Foundation: http://www.5aday.org

United States Department of Agriculture: http://www.usda.gov

University of California, Berkeley, School of Public Health Wellness Letter: http://www.wellnessletter.com

Originally published as Williams-Sonoma
New Healthy Kitchen series:

Grilling © 2007 Weldon Owen Inc. and Williams-Sonoma Inc.
Roasting © 2007 Weldon Owen Inc. and Williams-Sonoma Inc.
Sautéing © 2007 Weldon Owen Inc. and Williams-Sonoma Inc.

WILLIAMS-SONOMA
Founder & Vice-Chairman Chuck Williams

WELDON OWEN INC.

Chief Executive Officer, Weldon Owen Group John Owen
Chief Executive Officer and President Terry Newell
Vice President, Sales and New Business Development Amy Kaneko
Vice President and Creative Director Gaye Allen
Vice President and Publisher Hannah Rahill
Executive Editor Sarah Putman Clegg
Senior Editor Kim Goodfriend
Associate Editor Lauren Hancock
Assistant Editor Julia Humes
Art Director Marisa Kwek
Senior Designer Kara Church
Designer Ashley Martinez
Production Director Chris Hemesath
Production Manager Michelle Duggan
Color Manager Teri Bell
Co-edition and Reprint Coordinator Todd Rechner

THE WILLIAMS-SONOMA *EATING BY COLOR*

Conceived and produced by Weldon Owen Inc.
814 Montgomery Street, San Francisco, CA 94133
Telephone: 415 291 0100   Fax: 415 291 8841

In collaboration with Williams-Sonoma, Inc.
3250 Van Ness Avenue, San Francisco, CA 94109

A WELDON OWEN PRODUCTION
Copyright © 2007 by Weldon Owen Inc. and Williams-Sonoma Inc.

All rights reserved, including the right of reproduction in whole
or in part in any form.

Set in Vectora.

Color separations by Mission Productions Limited.
Printed and bound in China by Midas Printing.

First printed in 2007.

10 9 8 7 6 5 4 3 2 1

Library of Congress Cataloging-in-Publication data is available.

ISBN 13: 978-0-8487-3190-8
ISBN 10: 0-8487-3190-5

ACKNOWLEDGMENTS

Weldon Owen wishes to thank the following people for their generous support in producing this book:
Copy Editor Carrie Bradley; **Consulting Editor** Sharon Silva; **Proofreaders** Kate Washington and Lesli Neilson; **Indexer** Ken DellaPenta;
Photographer Dan Goldberg; **Photographer's Assistant** Shawn Convey; **Food Stylist** Jen Straus; **Assistant Food Stylist** Max La Rivière-Hedrick;
Heather Belt; Alexa Hyman; Carolyn Miller; Eduardo Navarro; Leigh Noe; Jackie Mills; and Ryan Phillips.

CREDITS

Recipes Georgeanne Brennan 27, 38, 42, 44, 45, 47, 61, 73, 74, 86, 87, 89, 90, 93 (bottom), 97, 106, 114, 123, 128, 130, 131, 138, 143, 147, 154, 167, 168, 170, 171, 173, 174, 188, 201, 211, 212, 216, 217, 224, 229, 230, 233 (bottom), 246, 251, 256, 257, 260, 263 (top), 264 (bottom), 274; Dana Jacobi 31, 32 (bottom), 48, 51, 52, 54, 55, 57, 62, 79, 80, 94, 98, 99, 101, 102, 105, 117, 124, 127, 137, 140, 141, 144, 157, 177, 178, 180, 181, 183, 184, 191, 202, 208, 215, 219, 226, 227, 234, 252, 255, 263 (bottom), 264 (top), 266, 267, 269, 270, 273; Annabel Langbein 28, 32 (top), 34, 35, 37, 41, 58, 69, 70, 76, 77, 83, 84, 93 (top), 113, 118, 120, 121, 133, 134, 153, 158, 160, 161, 163, 164, 187, 197, 198, 204, 205, 207, 220, 223, 233 (top), 241, 242, 245, 248, 249, 259.

Photography Ben Dearnley: pages 22 (top left), 148 (bottom left), 193 (top right)

Annabel Langbein would like to thank the BBQ Factory, New Zealand, for kindly lending
the Brinkmann barbecue used to test these recipes.

A NOTE ON WEIGHTS AND MEASURES

All recipes include customary U.S. and metric measurements. Metric conversions are based on
a standard developed for these books and have been rounded off. Actual weights may vary.